WHITE RURAL RAGE

WHITE RURAL RAGE

THE THREAT TO
AMERICAN DEMOCRACY

—

TOM SCHALLER and **PAUL WALDMAN**

RANDOM HOUSE | NEW YORK

Published in the United States by Random House,
an imprint and division of Penguin Random House LLC, New York.

RANDOM HOUSE and the HOUSE colophon are
registered trademarks of Penguin Random House LLC.

LIBRARY OF CONGRESS CATALOGING-IN-PUBLICATION DATA

NAMES: Schaller, Thomas F. author. | Waldman, Paul, author.
TITLE: White rural rage: the threat to American democracy /
Tom Schaller and Paul Waldman.
DESCRIPTION: First edition. | New York: Random House, [2024]. |
Includes bibliographical references and index.
IDENTIFIERS: LCCN 2023041429 (print) | LCCN 2023041430 (ebook) |
ISBN 9780593729144 (hardcover) | ISBN 9780593729151 (ebook)
SUBJECTS: LCSH: Proportional representation—United States. |
Rural population—Political activity—United States. |
Rural-urban relations—United States. | Democracy—United States. |
United States. Congress. Senate. | United States—Politics and government—2021–
CLASSIFICATION: LCC JF1075.U6 S36 2024 (print) | LCC JF1075.U6 (ebook) |
DDC 320.97309173/4—dc23/eng/20231213
LC record available at lccn.loc.gov/2023041429
LC ebook record available at lccn.loc.gov/2023041430

Printed in the United States of America on acid-free paper

randomhousebooks.com

2 4 6 8 9 7 5 3 1

FIRST EDITION

Book design by Barbara M. Bachman

To Dan, my closest and most trusted friend
for more than fifty years—and counting. (by TS)

To my children. (by PW)

CONTENTS

—

WHITE RURAL RAGE

SMALL TOWNS, BIG TROUBLE

—

"FRIEND, JASON ALDEAN RECORDED A SONG PRAISING SMALL-TOWN VALUES, and the Radical Left has canceled him for it. Why? Because they want every small town in America to look like the socialist disasters in California and New York."

This was the beginning of a fundraising email from the National Republican Congressional Committee in July 2023, responding to the controversy over "Try That in a Small Town," the single that country star Aldean had recently released. The song's lyrics present a list of alleged liberal urban horrors—people spitting in cops' faces, robbing liquor stores, burning American flags—as well as the specter of gun confiscation, and they issue a challenge: "Well, try that in a small town / See how far you make it down the road."

Aldean, whose oeuvre is heavy with well-worn tributes to rural life, was not "canceled." In fact, his fantasy of vigilante violence meted out against urbanites supposedly ready to bring their criminal mayhem to the idyll of rural America became his greatest success. Conservative media defended him, Republican politicians praised him, and "Try That in a Small Town" became Aldean's biggest crossover hit, shooting to No. 1 on the *Billboard* Hot 100.

Had Aldean released his ode to resentment and vigilantism a decade earlier, it might not have made the news, let alone become the controversy it did. But coming out when it did, with hostility between rural

and urban America intensifying as the country headed into a presidential election that promised an even more profound division between the
two, the song was bound to produce a fiery reaction. For Republicans, it
was a gift, yet another implement they could use to convince their rural
supporters that blue America was a "socialist disaster" to be feared and
hated. The criticism the song received from liberals only reinforced this
point.

The undercurrents that produced this controversy are the reason we
wrote this book. We stand at what may be the most dangerous moment
for American democracy since the Civil War. A great deal of attention
has been bestowed upon rural Whites since Donald Trump's ascension
in 2016, yet that discussion has overlooked a vital political truth this
book hopes to illuminate: The democratic attachments of rural White
Americans are faltering.

Rural America has suffered greatly in recent decades. Layered atop
cultural resentments that are nearly as old as our country, this suffering
has produced powerful antipathies that are aimed not just at certain
groups of Americans, but often at the American democratic system itself. Were rural White Americans as disempowered as they believe
themselves to be, their anger would be impotent. They would mutter
"Try that in a small town" to themselves, indulging in meaningless fan-
tasies of revenge against the liberals and urbanites they despise. But they
are not disempowered. In fact, in critical ways, they have more power
than any other large demographic group in America.

This power has already distorted the outcomes our system produces,
leaving us in an age of minority rule in which—to take just one example—
the party that won fewer votes in seven of the last eight presidential elections managed to assemble an activist 6–3 supermajority on the Supreme
Court, one that is now busy remaking the laws all of us live under to
conform to a right-wing policy vision that overwhelming majorities of
the public do not share. This minority rule is a consequence of the disproportionate power wielded by rural Whites, power that is often justified on the right by the insistence that these are the worthiest Americans,
the ones most possessed of virtue and "values," and that, therefore, it is
only proper that their votes count for more.

The fact that their votes do count for more is why Donald Trump became president in the first place, and if he should regain the White House, it will be rural Whites who return him there. Yet even as the threat to American democracy Trump represents has become the subject of enormous concern and debate, few have connected that threat to its essential source: rural White America.

Name a force or impulse that threatens the stability of the American political system—distrust in the fairness of elections, conspiracy theorizing, the embrace of authoritarianism—and it is almost always more prevalent among rural Whites than among those living elsewhere. Even as they are in some ways the greatest beneficiaries of democracy's distribution of influence, rural Whites are the least committed to our system.

While at various times in American history some extraordinarily creative and progressive movements began in rural areas, today most of rural America is gripped by a right-wing politics that is angry when it should be constructive and passive when it should be engaged. To many of the most cynical and malevolent characters in the political world, this is all part of the plan: Keep rural Americans bitter, and they'll be an easily manipulated force of destruction when democracy doesn't produce the proper results. The worse rural Americans feel, the better this plan works.

The devastating force of late-stage capitalism has inflicted enormous damage on rural Americans. But we are more concerned with how the political system responded and, specifically, why so few rural Americans have noticed that they've been exploited and lied to by the conservative politicians they elect. Their own leaders deploy a sophisticated propaganda system meant to ensure that every problem rural America faces will be blamed on faraway forces and people who have little if any actual influence on rural Americans' lives. It's the best way to stoke the voters' seething—that and telling them the solution to their problems will always be to elect more conservative Republicans, who will continue to spend more effort in ratcheting up rural anger than in addressing the problems confronting rural communities.

So, when urban America suffers from a spike in unemployment or violent crime, the right-wing noise machine quickly points its collective finger at liberals, minorities, and Democrats who dominate cities. Cities, they are told, are both nightmares of depravity and a threat to rural Americans. But when rural America suffers from precisely these same problems, who gets blamed? Those same liberals, minorities, and Democrats from faraway, scary cities. Almost daily—hourly on talk radio stations from Maine to Maui—those constituents hear Republican politicians and their conservative allies in the media redirect rural fury toward the boogeyman of the moment: immigrant caravans this month, critical race theorists next month, woke professors the month after that. Though most rural citizens are represented at all levels of government by conservative Republicans, those officials somehow bear no responsibility for their constituents' problems.

But Hollywood didn't kill the family farm and send manufacturing jobs overseas. College professors didn't pour mountains of opioids into rural communities. Immigrants didn't shutter rural hospitals and let rural infrastructure decay. The outsiders and liberals at whom so many rural Whites point their anger are not the ones who have held them back—and as long as they keep believing that they are, rural people won't be able to find their way to an effective form of politics.

This book is not intended to be mere polemic or a broadside critique of rural Americans or White rural citizens specifically. Rather, it is a warning about a growing problem that politicians and the media are reluctant to discuss. Rural voters—especially the White rural voters on whom Donald Trump heaps praise and upon whom he built his Make America Great Again movement—pose a growing threat to the world's oldest constitutional democracy. Rural discontent and grievances are hardly new. But more than at any point in modern history, the survival of the United States as a modern, stable, multi-ethnic democracy is threatened by a White rural minority that wields outsize electoral power.

In order to be complete, this story must be told from multiple vantage points, some high enough to view the entire country and decades of history and some directly on the ground. So, we have woven together data on economic and physical well-being and voting trends, and from public opinion surveys, with our own on-the-ground reporting from rural counties spread across the country, to describe the political reality of rural America today and what it portends for the rest of us. We examine not only what happens at the ballot box but also the underpinnings of rural culture and rural ideology. We journey from the Electoral College to West Virginia coal country, from the Affordable Care Act to the Arizona desert, and many places in between.

The story that results is often a disheartening one. Though the various parts of rural America differ in important ways, as a whole, they are weighed down by their struggles: resource economies where powerful interests extracted wealth and left the people who toiled to remove it with little or nothing to show for their decades of labor; manufacturing jobs that fled overseas; inadequate healthcare and physical infrastructure; limited opportunities that push talented young people to leave; and much more. And all this exists within a landscape of political emptiness in which a lack of real competition leaves Democrats believing there's no point in trying to win rural votes and Republicans knowing they can win those votes without even trying—and give the people who supply them nothing in return.

We have no illusions that the story we tell will be kindly received in most corners of rural America, nor by large swaths of the national media. Those media have spent years writing article after article in which customers at small-town diners explain what they're mad about, so many that pieces with headlines amounting to "In Trump Country, Trump Supporters Still Support Trump" have become a cliché. This coverage insists that the views these people express, no matter how alarming or repellent to coastal-dwelling cosmopolitans, demand consideration and respect. Rural sentiments, even undemocratic ones, must always be validated and amplified.

Some will surely respond to this book by charging that as two coastal cosmopolitans, we have no right to offer this critique of White rural politics. That is an understandable reaction, and there are certainly many fine books we would recommend from people who grew up in rural America exploring its past and present. But we set out on this project after years of thinking and talking with each other about how ordinary rural-urban tensions of the kind that have existed throughout the world for centuries have turned into something far more dangerous. Put simply, this is a problem that no American, no matter where they live, can ignore any longer.

This book asks some difficult questions: Is the support of White rural citizens for U.S. democracy conditional? If so, what conditions do they expect in return for remaining devoted to our democratic project? And what happens if the demands of the only group capable of holding America hostage are not met? Can our constitutional system survive, or even function, without the consent and cooperation of America's essential rural minority?

We conclude the book with preliminary answers to these questions. But we also argue that rural America can reimagine itself and its role in our democracy in a way that would not only offer a better future for rural people themselves but also make it possible for rural America to no longer be an anchor dragging down the rest of the country.

We do not offer ten-point plans for rural redevelopment. There are plenty of those around, in think tank white papers and government reports. But none of them can succeed on a national scale without a new political era for rural America, one that replaces self-perpetuating resentment with more constructive action built on demands for change.

Unfortunately, rural White Americans are told daily by the people they trust that what they really need is more rage and resentment. They're told that their fellow Americans who live in suburbs and cities look at them with disdain and that the answer is to look back with their own brand of belligerent contempt. This cycle of resentment leads nowhere but down—away from solutions to rural people's problems and away from a functioning democracy. Without a change, the politics of rural America will become meaner and more opposed to the foundations of American democracy—and more of a threat to all of us.

ESSENTIAL MINORITY,
EXISTENTIAL THREAT

—

WHEN WE VISITED TRUMAN CHAFIN IN HIS LAW OFFICE IN WIL-liamson, West Virginia, he regaled us with stories of the colorful and obviously guilty clients he had successfully defended over the years, then insisted we pose for a picture inside the jail cell, our hands gripping the bars as though we were small-time thieves nabbed by the sheriff. The former Democratic majority leader of the state senate, Chafin shares a sprawling suite with his wife, Letitia, herself a prominent attorney in the state, inside what used to be the courthouse. The cell is now used as a kitchen.

After running unopposed for years, Chafin was voted out of office in 2014, the victim of a Republican sweep that gave the GOP control of both houses of the state legislature. It was a key moment in West Virginia's transformation from one-party Democratic rule to one-party Republican rule,[1] but it was more than a transfer of power. The personal brand of politics that centered on the distribution of resources through the government was now just a memory.

The machine built by legendary West Virginia Democratic senator Robert Byrd is long gone, as is the importance of the county Democratic chair, a position Chafin held for many years in Mingo County. "The county chair was *the wheel* down here," he told us, the person who maintained all the critical relationships that not only provided services but kept people loyal to the Democratic Party. "Now you can't get anybody to take the job."

But the vacuum created by a withered local Democratic Party hasn't been filled by an active Republican Party. "Republicans don't have a good system, either," Letitia Chafin said, "but they don't really need one."[2]

Indeed they don't. For decades, the county was firmly Democratic, a streak that lasted through 2004, when John Kerry beat George W. Bush there by a comfortable margin. But Barack Obama's arrival brought a hard swing to the right, and in every election after, the Republican margin of victory increased. Today, no politician is more popular there than Donald Trump, and not because during his four years in office he turned rural America into a paradise or delivered on his promise to bring back all the lost coal jobs. He didn't. But in places like Mingo County, few seem to mind.

This paradox is part of what led us to write this book and what brought us to Mingo County, one of many rural places we visited during our research. It has a fascinating political and economic history, one that decades ago earned it the nickname "Bloody Mingo." The seminal period is referred to as the Mine Wars, a series of conflicts that took place over the first two decades of the twentieth century pitting miners asking for fair treatment against coal companies who often responded to those demands with murderous violence.[3]

That history is remembered by union members and their allies as a story of heroism and oppression. But it was the New Deal that began to bring what those miners fought for in the Mine Wars, and for a brief period after Franklin Roosevelt enacted his program of labor reform, it looked as though widely shared prosperity might come to the coalfields. Roosevelt had signed laws protecting collective bargaining rights and curtailing abuses from employers.[4] The United Mine Workers negotiated contracts that not only improved pay and working conditions but also offered health and pension benefits, and coal mining still required enormous numbers of men to go underground, which meant lots of jobs. In areas like Mingo County that had seen stifling poverty even before the Great Depression, a middle-class life was now attainable.

But things started to change in the 1950s. First, automation dramatically reduced the number of miners needed to collect the same amount of coal; with each new technological development, fewer miners were necessary.[5] As those good jobs with good benefits became less plentiful, union power began to recede. Then came Ronald Reagan and the war on collective bargaining, followed by the spread of mountaintop removal, carried out with explosives and massive machines, further reducing the number of miners needed to extract the coal as it turned large swaths of Appalachia's picturesque hills into a lunar-like landscape.

It wasn't just the economy and the topography that changed. "When the union was strong here, the voice was from the union," we were told by Raymond Chafin, a former miner who had a terrible fall in a mine decades ago, broke his pelvis, and nearly died. (He's not related to Truman Chafin; there are a lot of Chafins around there.) But today, that voice has gotten quieter and quieter. The industry created a public relations campaign called Friends of Coal to convince people that they were all united against environmentalists and other outsiders. Fox News and other conservative media came to dominate the informational landscape. Today, the traditional alliance between the Democratic Party and the unions has become all but irrelevant because both institutions are so much weaker in West Virginia. "The Republican stronghold that you've got now is a *strong hold*," Raymond Chafin said.[6]

There are fewer and fewer miners in Mingo County, as in so many places across Appalachia; according to the state of West Virginia, in 2021 there were just 296 people in the county employed by the coal industry,[7] or about 2 percent of the working-age population. Yet coal is an inescapable presence there, celebrated and venerated everywhere you look. The most notable building on the main drag in Williamson is the Coal House, a structure built out of coal. In the fall, you can participate in the Coal Dust 5K Run/Walk, where (fake) coal dust is tossed onto the runners at the finish line. Young girls can come to the firehouse for the Sweetheart of the Coalfields pageant. Mingo Central High School sits on King Coal Highway. Its sports teams are named "the Miners" and "the Lady Miners."

One might argue that coal has been more of a curse than a blessing to Appalachia, but that is not a conversation too many people there seem eager to have. The old conflict between workers and owners no longer means much, because in every way that matters, the owners won. That brief period when coal actually offered something like widely shared prosperity was made possible by union organizing and the actions of a Democratic government in Washington, but the current governor of West Virginia, Jim Justice, is a coal baron and the wealthiest man in the state—and one who switched his party affiliation from Democratic to Republican. Politicians who make dishonest promises to restore coal to its former glory—if you can call it that—are cheered and rewarded at the polls. Few people have ever done so with more lurid dishonesty than Donald Trump, and the voters in coal country ate it up; he didn't just win there, he won by astonishing margins. In 2016, Trump got 83 percent of the vote in Mingo County.[8] Four years later, they gave him 85 percent of their votes.

Although there are rural places that don't face the same grinding struggles that Mingo County does, it shares this devotion to the GOP with almost every other majority-White rural county in the country. If you look at where Trump got his most overwhelming support, the places are invariably rural and White. Rural Whites are the linchpin of Republican power at both the state and national level, yet in so many of the places where they live, there is a political void. Democrats can't compete there anymore, and Republicans can take lopsided victories for granted.

So, what do rural Whites get in return for all they bestow on the GOP? Almost nothing. The benefits they receive are nearly all emotional, not material. They're flattered and praised, and then they get whatever satisfaction can be had from watching their party win office and their enemies despair. Consider the opioid crisis, which took a devastating toll on Mingo Countians. Though some politicians try to pin the blame for America's addiction crisis on Mexican immigrants, look at the long list of companies that have now agreed to pay more than a billion dollars in settlements to West Virginia for this crisis. They include drugmakers like Purdue Pharma; the three major distributors McKesson, Cardinal, and AmeriSourceBergen; and frontline retailers including Food Lion, CVS, Walgreens, and Walmart.

Mingo County is suffering from a rash of economic, social, and health-related woes. As a small state, West Virginia is overrepresented in both the U.S. Senate and the Electoral College. With its large blue-collar, White population and deep mining traditions, West Virginia is the kind of "flyover" state routinely praised and glorified by the media as a repository of true "heartland" values. Unfortunately, politicians in the state—Democrats before, Republicans now—exploit West Virginians' worries that their way of life and their values are being replaced by those of citizens from more vibrant, racially diverse, and cosmopolitan cities and states.

The combined effect of these trends undoubtedly causes citizens from places like Mingo County to feel passed over, desperate, even angry despite winning elections. As they spread across the small towns and counties of the United States, these fears and resentments are undermining rural White Americans' democratic commitments to the world's oldest constitutional republic.

THE FOUR COMPOUNDING FACTORS

Since the rise of Donald Trump, few groups of citizens have received more fawning attention from hand-wringing journalists and pundits than rural Americans, especially disgruntled rural White voters. Over the same period, political observers began openly fretting over the fate and even the survival of American democracy. Somehow, almost nobody has noticed that these two phenomena are connected.

And they *are* connected. As we argue, the serious problems now plaguing rural White Americans are causing too many of them to lose faith in the American project, to the point where some are abandoning or even threatening the vital norms, traditions, and institutions that undergird the world's oldest constitutional democracy. Four compounding factors are causing a crisis in democratic support among rural Whites that, in turn, is undermining American democracy in potentially cata-strophic ways.

White despair

The first is that rural Whites—often, but not always, with cause—are increasingly dissatisfied with their lives and livelihoods. Population stagnation, economic decline, and healthcare problems have devastated thousands of the United States' small towns, cities, and counties. Pov-erty, unemployment, homelessness, crime, business closures, govern-mental failures, drug addiction and deaths, and a general despair are all rising across the so-called American heartland. So, too, are feelings of anger, helplessness, and desperation. As their desperation rises—and despite hundreds of state and federal programs specifically targeted to help rural communities—rural Whites have begun to question their commitments to an American political system many of them see as no longer sufficiently attuned to their needs.

Outsize political power

Unlike other demographic subgroups, however, rural Whites wield in-flated power in U.S. politics. This power is the second compounding factor because it grants rural Whites unusual leverage to bend politics and politicians to their will. Since the rise of Jacksonian democracy nearly two centuries ago, rural Whites have enjoyed what we call "es-sential minority" status because they have been able to extract conces-sions from state governments and especially the national government that no other group of citizens their size possibly could. By that we mean that both major parties too often have needed to please, or at least pacify, rural Whites if they entertained any hope of building and sustaining their governing agendas.

Indeed, thanks to a combination of slavery and the systematic suppression of Black male voters even after the Civil War ended and the Fifteenth Amendment was ratified, rural Whites retained immense power throughout the nineteenth century. Even after the United States ceased to be a majority-rural nation by the 1920 Census, rural Whites continued to comprise a formidable plurality that enjoyed malapportionment-inflated power for the remainder of the twentieth century. The U.S. Senate has long assigned greater voting power to rural states and rural voters within states. To a lesser degree, so, too, has the Electoral College process for selecting U.S. presidents. Meanwhile, to this day, gerrymandered districts often confer upon rural Whites voting power within state legislatures and the U.S. House of Representatives which their sheer numbers would not otherwise grant them. Only in recent decades has rural White electoral power begun to wane and only because the share of rural Whites is steadily shrinking. In a country that is roughly 20 percent rural—with about one-fourth of that 20 percent being non-White—rural Whites now constitute about 15 percent of the total U.S. population. Rural Whites exert power beyond their numbers, and surely could improve their communities were they to use this power judiciously.

Veneration of White culture and values

The third compounding factor is the incessant veneration of rural White culture and values as somehow superior to those of almost every other group of Americans. Small-town people are reflexively praised and revered by politicians and pundits alike. These "heartland" folks living in the "flyover" states and counties are repeatedly lionized as the "real Americans," yet also pitied as people who are unfairly disrespected, mocked, or condescended to despite their supposedly representing all that is noble and good about the United States. Unfortunately, the mythic status conferred upon rural citizens—and rural Whites especially—provides them a wider berth to engage in democratically transgressive behaviors that violate some of the core tenets of any pluralist, free, fair, and functioning political-electoral system.

Media triggering of Whites

Finally, the fourth factor derives from the repeated ways in which rural leaders, Republican politicians, and their conservative media allies trigger the worst instincts and most deep-seated fears of rural White Americans. Daily on cable news and hourly on talk radio stations, rural White citizens are warned that they are under siege. They are constantly told that horrible people who live in and govern our cities—racial and religious minorities, feminists, homosexuals, White liberals, and Democrats in general—threaten the survival of the traditionalist, White, Christian values venerated by so many who reside in the rural White heartland. Politicians ranging from Donald Trump to J. D. Vance to Marjorie Taylor Greene love to blame nearly every problem—local, state, or national—on scary people living in faraway cities whose lives and values, we're told, are destroying a nation built by small-town, god-fearing, flag-waving citizens.

TAKEN TOGETHER, THESE FOUR factors compound in ways that increasingly cause rural White Americans to question their commitment to the American project. Rural White citizens who are suffering economically and facing major health crises may justifiably despair of the situation they and their communities face. Armed with outsize electoral and mythic powers, they can, in theory, call local, state, and national politicians to heel. Unfortunately, too often rural Whites are pacified by culture war trinkets sold cheaply to them by the very politicians they elected and who ought to be addressing in more substantive ways the economic and health-related maladies crippling so many small, sparsely populated towns and counties—thereby perpetuating the cycle of despair. Rural Whites' willingness to trade away a substantive agenda of local improvement in favor of nursing cultural grievances is puzzling.

Sadly, rural non-Whites face worse economic and health challenges than rural Whites—not that many pundits or politicians care or even bother to notice. Indeed, with the exception of opioid addiction and gun suicides, the problems rural Whites confront pale by comparison to those of the one-quarter of rural Americans who are non-White. But the sufferings of Blacks, Latinos, and especially Native Americans who live in rural areas go largely unmentioned and unaddressed because these groups are not part of the "essential minority."

Angered by their very real problems, seething from slights both real and perceived, and all the while wielding their outsize political power, rural Whites, manipulated by the selfish motives of skilled authoritarians like Trump and a growing legion of copycats, now pose a rising threat to the state and fate of American democracy. Indeed, precisely because of their exalted power and status, when rural White citizens begin to question the validity or utility of democratic norms and traditions, the constitutional pillars of American democracy begin to buckle. From doubting the legitimacy of elections to spouting conspiratorial beliefs about vaccines and secret pedophile rings, from justifying the January 6 domestic terrorist attacks to holding xenophobic attitudes toward citizens who may look, speak, or pray differently from them, the undemocratic and sometimes violent impulses emanating from the rural White corners of the United States threaten to undermine and perhaps end America's democratic experiment.

A FOURFOLD THREAT

When we make claims about the threats posed by disgruntled, empowered, triggered rural White citizens, we do not do so casually. Nor do we offer such claims by mere assertion or without substantiation: In fact, over the course of this book, we cite a multitude of publicly available polls and studies to support our dire warnings about the rising anti-democratic impulses emanating from rural White America.

These threats, these impulses, take four related and interconnected forms.

Racism, xenophobia, anti-urban disdain, and anti-immigrant sentiment

First, rural Whites are the demographic group least likely to accept notions of pluralism and inclusion in a United States currently experiencing rapid demographic change. Rural Whites are uniquely hostile toward racial and religious minorities, recent immigrants, and urban residents generally.

Rural Whites express heightened fears about the growing cultural influence of immigrants, minorities, feminists, LGBTQ+ Americans, and people who live in cities. Compared with urban and suburban dwellers, a far lower share of rural Americans believes greater diversity has made the United States stronger,[9] and a far higher share describes immigrants as a "burden on our country."[10] Only four in ten rural White Republicans say they value diversity in their communities—the lowest share of any subgroup.[11] Rural Americans are less likely to believe systemic racism and White privilege exist in the United States.[12] Rural White men in particular harbor strong "place-based" resentments toward Americans who live in other parts of the country.[13] Rural citizens are more likely than those who live in cities and suburbs to claim that Americans who live in other parts of the country do not understand the problems their communities face or share their values.[14]

Acceptance of conspiracies as facts

Second, rural Whites are the most conspiratorial cohort in the nation, and their refusal to accept basic facts or scientific knowledge prevents the nation from having rational, informed discourse on a variety of issues. Rural Whites exhibit the highest support for election denialism, anti-science Covid-19 and vaccine resistance, Obama birtherism conspiracies, and unhinged QAnon claims.

Specifically, rural Whites are most likely to believe the 2020 election was stolen from Donald Trump.[15] They are more skeptical of science generally and of the safety and lifesaving power of vaccines like the ones for Covid-19. They are most likely to agree with QAnon claims that the government is controlled by nefarious "deep state" agents, some of whom kidnap and molest children.[16] And rural citizens were most likely to believe that Barack Obama was not born in the United States and was therefore an illegitimate president.[17]

Undemocratic and anti-democratic beliefs

Third, polls and studies confirm that rural Whites express the lowest levels of support for long-standing and essential democratic principles. They are least likely to endorse the twin constitutional principles of separated powers and checks and balances between the branches of government; are least supportive of basic voting rights and ballot access; and routinely reject established governing principles like state-level authority and national supremacy.

Unfortunately, rural Americans are less likely to support a free press, more likely to embrace authoritarian figures and unchecked presidential power,[18] and more supportive of aggressive policing and anti-immigrant policies.[19] They express greater support for White nationalist and White Christian nationalist movements.[20] Rogue sheriffs elected in rural counties increasingly believe they can and should operate outside the bounds of state or national law.[21]

Justification of violence

Finally, no group of Americans boasts a higher degree of support for, or justification of, violence as an appropriate means of public expression and decision making. From their defense of the domestic terrorists who attacked the U.S. Capitol on January 6, 2021, to their calls for Trump to be restored to the White House by undemocratic means, rural Whites are more likely to excuse and even applaud the use of political violence.

Indeed, too often, rural citizens' anti-democratic sentiments shade into violent reflexes. Rural residents are more likely to favor violence over democratic deliberation to solve political disputes[22] and were most likely to call for Donald Trump to be reinstated as president after January 2021—by force, if necessary.[23] According to one poll, rural Whites are most likely to say that "true American patriots may have to resort to violence in order to save our country."[24] Rural Whites are also quicker to excuse or justify the January 6 domestic terrorist attack on the U.S. Capitol.[25]

TAKEN SEPARATELY, EACH OF these threats is serious. But together, they pose an even bigger danger because they are often interconnected and mutually reinforcing. Attitudes or behaviors of one type often lead to, or bleed into, others.

Consider, for example, a person who harbors fears, whether realized or latent, toward immigrants. That's an expression of the first threat. Surely that person is more susceptible to false, conspiratorial claims that immigrants cast illegal votes. From there, that person may begin to question the legitimacy of elections, back undemocratic efforts to restrict ballot access, and perhaps hector election board officials. At that point, it becomes much easier for that person to endorse efforts to threaten, intimidate, or even harm those officials.

None of these threats exists in isolation. And not unlike the four compounding factors, each of the four threats holds the potential to magnify some or all of the others. This catalytic connection is perhaps the most perilous effect, for as scholars of democracy warn, once democratic antipathies are set into motion and begin to gain momentum, they can reach a point where they are impossible to reverse.

Moreover, these four impulses have caused millions of rural Whites to embrace radical and revanchist ideas, including but not limited to White nationalist and Christian nationalist solutions that, at worst, could lead to violence (and, in some instances, already have). The fourfold threat rural Whites pose to American democracy is serious and growing.

THE STATE AND FATE OF
U.S. DEMOCRACY

Yes, rural America is struggling. Population decline, economic stagnation, and crippling health problems threaten the lives and livelihoods of people from the nation's small towns and sparsely populated counties. Large numbers of young people are leaving the rural hometowns where they were raised in search of new opportunities. This is the crisis happening in rural America, and the responsibility to fix it belongs to every citizen, regardless of race or place. Unfortunately, the crisis happening *in* rural White America is exacerbating the crisis emanating *from* it. Illiberal ideas and tendencies are not confined to rural areas, and of course millions of rural citizens revere the United States' democratic institutions and traditions. But the threats today to U.S. democracy have a distinctly rural tint. Exacerbated by the economic and healthcare problems wreaking havoc across the heartland, rural resentment has become a civic and constitutional powder keg. Thanks to their twinned powers—their mathematically inflated electoral power and the mythology-based political deference they enjoy—rural White citizens are equipped to undermine our constitutional democracy, or at least wreak serious havoc on long-standing and widely accepted democratic norms and traditions.

It helps nobody, rural or otherwise, that Republican politicians—including but not limited to those who represent rural counties, districts, and states—routinely stoke rural White resentments to serve their own selfish agendas. In pursuit of votes, campaign contributions, media attention, and re-election, these politicians willfully exacerbate rural resentments. The sad fact is that their manipulative and destructive behaviors work, exempting rural politicians from developing and implementing policies to cure what ails rural communities. Politically, it's much easier and far more effective for these politicians to use culture war triggers to frighten and anger their rural electorate into supporting them than it would be to actually earn their votes and trust by improving their constituents' everyday lives.

Rarely mentioned after the 2020 presidential election is that, in defeat, Donald Trump lost ground with almost every demographic subgroup since his 2016 election victory except rural Whites, among whom his support grew during the intervening four years. Trump's rural-based, authoritarian challenge to the constitutional order is nothing less than an existential threat to the state and fate of American democracy.

Yet, until now—and despite ample public evidence documenting

how rural White citizens' rising antipathy threatens American governance and our pluralist society—few if any political observers have dared
to identify or warn the nation about the impending danger posed by the
"essential" rural White minority. If the survival of the American political
system matters, the collective silence of these politicians and pundits—
their near-universal reluctance if not refusal to identify this existential
threat by name—can no longer be abided.

CHAPTER

2

RURAL RUIN

—

I N UPSTATE NEW YORK, WILMINGTON'S ROY HOLZER AND WILLSBORO'S
Shaun Gillilland are archetypal rural town supervisors. Their offices in
Essex County are understated and devoid of the sort of "glory wall"
photos of them posing with notable state or national politicians that
many elected officials favor. Supervisor is a mostly thankless job on the
front lines of local governance: You maintain public services, fight for
scarce revenue, and solve local political disputes. Most of your constituents are first-name-basis neighbors, and some have known you since you
were a kid. When you show up for work at the town hall, it's best to
check your ego at the door.

Wilmington and Willsboro are two of eighteen townships in Essex
County. Twelve miles east of Lake Placid, Wilmington is nestled in the
shadow of Whiteface Mountain, the downhill skiing venue for the 1932
and 1980 Winter Olympics and a perennial attraction for winter skiers
and summer hikers. On the eastern side of the county, perched on the
idyllic shores of Lake Champlain, Willsboro's marinas and lakefront
launches are popular havens for recreational boaters and fishing enthusiasts.

Essex is a swing county in presidential politics: In fact, it is one of
only eight U.S. counties carried by every presidential winner during the
past seven consecutive election cycles, from Bill Clinton's re-election
victory in 1996 through Joe Biden's 2020 win. (Only three counties cur-

rently have longer active streaks.[1]) Holzer and Gillilland are Republicans who support U.S. representative Elise Stefanik and President Donald Trump. But neither is an ideological firebrand. Management and policy, not divisive partisanship, animate their daily routines. "Wilmington's the kind of town a lot of people are longing for, especially now, the way our country is," Holzer says proudly, noting that his town features a cordial mix of Republicans, Democrats, and independents. "You can still go to a local coffee shop and have a disagreement with somebody and then spend the day fishing with them. In the end, if you are having a personal problem, people are going to come to your aid. That's what's so great about living up here in Wilmington."[2]

Born-and-bred locals, Holzer and Gillilland have deep familial roots within their respective towns. Holzer's great-great-great-great-grandfather was town supervisor in the 1800s. By age eighteen, Holzer had started a local newspaper and won election to the Wilmington town board. He and his wife owned and operated a small grocery for twenty-two years, which they recently sold to Holzer's nephew rather than to a corporate chain. Gillilland's roots run even deeper. The Gillillands still own a farm on a road bearing the family name, and Shaun's ancestors literally settled the town: The "Will" from which "Willsboro" is derived is from its first European settler, William Gilliland (his name spelled with one fewer *l*), who arrived in 1765. His portrait adorns the town hall's main room, site of local court hearings and town council meetings.

Emergency services are a concern for Holzer and Gillilland, but their situations differ somewhat because of their two towns' proximity to vital healthcare services. In October 2022, Adirondack Health announced that it wanted to close its Lake Placid Memorial Hospital emergency room, which had already scaled back to half-day operations. Holzer was understandably panicked about what this decision would mean for his constituents. "I've been leading the charge on this because it really pisses me off," he said. Holzer rejects Adirondack Health's claims that the ER is losing money. He even cornered New York State governor Kathy Hochul, two months before we sat with him, when she visited Lake Placid to attend the University Games. As a former EMT, Holzer knows that if LPMH closes its emergency room, ambulances and the

area's residents will be forced to drive either forty minutes west, to Saranac Lake; thirty minutes southeast, to Elizabethtown, home to a Champlain Valley Physicians Hospital satellite facility; or nearly an hour to
reach CVPH's regional hospital complex in Plattsburgh, in neighboring
Clinton County. Gillilland's constituents in Willsboro, by contrast, are
fortunate to live closer to the Elizabethtown and Plattsburgh facilities.
(CVPH is not even a New York chain; it's owned and operated by the
University of Vermont system, based in Burlington, across Lake Champlain.)

However close their constituents live to the nearest hospital, both
Holzer and Gillilland are dealing with the problem of retaining qualified
emergency services personnel. The two towns have long relied upon
volunteers, but the number of volunteers is shrinking and aging out.
"You can't have a bunch of seventy-five-year-olds doing it," Gillilland
said with a shrug. But Essex County simply cannot afford the millions it
would take to hire an all-professional, full-time EMT staff. So it applied
for and won a six-million-dollar grant from New York State to implement a transitional pilot program, focused initially on four of the county's eighteen towns. (Wilmington is one of the four; Willsboro is not.)
When money from that short-term grant expires, Essex will implement
a shared-funding model wherein the county will cover the cost of emergency medical technicians' benefits (pension contributions, healthcare
premiums), but each of Essex County's towns will cover the hourly
wages of the EMTs when they work in their town. "It's a helluva lot
cheaper than hiring a full-time employee," Gillilland explained.

Rural leaders across the United States grapple with many of the same
problems that Supervisors Roy Holzer and Shaun Gillilland do—from
finding creative fiscal solutions to maintaining quality facilities and services. More than half of rural hospitals nationwide currently operate in
the red, and hundreds more have closed entirely. A single emergency
room closure, or the inability of ambulatory services to quickly retrieve
and deliver citizens to an ER, can have life-or-death consequences. Even
in rural places blessed with assets other rural towns envy (like Wilmington and Willsboro), battling public and private entities to maintain vital
services is commonplace.

Think tanks, advocacy groups, and government agencies have issued countless reports on the devastation of rural America. Many of these studies pre-date Donald Trump's presidential bid, which itself occasioned a new round of attention to rural crises from public officials and the media. A variety of painful and sometimes lethal socioeconomic problems now confronts the nation's small towns and counties: shrinking populations, economic distress, crumbling infrastructure, and an epidemic of "deaths of despair" from gun suicides and opioid overdoses.

In this chapter, we chronicle the problems confronting contemporary rural America. The economic and health-related struggles that rural Americans face matter directly but also indirectly, because the decline of so many rural communities has caused many rural Whites to question whether the U.S. political system properly and sufficiently serves them.

STAGNANT POPULATIONS

Let's begin with population decline. The population in rural areas is either shrinking or growing at a far slower rate than that of the rest of the nation. At just 7.4 percent, population growth in the United States during the 2010s was the slowest of any decade since the 1930s. But growth was not uniform: Urban and suburban areas gained a net of 21 million people, while rural areas shrank by 226,000 people.[3] The five states with the largest declines in nonmetropolitan populations during the 2010s were, in descending order, West Virginia, Illinois, Louisiana, Arkansas, and Pennsylvania.[4]

Between 2010 and 2020, more than half of all U.S. counties, 53 percent, lost population. Because 81 percent of metro areas grew during that period, most of the shrinking counties were rural. In fact, two-thirds of rural counties—1,326 in all—lost population over the last decade.[5] Most of these population losses occurred in "persistently poor" rural counties that the U.S. Department of Agriculture classifies as having at least 20 percent of residents living persistently below the national poverty level since 1980.

Six decades ago, the term *white flight* entered the American political

lexicon. In response to racial integration, urban Whites fled to the suburbs in search of more land, bigger houses, and lower taxes, and to re-
create the urban White communities that existed before the Great
Migration brought millions of African Americans northward. Today,
white flight takes a new form and direction: Hundreds of thousands of
rural Whites are relocating to more diverse and densely populated suburbs and cities. In fact, 42 percent of rural residents report knowing
somebody who has recently moved away from their community.[6]

Young Americans are abandoning rural areas, draining rural America of its most precious asset: its future. In 2010, sociologists Patrick Carr
and Maria Kefalas published *Hollowing Out the Middle: The Rural
Brain Drain and What It Means for America.* They interviewed hundreds of people in a small, rural Iowa town and found that rural parents
and schoolteachers invest unusual resources in their most promising
teenagers, the ones most likely to get into good colleges and never return
home. "Fueling the out-migration is a regional filtering system pushing
some young people to stay and others to go," Carr and Kefalas concluded. "Teachers, parents, and other influential adults cherry-pick the
young people destined to leave and ignore the ones most likely to stay or
return."[7]

A national survey conducted by the University of New Hampshire in
2018 revealed that 61 percent of nonmetro adult respondents said they
would "advise teens to move away." Only 40 percent of metro adults say
the same.[8] Nobody can blame self-interested parents and teachers for
urging their best and brightest youngsters to seek more promising fu-
tures, even if that means exporting rural America's best human resources
to cities. "When one considers the blighted and aging nature of many
American towns, it's obvious that there are no easy solutions ahead,"
writes Gracy Olmstead, an Idaho journalist and author of *Uprooted: Recovering the Legacy of the Places We Left Behind.* "But one thing is certain: Unless we can begin convincing some of these young people to stay,
to move in, or to move back, we won't get the chance to find those solutions."[9]

We heard similar stories during our travels. Mila Besich shared her
experience as a high school senior in Superior, Arizona, the small,

majority-Latino rural city in the state's so-called Copper Corridor region, over which she now presides as the city's mayor. "If you would have come to Superior a decade ago, everything was boarded up. When I graduated from high school, this town was blighted. It was in decay," Besich told us. "My high school guidance counselor was like, 'BHP [one of the mining companies that operates in the area] is shutting everything down. There's not going to be any mining going on here at all. You guys are the top of your class. Get the hell out of here. We'll get you as many scholarships as we can. There's not going to be anything for you here.'"[10]

A few hundred miles northeast, in Arizona's Apache County, on Election Day 2022, Navajo Nation Council candidate Shawna Ann Claw talked to us while greeting voters on their way to cast ballots at her local polling place in Chinle. When we asked if brain drain was a problem on the reservation, she said, "Yes, it is. And I speak personally because I have a son and a daughter, and they both reside off the reservation." Her son is in the U.S. Air Force, and her daughter lives in Phoenix. "She wants to open a business. She's going to school for cosmetology. She sees the service industry is something that we don't have here on the Navajo Nation [Reservation]. We don't have a salon, we don't have a barbershop."

But Claw is sure her kids will return. "I really feel like they are rooted," she said wistfully. "I have no doubt they're going to return. And when my son returns, he's going to just take my place here as a leader and guide his people. That's how much faith I have. Because I was raised in a traditional way by my grandmother and my grandfather in a dirt floor hogan [a traditional Navajo log-and-mud dwelling]. So that commitment to service, to community, and family is very important for us."[11] Claw won her election from the Chinle Chapter and now holds one of twenty-four seats on the Navajo Council.[12]

In Malone, a small city of about fifteen thousand people in Franklin County, New York, we asked town supervisor Andrea Stewart about the four kids she and her husband raised together. None still resides in the area, she told us.[13] The common thread connecting the stories from Besich, Claw, and Stewart is that they are middle-class, educated local leaders. The children of less fortunate rural parents may also leave home, but surely they are less likely to have the encouragement and resources to do so.

Covid-19 caused enough Americans to rethink their living arrangements that demographers wondered if the pandemic might trigger a rural revitalization. Reporters filed stories about affluent retirees and remote-work professionals trading expensive urban condos for bucolic rural homes. But the effects of these new arrivals have been mixed. On the one hand, residential and commercial property sales raise values for existing homeowners and businesses, creating windfalls for local real estate agents, builders, and retailers. On the other hand, new arrivals rarely bring children to fill the empty seats of rural classrooms.

The same story repeats itself across the country: However much affection rural people have for their homes, they doubt that young people can build a prosperous future if they don't leave. Across the United States, rural population declines have forced many communities to close and consolidate their school districts. But school consolidation is uniquely complicated for rural parents and communities for one simple reason: Their school-age kids live farther apart from one another than do students in more densely populated suburban and urban areas. Rural school consolidation thus forces students from closed facilities to travel long distances.

Upon becoming West Virginia's new governor in January 2005, conservative Democrat Joe Manchin—who grew up in Farmington, a town of about eight hundred people when Manchin was a boy—immediately established guidelines to protect rural students from spending too much time on school buses. Manchin's rules restricted the one-way bus commutes for elementary school children to no more than thirty minutes, forty-five minutes for middle-schoolers, and an hour for high school students.[14]

West Virginia's Mingo County had no choice but to consolidate. Like so many rural counties, Mingo lost population over each of the past seven decades. Today, its roughly 23,000 residents represent half the number who lived there in 1950, when the county reached its peak population. (By comparison, the national population has more than doubled since 1950.) With plenty of empty seats in each of the county's four high schools, the costs of staffing and maintaining all four facilities became too burdensome, and in 2014, Mingo County consolidated its high schools in Burch, Gilbert, Matewan, and Williamson, the county seat, into one. The new Mingo Central High School, formed from remnants of the four shuttered high schools, was constructed on a reclaimed surface mining site in Newtown. A town built on coal built its new high school atop a former coal mine.

To stem the tide of shrinking populations, rural leaders are getting creative. At least fifty rural communities across the United States have enacted programs designed to lure new residents with a mix of tax credits, housing subsidies, and other relocation incentives.[15] The West Virginia Legislature is considering a bill that would provide up to $25,000 in tax credits to former residents willing to move back to the Mountaineer State.[16] During the height of the pandemic, these efforts seemed to have an effect, if only temporarily: In 2021, rural areas made slight population gains of 0.13 percent—a small bump, but better than continued decline.[17]

For most of the two-thirds of rural counties that have lost population since 2010, declines have been modest, typically under 3 percent. Majority-Black rural towns and counties have experienced above-average population losses.[18] Still, except for select communities blessed with outdoor and recreational attractions, or a sudden economic boom caused by oil or fracking discoveries, most rural towns and counties are slowly but steadily losing residents as the rest of America continues to grow.

ECONOMIC DECAY

What are rural Americans who abandon their hometowns leaving behind? The short answer is economic contraction and decay defined by declining wages, rising unemployment, persistent poverty, and increased government dependency.

Almost all rural problems are rooted in struggling local economies. Industries like farming and mining have suffered from a variety of assaults, both domestic and foreign, including but not limited to greater competition from global markets, corporate consolidation, the rising power of giant agribusiness, and a dramatic shift in the U.S. economy toward the healthcare, education, and service sector industries. Stagnant rural populations compound rural economic travails: More than a third of owners of rural small businesses say they cannot find enough qualified local employees.[19]

In the two years following the 2008 Great Recession, unemployment surged across the United States, but during the 2010s, metro-area jobs eventually returned to pre-crisis levels. Nonmetro areas, however, never fully rebounded: Counties with populations of 100,000 people or fewer lost a net 175,000 jobs after 2008. Shockingly, there are fewer rural businesses today than there were before the recession began a decade and a half ago. Economic mobility in the United States is now lowest in the rural counties of the South and Midwest.[20] This failure of rural areas to rebound post-recession contrasts sharply with the years 1992–96, when one-third of new small businesses formed after the 1991 recession opened in small counties.[21]

Globalization certainly contributed to the collapse of rural economies. Politicians ranging from Republican president Donald Trump to former Ohio Democratic congressman Tim Ryan routinely blame emerging economies like China for stealing blue-collar American jobs that once paid well and included decent benefits. But for decades, Republicans promised that if workers surrendered their labor union advantages—better wages, healthcare coverage, and retirement benefits—U.S. companies would be able to compete. This was a lie: Union membership plunged over the past forty years, yet millions of industrial jobs vanished anyway.

These job losses have not dissuaded rural constituents from voting every two years to re-elect politicians promoting "right-to-work" laws that make it harder for unions to organize, even as those rural constituents struggle to survive on the meager wages and health benefits their nonunion jobs provide. It's not because people are opposed to unions: In the summer of 2022, Gallup reported that support for unions had risen to 71 percent, the highest level since 1965.[22] Yet Republican state legislators or members of Congress from rural, overwhelmingly White communities who support unions, a living wage, or universal healthcare are rare. Their opposition to paid sick leave is a perfect example of how rural voters elect politicians who vote against their material interests. "While a growing number of states, cities, and counties have passed paid sick leave or general paid time off laws in recent years, most states where more than 20% of the population is rural haven't, leaving workers vulnerable," reports Jazmin Orozco Rodriguez of *Kaiser Health News.* "Vermont and New Mexico are the only states with a sizable rural population that have passed laws requiring some form of paid sick leave."[23]

Didn't bad trade deals negotiated by the federal government destroy rural America's agricultural economy? That's the narrative peddled by self-styled economic nationalists like Steve Bannon, who repeatedly blame the North American Free Trade Agreement and other trade deals for the existential crisis facing rural America. In almost every 2016 campaign speech, Donald Trump called NAFTA the worst trade agreement the United States ever negotiated. As president, he enacted new tariffs.

NAFTA, however, cannot be blamed for the steep drop in U.S. crop prices in the postwar period. Although crop prices rose 41 percent between 1945 and 1970, in relative terms, they shrank compared to the 116 percent increase in the price of consumer goods over that same period.[24] The next two decades were worse: Between 1970 and 1990, the inflation-adjusted prices for wheat, soybeans, and corn cratered by two-thirds or more.[25] Ratified by the United States, Canada, and Mexico in 1994, NAFTA obviously did not cause the steep plunge in agriculture prices during the five decades *before* it took effect.[26]

Corporate consolidation at home exacerbates market pressures from abroad. Supposedly free-market politicians rarely admit that monopolies and oligopolies transformed the agricultural economy, making the family farm an endangered species. In 2018, the four largest meatpacking firms controlled 85 percent of the beef market. The four largest hog processors accounted for 70 percent of the pork market. Likewise, four firms held 85 percent of the market in corn seeds.[27] In the United States, the number of large farms—those of one thousand acres or larger—

doubled between 1978 and 2017.[28] In 1940, 53 percent of rural Americans lived on farms, but now only 6 percent do.[29]

The uncomfortable truth is that small family farms that once fed the nation and enriched local farmers were gobbled up by ConAgra, not China. To cite one notably sad example, 44 percent of small dairy farms in Vermont—a state that rivals Wisconsin in its cheese and dairy product production—have shut down just since 2012.[30] Frustration is growing: In 2023, fifty activists met at the Rural Policy Action Summit in Omaha, Nebraska, to develop strategies to protect family farmers from agribusiness monopolies.[31] Rural folks are gradually realizing that corporate consolidation, not socialism, is destroying their local economies.

Peanut farming in the Albemarle region of Eastern North Carolina typifies the transformation of rural agriculture. Northampton County is home to lumber companies Georgia-Pacific and Clary, plus a Lowe's Home Improvement distribution warehouse. But the county—which not long ago led North Carolina in peanut production and ranked thirteenth nationally—has long depended upon peanut farming and still ranks fifth in the state in peanut production.[32] In operation since 1945, Aunt Ruby's Peanuts is the oldest retail business in Enfield, a small town with mostly boarded-up storefronts in neighboring majority-Black, rural Halifax County. Bob Allsbrook, the founder Ruby Allsbrook's son, told us that like so many other agricultural commodities, peanut farming has become increasingly consolidated: Aunt Ruby's now sources its peanuts from a smaller number of larger operations than it used to. "Small farmers, family farms, is a thing of the past," Allsbrook lamented.[33]

The rise of large agribusiness farming has also transformed rural partisanship. In their analysis of Great Plains farming, political scientists Aditya Dasgupta and Elena Ruiz Ramirez conclude that technological changes (especially center-pivot irrigation systems) accelerated the conversion of postwar Democratic-leaning rural communities into the Republican strongholds they are today. How? As Dasgupta and Ramirez explain, agribusiness lobbyists pushed legislators to link federal farm subsidies to *total* output, with large farms favored over family farmers. "Large-scale farms and agribusinesses have also sought over time to reshape the farm subsidy system, seeking to delink subsidies from production controls—the lynchpin of the New Deal–era farm policies—in favor of a 'market-oriented' regime linking subsidies to the quantity of a farm's output, concentrating subsidies in the largest farms," they conclude. Big Ag consolidated land and rural power by forging alliances with local and state Farm Bureau chapters to build a Republican coalition that wields power exceeding its numbers.[34]

Environmental historian Curt Meine agrees. Rather than drive small farmers into the arms of the Democratic Party, Meine contends that Big Ag destroyed family farmers and empowered Republicans by exacerbating rural antagonisms. "Concentration fed and fueled the politics of resentment, entrenched corporate power, depopulated the landscape, and weakened the autonomy and agency of farmers, consumers, local governments, and communities," Meine said in *The New Yorker*. "I think this is at the very heart of the rural-urban political divide." According to a 2020 Family Farm Action poll, a stunning 81 percent of rural Americans would be more likely to support a candidate who believed that "a handful of corporate monopolies now run our entire food system" and who would impose "a moratorium on factory farms and corporate monopolies in food and agriculture."[35] Yet rural White voters continue to elect corporate-friendly Republican politicians. The glaring disconnect between the economic realities that farmers openly concede and their electoral behavior is perhaps the most puzzling feature of contemporary rural politics.

During his first term, President Barack Obama and his agriculture secretary, Tom Vilsack, pushed for major changes to the 1921 Packers and Stockyards Act, a law originally passed to protect small farmers and prevent agricultural consolidation. Beginning with the Reagan administration, conservative judges devoted to the Chicago School's free-market theories had steadily destroyed the act's antitrust protections. By the time of George W. Bush's presidency, the federal agency tasked with enforcing antitrust regulations was "deliberately suppressing investigations and blocking penalties on companies violating the law," reported Lina Khan in her investigation of how Big Ag got so big. (Khan was later appointed by Joe Biden to chair the Federal Trade Commission, where she became a regular target of Republican attacks for her efforts to push back on corporate consolidation.) When Obama and Vilsack in 2010 demanded that Congress revive the law's antitrust protections, a bipartisan group of members—most with close ties to Big Ag trade associations like the National Cattlemen's Beef Association, National Chicken Council, and National Meat Association—watered down the Obama administration's attempts to limit the degree to which commodity markets could consolidate, an effort that might have leveled the playing field for small farmers.[36]

In her study of rural resentment in Wisconsin, political scientist Katherine Cramer met local farmers who had been devastated by agribusiness domination and the predatory corporate practices crushing family farms. But Cramer found that these farmers were far angrier with urbanites, liberals, and Democrats than they were with conservative Republicans who raised gobs of Big Ag campaign cash rather than raise policy objections to consolidation.[37]

Natural resource extraction, a core component of many rural economies, is also in decline. In 1985, there were 178,000 coal mining jobs in America.[38] But the industry fell into steep decline—not, as Republicans told people, because of environmental regulations, but mostly due to automation and competition from natural gas and, eventually, renewables that are cleaner and cheaper than coal. What were people from rural coal states like Wyoming, West Virginia, and Pennsylvania left with? Fewer jobs, their previously beautiful landscapes scarred by mountaintop removal, and a bunch of empty promises.

Still, voters wanted politicians to keep lying to them about a coal revival that was always just the next "red wave" election away. In the 2016 presidential election, Hillary Clinton risked her candidacy when she told a CNN town hall that "we're going to put a lot of coal miners and coal companies out of business." Folks in coal country took this as proof that Clinton was hostile to them and their interests. Her quote was repeated endlessly to show what an out-of-touch elitist she was. But few people heard and fewer remember the rest of what she said: "And we're going to make it clear that we don't want to forget those people. Those people labored in those mines for generations, losing their health, often losing their lives to turn on our lights and power our factories. Now we've got to move away from coal and all the other fossil fuels, but I don't want to move away from the people who did the best they could to produce the energy that we relied on."[39]

Contrast Clinton, and her candor, with Donald Trump, who went to West Virginia, put on a hard hat, and told the easiest of campaign lies: "For those miners, get ready because you're going to be working your asses off," he told a cheering crowd.[40] But Trump didn't revive the coal industry. In fact, he failed to stop its continuing decline. Only 50,000 coal jobs remained in the United States when he took office, and by the time his term ended, that number had fallen to 38,000—a 25 percent decline during his four years in office.[41]

Did voters in coal country punish Trump for letting them down? No. In 2016, the two biggest coal-producing states, Wyoming and West Virginia, voted more heavily for him than any other state: They favored him by margins of 46 and 42 points, respectively. Four years later, they voted for him by margins of 43 and 39 points, that small decline mirroring exactly the three-point drop between 2016 and 2020 in the margins by which Trump lost the national popular vote.

For all that environmentalists have warned about the climate change effects of burning coal, in the end, coal's demise is being driven by free-market capitalism more than anything else. And true to form, capitalism doesn't care what it leaves behind when it departs; that's the problem coal country faces. Given domestic and global market forces, Trump cannot be blamed for the continuing decline of coal or other U.S. mining sectors. It is fair, however, to blame him for making outlandish promises that neither he nor any other president could deliver.

What's ironic about the transformation of rural economies is that most locals grasp the hard realities. In a 2017 survey conducted by *The Washington Post* and the Kaiser Family Foundation, rural voters who said their communities had not recovered from recent job losses were asked if they thought it would be better to bring back "the same types of jobs" recently lost or to "create jobs in new industries." By a two-to-one margin, 61 percent to 30 percent, rural residents advocated for creating jobs in new employment sectors.[42] In other words, a solid majority of rural citizens agrees with the economic solution that Hillary Clinton, not Donald Trump, promised those beleaguered West Virginia coal miners in 2016. Confirming what rural voters already knew to be true did not, however, help Clinton come Election Day.

University of Oregon historian Steven Beda explains that the steady conversion of extraction-based rural jobs into service sector employment wreaks more than economic havoc on rural communities. Transitioning, struggling rural economies also experience a "Walmart effect" that destroys the core identity upon which many rural communities were built. "The identity of rural communities used to be rooted in work. The signs at the entrances of their towns welcomed visitors to coal country or timber country. Towns named their high school mascots after the work that sustained them, like the Jordan Beetpickers [sic] in Utah or the Camas Papermakers in Washington," writes Beda. "How do you communicate your communal identity when the work once at the center of that identity is gone, and calling the local high school football team the 'Walmart Greeters' simply doesn't have the same ring to it?"[43] Tectonic economic forces are decimating rural economies, but economic decline is having an even more nefarious impact: It is erasing rural identities.

PROXIMITY IS PROSPERITY

Family farming and extractive resource economies in rural America are cratering, but one rural business sector is booming: discount retailers like Family Dollar and Dollar General, which sell off-brand goods at rock-bottom prices. Discount retailers pop up where economies turn down, so their arrival is no sign of revival. Quite the opposite, in fact. "They serve a part of the country that Walmart doesn't serve directly," Al Cross, director of the University of Kentucky's Institute for Rural Journalism, told NPR. "You have to maybe drive twenty miles to get to a Walmart. You might only have to drive five miles to get to a Dollar General."[44]

You can see the discount economy when you traverse the rural, majority-Black counties of North Carolina's Albemarle region. Scattered across Bertie, Edgecombe, Halifax, and Northampton counties are more Family Dollar and Dollar General stores than you can count. Of course, with so many of the main street storefronts shuttered in rural small towns like Enfield, Rich Square, Tarboro, and Windsor, the wares once peddled by local merchants must now be purchased from the same retail chains whose predatory business practices drove the mom-and-pop stores out of town in the first place.

Dollar stores make life for cash-strapped rural consumers a bit more affordable and convenient. But because they drive out local businesses, discount retailers cripple rural economies in two related ways. First, when mom-and-pop stores shutter, profits shift from local business owners to distant corporations. Second, dollar stores create so-called food deserts, where fresh fruits, vegetables, and meats are replaced with processed foods, in places where obesity and diabetes are common. And the share of rural Americans living within ten miles of a store selling fresh produce is dwindling.[45] One study found that citizens from rural and low-income areas spend more than 5 percent of their food budgets at dollar stores—nearly 12 percent for rural Black households.[46] Obesity rates in rural counties are one-sixth higher than in metropolitan areas.[47]

Living near a discount retailer may be convenient, but it is often a sign of economic peril. The retailers all pay very low wages; in 2023, the U.S. Department of Labor singled out Dollar General as a "serial violator" of labor laws that protect workers.[48] And of course, these chains react to the barest whiff of union organizing at one of their stores with all the fury of a nineteenth-century mining company.[49] Hoping to keep local businesses from folding, a growing number of rural officials has joined forces to try to prevent dollar stores from opening in their communities.[50] In rural Ebony, Virginia, a coalition of White and Black residents is fighting its town board's narrow 3–2 vote to approve a new Dollar General franchise in its town that opponents say will destroy locally owned proprietors and blight the bucolic landscape.[51]

Distance, not discounts, is even more critical to rural prosperity. Why? Because the closer and more connected a rural county is to a medium-size or large metro area, the better it performs across a range of measures, from educational attainment to high-wage jobs. For rural

Americans, proximity to more thriving small cities or large urban areas
is prosperity.

At the Bozeman, Montana–based think tank Headwaters Economics,
researchers in 2009 compared the prosperity of rural communities in
the western states with their proximity to metropolitan areas. They
found that "isolated" rural counties without airport access lag behind
"connected" rural counties that either are a shorter drive from city markets or can ship goods via local airports to those markets. "The ability of
a community to create or retain jobs in manufacturing or service and
professional industries is limited by distance and access to markets,"
their report concluded. "These sectors are therefore least likely to be
found in isolated counties, more likely to be in counties that are connected via airports, and most likely to exist in [rural areas within] metropolitan counties."[52]

Distance from their workplaces also matters to rural commuters. As
rural industries shutter, residents are forced to commute longer distances for work. Some federal programs support rural transportation,
but commuting requires most rural workers either to own or to have
access to a car. Rural workers are uniquely dependent on their automobiles, explains Strong Towns reporter Aubrey Byron. "The pivotal
question on job applications, 'Do you have reliable means of transportation?' may be one you overlook, but if you're without a car in the country, the answer is a resounding, disqualifying 'No,'" Byron writes.
"Whether because of finance or circumstance, the situation of not having or being able to drive a car becomes a constant need to beg rides
from friends and loved ones, many of whom have their own sizable commutes to attend to."[53]

Not surprisingly, rural Americans endure longer average daily commutes and spend more on automobiles, a higher share of which are used
cars that may need more frequent repairs.[54] Rural drivers inclined to
save both the environment and gas money by purchasing electric vehicles are also hamstrung by the fact that large, sparsely populated states
struggle to provide sufficient EV charging stations. Indeed, Upper Midwest and Plains states feature the fewest electric vehicles.[55]

It's important to understand that most people wouldn't trade their rural lifestyles away. Bucolic rural spaces offer incomparable charms. Far from light-polluted cities, rural residents can gaze at the stars overhead on cloudless nights. Many pastoral areas are otherwise so quiet that symphonies of chirping crickets count as noise pollution. But peace and quiet can also be liabilities for rural citizens, who are more likely to suffer the detrimental effects of social isolation. That is, distance from one's friends and neighbors matters too, because being too distant can be isolating. That isolation leads not only to loneliness but also to physical risks like higher rates of stroke and heart disease. For rural seniors, especially those who are immobile, social isolation can be debilitating: Roughly three in ten rural seniors report that most days, they do not see a single friend or family member. "One of the greatest strengths of rural America has always been the sense of community, but when that breaks, it breaks bad," Alan Morgan, president of the National Rural Health Association, argues. "In an urban setting, you might have social services to fall back on, but that's nonexistent in rural [areas]."[56]

Distance to recreational attractions also matters because proximity to tourist-friendly outdoor areas can mitigate the economic challenges of the post-industrial and post-extraction U.S. economy, but only for those communities fortunate enough to be close to those attractions. The Adirondacks of Upstate New York and the rugged hills of Southern West Virginia are perfect examples of how the blessings of recreational resources give certain rural communities the opportunity to capitalize on their natural resource advantages.

Site of the "Miracle on Ice" U.S. men's hockey title team in 1980, the Lake Placid region is blessed with stunning mountains and lakes that would draw hikers, skiers, and cyclists even if this quaint Adirondack town had not hosted the 1932 and 1980 Winter Olympic Games. But the Olympic facilities there—hockey rinks, ski jumps, toboggan and luge tracks—can be an added draw for both tourists and world-class competitors only if they are maintained. To that end, in recent years New York State has appropriated more than $500 million for the Olympic Regional Development Authority to upgrade these facilities. In nearby Saranac Lake, the state also spent $8.5 million in 2022 to upgrade the

Adirondack Regional Airport (SLK) and nearly $7 million to upgrade the local civic center, including its new curling facility.[57]

SLK airport is located in the township of Harrietstown, New York. Town supervisor Jordanna Mallach explained to us how SLK serves as an economic driver. The state-funded upgrades created short-term construction jobs directly and ongoing income indirectly for workers who staff the airport's new café. Cape Air offers regular round-trip service from SLK to Boston and New York City. These routes are heavily subsidized by the federal government's Essential Air Service program, making these flights more affordable for locals. But SLK also serves wealthy visitors who arrive via private charters or personal jets to gain quick access to lavish Adirondack vacation homes or exclusive resorts like Lake Placid Lodge or the Point, on Upper Saranac Lake. For local residents to reap the economic benefits of the natural environment, they need extensive involvement—and lots of money—from the state and federal governments.

Like Mallach, Willsboro's Shaun Gillilland and Wilmington's Roy Holzer benefit from the revenues that short-term visitors and owners of second homes bring to the Adirondacks. But seasonal residents often complicate local governance for these understaffed town supervisors. For example, visitors increasingly use Airbnb or other short-term rental platforms to book rooms and houses (rather than traditional, business-zoned hotels and motels) in many Adirondack residential areas. The towns and counties benefit from taxes levied on these short-term rentals, but renters sometimes create noise and generate nuisance complaints or fail to observe garbage and recycling policies. Tensions between the locals who reap the rental income and their neighbors who deal with the consequences inevitably ensue.

Gillilland and Holzer told us they are working to find ways to balance these trade-offs. For example, Holzer is developing a plan to cordon off a section of town where short-term rentals would be banned. Gillilland has similar issues to manage in Willsboro, a town of 1,900 year-round residents whose population swells to more than 5,000 during summers. Because the Willsboro Point peninsula juts out into Lake

Champlain, Willsboro is blessed with more lakefront property than other lakeside municipalities. "Therefore, we generate a lot of building permits for residential second homes," Gillilland says, noting that buyers hail not only from nearby northeastern states but also from as far away as Texas, California, and even France.[58]

In Southern West Virginia, local governments and entrepreneurs are taking advantage of the rugged mountain terrain to lure off-road vehicle enthusiasts. Hatfield-McCoy Trails is a network of more than nine hundred miles of trails for use by all-terrain vehicles (ATVs), larger utility terrain vehicles (UTVs), off-road jeeps, and motorcycles. Trails are open sunrise to sunset every day of the year, and riders must have permits and adhere to strict safety standards, including mandated safety equipment for vehicles, drivers, and passengers.

The trail system has quickly emerged as a significant cottage industry that generates income for local merchants in lodging rentals, food and beverage receipts, and equipment sales. According to a report prepared by Marshall University for the Hatfield-McCoy Regional Recreation Authority, those economic impacts are substantial. Although many locals in West Virginia and border counties in Kentucky and Virginia use the trails, the annual report estimates that nonlocals spend an average of $535 more during their visits, generating $53.4 million in 2021 for the fourteen West Virginia counties (including the five that contain trail segments) that benefit from tourist spending.[59]

Devil's Backbone Adventure Resort in Matewan, Mingo County, is a perfect example of how off-road trail riders are infusing needed capital into Southern West Virginia. Perched on a hill at the entrance to Devil Anse Trail 59, the resort, which opened in 2019, was named in honor of Devil Anse Hatfield, patriarch of the family that waged war against its rivals, the McCoys. The sprawling facility offers modern cabins to rent, a great restaurant, and an outdoor swimming pool. The parking spots arrayed around the Tipple Tavern are reserved for ATVs and UTVs, and although we had to park our car elsewhere nearby, the food was worth the walk. The facility has a mini-mart that sells trail permits and maps, snacks, beverages including wine and beer, firewood, ice, and other supplies. We stopped in after dinner to grab a couple of ice-cream novelties and examined the pin-filled map showing visitors' hometowns. Though it was not a scientific sample, we saw that an impressive number of Ohioans come to Matewan to ride the trails.

But the development around the Hatfield-McCoy Trails shows the challenges of creating a recreation-based revitalization. As we've seen in other places hoping to develop recreational resources, this attraction required investment from both the federal and state governments—in this case, to clean and update the trails. The hope that the trails would create thousands of jobs and be the key to replacing the departing coal industry in the area has not come to fruition; instead, the trails have created only a few hundred jobs, spread out over those fourteen counties.[60] While every tourism dollar helps, the struggling people in Southern West Virginia will need a good deal more to bring their economy to where they want it to be.

Rural leaders not blessed with the recreational allure of the Adirondacks or the West Virginia mountains may not have to deal with the complications of visiting tourists. But most would happily endure a few added governing headaches in exchange for the economic windfall tourists bring. The alternative—not having a natural resource upon which to capitalize—is far worse.

A familiar small-town boast is that rural folks know their neighbors by name and can leave their front doors unlocked—advantages that anonymous urbanites packed into high-rise apartments and condo buildings can only imagine. This is true. Rural communities closely connected to recreational hubs can enjoy quaint rural spaces and still prosper. That's proximity's upside.

On the other extreme is isolation. The proliferation of economic deserts dotted by discount retail stores, when coupled with rising social isolation, can turn rural communities into cultural deserts. If interacting with one's neighbors is reduced to a weekly church service or the chance encounter at the local dollar store, rural American lives and livelihoods become diminished.

THE PUBLIC REVENUE SQUEEZE

Declining populations and withering economies pose another problem for rural communities: how to generate sufficient tax revenues to fund local governance.

For starters, the taxes generated from rising farm values provide local officials with short-term budgetary relief at best. A 2020 study conducted by agricultural economist Larry DeBoer found that since 2002, rural population losses in Indiana did not initially deplete local tax revenues because rising farmland values offset the losses from shrinking populations—at least in the short term. "Costs per person go up when rural populations fall, but the farmland remains to be taxed, and we increased farmland assessments a lot in the past 20 years," DeBoer writes. "But as those people move to cities and urban areas, they increase costs in those places without doing as much for expanding the tax base."[61]

The ability to fund local priorities through taxes on farmland or extractive industries—rather than from property, income, or sales taxes levied directly on residents—is what public finance experts call "tax substitution." As substitution options dwindle, rural leaders face three unpleasant fiscal options.

The first option is to double down by raising tax rates on extractive industries. Given the changing nature of rural economies, this option may be untenable. A 2020 report issued by the Center for American Progress (CAP) warns that rural governments long reliant on taxes levied upon resource-based commodities, ranging from corn to coal, must adapt to new fiscal realities. "Although agriculture, manufacturing, and mining have been the mainstays of the rural economy, due to increasing concentration of industries creating firms with extreme market power, this is no longer the case," CAP policy analysts Olugbenga Ajilore and Caius Z. Willingham write. "In fact, the largest sector in rural communities in terms of employment is the service sector, specifically in health, education, and social services."[62] Local leaders can squeeze only so many tax dollars from the farms and mines that traditionally financed rural prerogatives.

The second option is to raise taxes on residents. Given rural voters' stagnant incomes and resistance to higher taxes, this choice is electorally risky. It is also fiscally treacherous because higher property or income taxes may encourage longtime locals to leave and may deter potential newcomers from buying rural retirement or vacation homes. Even if rural officials wanted to target residential property tax hikes to wealthy carpetbaggers, they would run afoul of the statewide tax limits that followed the tax revolts led by conservative Republicans like Ronald Reagan that began in the late 1970s. "Resource-dependent communities are not blind to the dilemma of reliance on fossil fuel, timber, and mining revenue to pay the bills. But they remain trapped by it because of fiscal policy crafted at state and federal levels," a Headwaters Economics think tank report concludes. "It is easier for Wyoming community leaders to protect the fossil-fuel industry from climate policy or public land protection . . . than to ask their constituents to raise taxes on themselves. These dynamics are not lost on politicians seeking to remain in office."[63] Superior, Arizona, mayor Mila Besich told us her county tried to pass a local tax increase, but the Goldwater Institute, the Phoenix-based anti-tax think tank, helped block the measure.[64]

This leaves the third and perhaps most painful option, even if it makes the most sense given stagnant or declining rural populations: cut spending and reduce public services. Many local governments have chosen to reduce or eliminate spending on municipal projects and programs, hoping state or federal officials can somehow offset these losses. State and federal governments often step in, which is why rural Americans increasingly depend on a variety of targeted welfare programs, subsidies, and tax benefits.

Polls repeatedly confirm that many rural Whites believe federal policies favor minorities living in cities. This is a comforting delusion. The truth about federal largesse is obvious to anyone who spends even a few minutes on the U.S. Department of Agriculture's rural development homepage, which lists seventy programs focused exclusively on rural communities. These programs include loans, grants, subsidies, or training resources for individuals, businesses, agencies, and local governments to support housing, healthcare, energy, small business development, agriculture, community facilities, infrastructure, water quality management, and sewage treatment.[65]

Those are just programs at the USDA, a single cabinet-level agency. All told, twenty-three federal departments or agencies administer approximately four hundred rural-targeted programs. More than a dozen congressional committees are empowered to create programs that serve rural businesses or constituents.[66] Then there are the various tax credits, available to the public at large, but upon which rural Americans increasingly rely.[67]

For example, a rising share of rural citizens qualifies for either the Earned Income Tax Credit, the Child Tax Credit, or both.[68] According to the American Community Survey five-year summary for the years 2014–18, the 17.9 percent of rural Americans (i.e., those from "non-core" counties) who receive Social Security disability payments is higher than the share of those living in either micropolitan counties (15.9 percent) or metropolitan counties (12.0 percent).[69] Subsidized and welfare-dependent rural Americans are neither ignored nor neglected by the federal and state governments. Contrary to what many rural people believe, federal funds don't flow disproportionately to cities. In fact, metro and nonmetro areas have traditionally received about the same amount of federal spending per capita.[70]

Those streams of funding can make a difference on the ground. To take one example, the county court complex and police headquarters in rural, majority-Black Northampton County had deteriorated to the point where bats were living in the cupola of the courthouse building. But thanks to an infusion of funds from both the state and federal government, the county is completing a new governmental complex, slated to open in 2024.[71]

Stories like Northampton's illustrate an important point: Much of the time, when services are expected to improve and economic opportunity begins to arrive in rural areas, it's because the government at higher levels stepped in to make it happen. Rural economies are under intense pressure, and local officials face budgetary squeezes. The collapse of rural economies has had many spillover effects, few of which are beneficial or welcome. Tough times are compounded by even tougher fiscal challenges.

UNHEALTHY HEARTLAND

As go local economies and budgets, so go vital healthcare resources. When combined with a variety of poor lifestyle choices—some undoubtedly caused by their environment—the loss of health services and providers causes rural illness and premature deaths to surge. Rural America is increasingly sick and dying.

Healthcare facilities are disappearing from rural communities. In just the dozen years comprising 2010 through 2021, 136 rural hospitals either closed completely or became "converted closure sites" that no longer provided inpatient care.[72] Because they serve older, sicker, and poorer populations that often lack insurance coverage, rural hospitals are less profitable, more fiscally vulnerable, and therefore at greater risk of closure.[73] Physician shortages are also projected to hit rural communities harder than the nation overall.[74] In rural America, a place where politicians routinely espouse support for the "pro-life" agenda, fewer than half of all hospitals offer labor and delivery services.[75]

Rural hospitals that are part of statewide or regional chains are more likely than independent hospitals to remain open, but their survival is hardly guaranteed. One study found that for-profit chains sometimes close stable, if less profitable, rural hospitals purely as a "business decision that did not prioritize community needs."[76] Translation: Capitalism, not some nefarious socialist boogeyman, is shuttering rural hospitals.

When hospitals close, rural communities lose access not only to quality healthcare and emergency services but also to a vital employer and economic engine; in many rural places, the biggest employers are the school district and the nearest hospital. Given the high-quality jobs with good benefits that hospitals provide, rural hospital closures can devastate the surrounding community, according to a report issued by the University of North Carolina's Cecil G. Sheps Center for Health Services Research.[77] Healthcare access also affects the real estate choices of seniors, who are more likely to retire in rural communities that feature decent healthcare facilities.[78] In conservative states especially, rural areas may well become less attractive to obstetric/gynecological doctors and others who provide family planning and pregnancy services in the wake of the Supreme Court's 2022 *Dobbs* decision.

When your local hospital or clinic closes, it means you'll need to travel even farther to get care. For general inpatient and emergency departments in rural areas, the median travel distance in the seven-year period between 2012 and 2018 rose sevenfold, from roughly 3.5 miles to about 24 miles. In the middle of the opioid crisis, the distance to reach an alcohol or drug treatment clinic increased eightfold, from 5.5 miles to 44.6 miles.[79] Compounded by weaker cell phone service, dangerous driving conditions, and lower seatbelt use in rural communities, the extended distances that ambulances must drive to retrieve rural car accident victims and deliver them to emergency rooms are why nearly half of all car crash fatalities in the United States occur on rural roadways.[80]

Rural pharmacies are vanishing, too. Between 2003 and 2018, one-sixth of independent rural pharmacies closed.[81] Closure rates eventually slowed, but a 2017 study by the Center for Rural Health Policy Analysis of the Rural Policy Research Institute identified a series of connected problems that make prescriptions unaffordable for rural citizens.[82] One in eight Americans—and majorities in 40 percent of U.S. counties, most of them rural—must drive at least fifteen minutes to reach a pharmacy.[83]

As *The Washington Post*'s Markian Hawryluk explains, rural pharmacies are disappearing for the same reason local grocers did: "Independent pharmacies are struggling due to the vertical integration among drugstore chains, insurance companies and pharmaceutical benefit managers, which gives those companies market power that community drugstores can't match."[84] In other words, giant pharmacy chains have devoured the little guys. Yet again, unfettered capitalism is making life more difficult for rural residents.

Despite national trends, we encountered some notable success stories. Thanks to two million dollars in federal aid secured by Democratic senator Joe Manchin, Williamson Memorial Hospital in Mingo County, West Virginia, is slated to reopen after being closed since the middle of the coronavirus pandemic in 2020.[85] In rural Eastern North Carolina, the locally owned Futrell Pharmacy chain has kept open all four of its branches—two in Northampton County and one each in Halifax and Warren counties.[86] In the five Texas Hill Country counties it serves, regional healthcare provider Baylor Scott and White Health has kept open all ten of its family medicine facilities, including the medical center, seven local clinics, and two specialty facilities.[87] And in New York, the Citizens Advocates chain supervises developmental disability, mental health, and substance abuse facilities across five rural counties in the Adirondacks.[88]

Even as medical facilities in rural areas depend on support from the federal government, especially through Medicare and Medicaid, rural resistance to expanded federal government–provided health remains a cause of declining health outcomes for rural Americans. If that claim sounds hyperbolic, read Jonathan Metzl's book *Dying of Whiteness: How the Politics of Racial Resentment Is Killing America's Heartland.* In the book, Metzl shares his encounter with Trevor, a forty-one-year-old former cabbie living in a low-income housing complex outside Nashville. When his years of hard partying and a hepatitis C infection caught up with him, Trevor could no longer work. By the time Metzl found him, his complexion was yellow with jaundice and he needed the help of an aluminum walker.

Metzl asked Trevor if he was upset that state Republicans had blocked implementation of the Affordable Care Act in Tennessee. Nope. "Ain't no way I would ever support Obamacare or sign up for it," Trevor said. "We don't need any more government in our lives. And in any case, no way I want my tax dollars paying for Mexicans or welfare queens." Never mind that, unemployed and disabled, Trevor almost certainly drained more from public coffers than he ever contributed in state or federal taxes. Nor would any of his tax dollars be spent on Mexicans. What mattered most to Trevor was his willingness, literally, to die in defense of his reflexive hatred of big government and socialized medicine.

At least Trevor's resistance was a principled, conservative policy objection to Obamacare, right? Not likely. Repeated polling by the Kaiser

Family Foundation shows that when asked about various national healthcare policies, Republicans support almost every one of the ten major provisions of the Affordable Care Act, often by solid margins.[89] (The individual mandate provision is an exception.) Only when asked if they backed "Obamacare" did GOP support evaporate. Even White *Democrats* are less likely to support healthcare reforms when told that Obama was connected to these policies.[90] In the years following the Obamacare debate, multiple studies showed that racial resentments drove opposition to the ACA even when factors like party identification and political ideology are held constant.[91] White voters' knee-jerk opposition to Obamacare was always more about the "Obama" part than the "care" part.

How did millions of people come to hate a law despite approving nearly every major provision in it? The short answer is that Republican politicians railed against Obamacare, vowing repeatedly to "repeal and replace" it. These incessant attacks created hatred among White Americans toward healthcare policies they actually support and from which they stood to benefit. Though hardly perfect, the Affordable Care Act offered numerous protections, guarantees, and options for citizens like Trevor in need of insurance. In fact, Obamacare led to two very profound changes in U.S. health insurance coverage that benefit rural communities.

First, as with Medicare and Medicaid, the law decouples insurance coverage from employment status. Decoupling reduces what economists call "job lock," thereby giving workers greater flexibility to seek new opportunities: change careers, retrain themselves, or even relocate to take a better-paying or more rewarding job without fear of losing their coverage. Because it liberates workers to pursue their own best interests in the labor marketplace, Obamacare is quite the opposite of socialism. And who suffers most from job lock? Surprise, surprise: Rural Americans do, as they have fewer employment options than people who live in more densely populated areas.[92]

Second, the ACA significantly reduced the share of uninsured rural citizens. In fact, rural uninsured rates for non-seniors fell from 24 percent to 16 percent in just nine years following passage of the Affordable Care Act. But the effects diverge between urban and rural areas because so many rural Republican states in the Southeast and Plains regions rejected the ACA's Medicaid expansion provision, thus denying their most vulnerable citizens the opportunity to acquire health insurance.[93] Some of the very same rural voters who fumed about Obamacare were prevented from benefiting from the law only by the Republicans they elected.

The fight over expanding Medicaid was of particular importance to rural America, where uninsured rates are high and medical facilities rely heavily on Medicaid funds to stay open. Until the passage of the Affordable Care Act in 2010, the cost of covering low-income Americans was split evenly between the federal government and the states. Each state was allowed to set its own eligibility criteria, and in practice, conservative states—most of which have large rural populations—were unusually stingy with Medicaid, such that a family had to be desperately poor to qualify. The ACA changed this by setting a single and more generous standard for eligibility.

But the conservative majority on the U.S. Supreme Court ruled in 2012 that states could refuse the expansion if they wished, and many Republican-run states did just that, even though under the law, the federal government would pay 100 percent of the cost of newly eligible recipients, a percentage that declined to 90 over the course of a few years. It was an extraordinarily good deal for states: They'd get a healthier population, an improved economy, and a stabler healthcare system while paying only a fraction of the cost. But for multiple states, the opportunity to give the finger to Barack Obama outweighed all this. By 2023, there were only eleven resister states remaining; in a number of right-leaning states, the public defied the GOP-controlled legislature and passed referenda accepting the Medicaid expansion.

Rejecting the ACA's Medicaid provision offers yet another example of rural White conservatives voting against their own material interests. Rural Whites, after all, are uninsured at higher rates than their urban White counterparts. Rural inequalities tend to be especially punitive for rural non-Whites, and health insurance coverage is no exception: Although 24 percent of rural citizens are non-White, they account for 44 percent of the rural uninsured.[94]

Republican-controlled states' rejection of Medicaid expansion is perhaps the most glaring example of self-inflicted healthcare policy failure. The effects on rural residents are painfully clear: The 11.8 percent rural uninsured rate in states that approved expanded federal Medicaid coverage is *nearly half* the 21.5 percent for rural folks in the states that rejected Medicaid expansion. Yet Mississippi governor Tate Reeves and Republican legislators in 2023 reiterated their opposition to Medicaid expansion, even though federal help would have mitigated the catastrophic healthcare impacts expected to be suffered by rural Mississippians. In his State of the State address, Reeves urged lawmakers not to "cave under the pressure of Democrats and their allies in the media who are pushing for the expansion of Obamacare, welfare, and socialized medicine." The state had a $3.9 billion surplus, which Reeves said should be used for tax cuts, including eliminating the state's income tax.[95] Just a few months earlier, the state's health administrator had warned that as many as 54 percent of Mississippi's rural hospitals may close.[96] In rural America, a place where half of all hospitals now operate in the red, the share of money-losing hospitals in states that refused to expand Medicaid, 51 percent, is twelve points higher than the 39 percent in states that did.[97]

Rural opposition to Obamacare and Medicaid expansion was the third and final act of a self-destructive political-electoral drama. First, rural Whites voted for national and state politicians who sided with the corporate interests that decimated their industries and healthcare infrastructure. Next, they rewarded those same politicians for opposing life-saving and life-changing healthcare reforms. In the final and fatal act, many got sick, and some even died from lack of care or coverage.

Drug use and drug-related deaths are also decimating rural communities. Experts debate whether drug-related deaths in the United States surged because of a greater supply of potent opioids or because of deteriorating economic conditions. The effects differ between urban and rural Whites. According to public health expert Shannon Monnat, drug mortality rates among urban Whites are more closely linked to supply levels, whereas economic circumstances better predict per capita drug-related deaths for rural Whites. Of course, the combination of greater supply plus economic distress is especially lethal. "The highest drug mortality rates are disproportionately concentrated in economically-distressed mining and service sector dependent counties with high exposure to prescription opioids and fentanyl," Monnat concludes.[98]

Beth Macy's chronicle of the opioid crisis, *Dopesick*, in part focuses on Virginia's Lee County, one of many rural counties devastated by Purdue Pharma's OxyContin. *New Republic* staff writer and Virginia native Sarah Jones draws a powerful parallel between the devastation that coal and drugs have had on coal miners in places like Southwest Virginia, West Virginia, and Western Pennsylvania. "Coal enriched its tycoons. Oxycontin enriched the Sacklers. Coal gave people work. Oxycontin allegedly gave them relief from pain," Jones writes. "But while the coal industry extracted resources from the land and labor from the people who lived on the land, Purdue accomplished a particularly sinister feat. It extracted something essential from the people themselves: their will."[99]

We heard harrowing stories of how opioids destroyed so many lives in Mingo County, West Virginia. Mingo is the seventh-most lethal county in the most lethal state for opioid death rates, and its experience with drug addiction and overdose deaths is almost too tragic to fully comprehend. According to a 2018 congressional report, between 2008 and 2015, drug distributors sent more than 20 million doses of pain pills to Mingo's county seat of Williamson, or about 6,500 doses for every man, woman, and child in the town.[100] Residents told us about mile-long lines of cars stretching out from the pill mills, bearing license plates from all the surrounding states.

Guns also contribute significantly to rural death rates. This might come as a surprise to those who get their news from cable networks and talk radio, where conservative talking heads pretend to lament the scourge of urban violence. Here's what those pundits rarely if ever tell their viewers and listeners: In 2020, the age-adjusted gun death rate in rural communities was *40 percent higher* than that for large metropolitan areas.[101] That same year, the murder rate in rural America surged 25 percent.[102] Donald Trump was still president in 2020, yet somehow the same media that blame liberals and Joe Biden for urban crime never held Trump to account for the rural crime surge during his presidency.

In a detailed examination of the geography of gun violence, *Politico Magazine*'s Colin Woodard showed that gun death rates were lower per capita in New York City than in "red America" enclaves where Second Amendment advocates repeat "more guns equals less crime" talking points. Gun death rates vary widely among rural communities, too. "If you grew up in the coal mining region of eastern Pennsylvania your chance of dying of a gunshot is about half that if you grew up in the coalfields of West Virginia, three hundred miles to the southwest," Woodard explains. "Someone living in the most rural counties of South Carolina is more than three times as likely to be killed by gunshot than someone living in the equally rural counties of New York's Adirondacks or the impoverished rural counties facing Mexico across the lower reaches of the Rio Grande."[103]

Total gun deaths, of course, includes suicides. In 2021, more than half of U.S. gun deaths, 54 percent, were suicides. Unlike other forms of attempted suicide, gun suicides succeed 83 percent of the time.[104] Nine out of every ten Americans who kill themselves with a gun are White.[105]

And rural Whites are most likely to have access to guns and to die from gun suicides. Surging rural gun suicides are the result of higher gun ownership rates and lax gun control laws in rural red states. Polls show that 59 percent of rural Americans either own a gun or live in a home with a gun owner. Comparable rates are 40 percent in the suburbs and just 28 percent in cities.[106]

To understand how much guns contribute to suicide rates, consider that suicide by all methods *other* than guns varies nationwide within a tight range, from a low among all fifty U.S. states of 4.6 suicides per 100,000 people in Mississippi to a high of 11.4 in South Dakota—a difference of just 6.8 percentage points. State gun suicide rates, by contrast, range from rural Wyoming's 20.9 per 100,000 to most densely populated New Jersey's 1.8—a whopping 19.1-point difference. In fact, the nation's eighteen most rural states, those with at least 30 percent rural population shares statewide, all rank among the thirty states with the highest number of gun suicides per capita, including six of the seven highest, from Wyoming through West Virginia.[107]

Non-rural residents in these states commit suicide, too. But gun culture is a lethal contributor to the higher suicide rates in rural states and communities. Second Amendment advocates love to say that "guns don't kill people, people kill people." In rural America, the more apt phrase might be, "Guns don't kill people, but people with easy access to guns too often kill themselves."

Like guns, abortion is a powerful culture war issue in rural America. Given that rural voters are Whiter, more evangelical, and more conservative, they are less likely to support abortion rights and reproductive health services for women seeking abortions. But the consequences of their opposition are often fatal, with rural communities suffering from both diminished access to pregnancy-related services and the highest rate of pregnancy-related deaths. Rural hostility to government-subsidized health insurance is also punitive for pregnant rural women, half of whom depend upon Medicaid for prenatal care.[108] "The consequence of a lack of access to maternal care services, research shows, is that women living in rural areas often forgo prenatal, emergency and delivery care—which can have serious health consequences, such as severe hypertension and hemorrhaging," write rural reporters Shelby Harris and Sarah Melotte of *The Daily Yonder*.[109] There's nothing "pro-life" about rural conservative leaders allowing pregnant rural women to give birth without healthcare coverage.

According to data reported by the CDC's Pregnancy Mortality Surveillance System, pregnant women from rural areas are also far more likely to die during childbirth. Although outcomes vary from year to year, the roughly 26 deaths per 100,000 in rural or micropolitan areas is significantly higher than the approximately 16 women per 100,000 from urban areas who die giving birth.[110] Maternal healthcare statistics in Texas are the worst in the nation; as one family doctor in West Texas said, "The lack of funding for rural healthcare—what we're putting patients through because of this—to me, I think it's unconscionable."[111] Fatality rates are higher for Black, Native American, and Asian American women than for Whites and Latinos. Like other rural crises, this problem seems to attract less public attention and media scrutiny because it disproportionately affects non-White rural women, who are tragic victims of their White neighbors' policy choices.

According to a bombshell 2019 report by the *Journal of the American Medical Association*,[112] for the first time in U.S. history the average lifespan for White citizens during non-wartime declined for three straight years beginning in 2014. This lethal pattern was especially prevalent in America's smallest, most sparsely populated communities. In fact, fully one-third of all excess deaths during that three-year period came in just four states with significant rural White populations: Indiana, Kentucky, Ohio, and Pennsylvania.[113]

These life expectancy declines occurred *before* the Covid-19 pandemic began. Disappearing health services and pervasive conspiracy theories about science and scientists set the stage for the next rural tragedy: heartland America's disastrous response to the coronavirus pandemic.

Covid-19 did not hit rural America first, but it hit rural communities hardest. When the SARS-CoV2 virus arrived in the winter of 2020, urban areas suffered more because there were no vaccines and because most infected persons had arrived in the United States from abroad via airports in Boston, New York, Philadelphia, Seattle, and other major cities that are densely populated and more reliant on public transportation. Not surprisingly, for more than the first year of the pandemic, New York and New Jersey led the nation in per capita positivity rates and deaths.

By contrast, rural Americans enjoyed the geographic advantage of living in sparsely populated communities far from big-city airports. On March 17, 2020, President Trump tried to downplay Covid-19's danger by noting that West Virginia, one of the nation's Whitest rural states, had yet to report a single confirmed case.[114] The president's implicit message to his rural supporters was "Don't worry, you're safe."

By December 2020, however, per capita fatality rates in rural areas caught up with urban rates. And the urban-rural disparity reversed dramatically after the Food and Drug Administration approved vaccines in January 2021. That summer, the lethal Delta variant of the virus arrived.

By mid-2021, distance from major airports no longer conferred an advantage. What mattered most were vaccination rates.

As Americans lined up to be vaccinated in early 2021, higher shares of rural residents refused to receive the free, safe vaccines. The gap between rural and urban vaccination rates doubled from seven points in April 2021 (46 percent urban versus 39 percent rural) to sixteen points by January 2022 (75 percent versus 59 percent).[115] Vaccine resistance also had a distinctly partisan pattern: Because rurality correlates highly with Trump support, the counties where Trump performed best tended to have the lowest countywide vaccination rates.[116] Those lower vaccination rates in rural, Trump-loving areas inevitably translated into higher shares of rural residents testing positive, becoming hospitalized, and dying from the Delta variant.

In fact, per capita Delta cases were 2.4 times higher in rural counties than the national average and *3 to 4 times those of urban counties.* And the less densely populated the county, the higher the per capita death rate.[117] "During the first wave, the coronavirus death rate in the 10% of the country that lives in the most densely populated counties was more than nine times that of the death rate among the 10% of the population living in the least densely populated counties," writes Bradley Jones of the Pew Research Center. "In each subsequent wave, however, the nation's least dense counties have registered higher death rates than the most densely populated places."[118]

Monica Potts, a journalist who chronicles life in rural America, reviewed several studies that connect rural identity to vaccine skepticism. Rural citizens, Potts writes, tend to be more wary of science and "booksmart" experts at universities, preferring to trust their "gut" over the advice of such experts. Consequently, vaccine resistance became the latest manifestation of the skeptical rural mindset, preventing millions of rural folks from taking added precautions to guard against the virus. Perhaps most stunning, Potts found, the power of anti-science skepticism in rural communities even extended to rural physicians, who were more likely to question the validity and safety of the Covid-19 vaccine. "The vaccine-hesitant doctors shared many of the same characteristics as other vaccine skeptics: They were more likely to be rural and conservative," Potts writes. "For rural areas especially, this data suggests a vicious feedback loop. People who were suspicious of the vaccines had doctors who were suspicious, too."[119]

The 2021 Delta wave's geographic effects were predictable and tragic. Despite a huge geographic head start, rural counties managed to match and then eclipse the death rates in urban counties; by mid-2022, in fact, the cumulative death rate of 401.9 per 100,000 people in rural areas was 37 percent higher than the 293.1 rate in urban areas.[120] Most of these surplus rural deaths were avoidable. And West Virginia, the state Donald Trump boasted of being the last to have an official Covid-19 case? By May 2023, it ranked second nationally in per capita deaths, with 454 for every 100,000 citizens, barely behind Arizona's rate of 456.[121] Put simply, in just two years, West Virginia fell from first to worst.

Conspiracists claim that hospitals exaggerated Covid-19 death rates by counting persons who died *with* the virus as having died *from* it. Comorbidities contribute to Covid-19 fatalities, of course. But there is no evidence that hospitals lied about coronavirus-caused deaths. In fact, Covid-19 deaths were most likely *undercounted*, by some estimates as much as 36 percent.[122] The most lethal co-morbidity—one never reported on a single death certificate—was the refusal to get a free, safe vaccine. The stubborn, conspiratorial-minded rejection of vaccine science was not confined to rural White communities, but it was most prevalent there.

Perhaps the most painful irony is that the rural White electorate, who voted for Donald Trump at even higher rates in 2020 than in 2016, were a specific target group for Joe Biden's Covid-19 vaccine policy. After a year of President Trump peddling snake oil solutions like ivermectin and hydroxychloroquine, his successor's vaccine campaign was almost certain to be greeted with skepticism by many rural citizens. Recognizing this obstacle, the Biden administration made rural communities a priority target for vaccines. Biden's program deployed and funded faith-based groups and other organizations with rural credentials like the National Milk Producers Federation to persuade wary, misinformed rural voters to get vaccinated.[123]

The excess coronavirus deaths in rural counties should be classified as suicides by scientific skepticism. By rejecting proven vaccines, conspiracy-addled rural Americans, though living in communities where social distancing was easier than in densely populated cities, squandered their geographic advantage.

All told, premature deaths from reduced healthcare access and facility closures, healthcare ignorance and scientific skepticism, and a fatal devotion to guns and drugs are killing rural White Americans—especially downscale rural Whites. In some cases, these problems are reaching epidemic levels and should concern every American, whatever their race and wherever they live.

BROKE AND BROKEN

Donald Trump won about five-sixths of all U.S. counties in the 2020 election, a statistic his supporters love to cite. Yet the one-sixth of counties Joe Biden carried produced an estimated 70 percent of the nation's gross domestic product; the disproportionately rural Trump counties produced the remaining 30 percent. Four years earlier, the GDP split was 64–36 percent for Hillary Clinton–won counties. In 2000, the GDP tilt was only 56–44 percent for the counties Al Gore won. Counties with declining health metrics also swung significantly to Donald Trump in 2016.[124] Blue counties are becoming more vibrant, healthier, and productive while red counties wither.[125]

The economic and healthcare woes of rural Americans, and especially downscale White rural citizens, are real and consequential. In a piece about what he calls the "hard truths" of saving rural America, *New York Times* economics correspondent Eduardo Porter offers a powerful, if grim, summary of the malaise facing small towns and counties in the United States. "Rural America is getting old. The median age is 43, seven years older than city dwellers. Its productivity, defined as output per worker, is lower than urban America's. Its families have lower incomes. And its share of the population is shrinking."[126]

So-called heartland America is embattled and beleaguered. Rural citizens are losing population, economic power, and other tangible signs of vitality, including a brain drain that is depleting communities of their most talented youth. They are becoming sicker and dying younger and often unnecessarily, sometimes by self-inflicted means. Some might be tempted to say this grim picture is entirely the fault of the people who live in these places, but the truth is far more complex. People make their own choices, but they can also be the victims of impersonal financial forces, amoral corporate profiteering, changing political realities, and the occasional global pandemic. What is beyond dispute is that with each passing year, the most deeply red, rural American places become more endangered. And there are few signs that rural decline will abate, no less reverse, anytime soon.

CHAPTER

3

THE GREATEST POLITICAL HAND
EVER DEALT

—

T HE THIRTY-EIGHT-YEAR-OLD FAMILY FARMER WAS FRUSTRATED AND restless. A U.S. Naval Academy graduate who had traveled the world, he was fascinated by politics and itching to get involved. But he and his wife were busy managing the family farm he had inherited from his father while raising their four kids in his rural hometown of 860 people.

Then, in 1962, the U.S. Supreme Court ruled that state legislative districts had to be redrawn to account for population changes. No longer could state legislatures be malapportioned so that small rural counties wielded more voting power than large urban counties. No longer could party bosses—especially from those rural White counties—use their magnified voting power to dominate primary and general elections. No longer would racial minorities from urban areas have their votes diluted by a system that assigned greater power to rural Whites.

A month before the election that year, the ambitious small-town farmer filed to run for the open seat in his senate district. "I decided to run for office in 1962, after the Supreme Court ruled in *Baker v. Carr* that all votes had to be weighted as equally as possible. This resulted in the termination of Georgia's 'county unit' system, where some rural votes equaled 100 votes in urban areas," he wrote later.[1] He lost, but a powerful party boss from a neighboring county had rigged the vote. Undeterred, the navy veteran with a deep commitment to justice challenged the election in court. A judge threw the results out and ordered a second election.

This time, James Earl Carter won.

Eight years later, Georgians chose him to be their governor, and six years after that, he was elected president of the United States. A rural southern Democrat who cut his political teeth by taking on a corrupt, unfair system that for two centuries had favored rural southern Democrats like him and his forebears was in the White House.

The end of the "county unit system" that aggregated votes and power by county triggered a revolution that, with time, expanded the representation and influence of racial minorities, particularly African Americans in the former Confederate states. In the South and across the country, this revolution transformed both political parties: Democrats embraced Black voters, and Republicans increasingly appealed to White Democrats who could no longer abide a party advocating racial equality. Thirty years after his state senate run, former president Carter reflected on the meaning of that fateful campaign in his book *Turning Point:* "The 1962 campaign marked a turning point—the first real defeat for the old system on its own turf—that helped to end the legalized system of White supremacy, rural domination of government, and deprivation of civil rights among our neighbors."[2]

Six decades have passed since Jimmy Carter's court-aided election victory. Rural Americans can legitimately complain about countless aspects of their current economic and healthcare predicaments. They cannot complain about a lack of representation or electoral power. The old county unit system is gone, but voters from rural counties and states continue to enjoy a form of super-enfranchisement that assigns them electoral power that urbanites have never enjoyed and can only imagine.

Because it violates the "one person, one vote" standard, malapportionment in the Electoral College and especially the U.S. Senate is the primary means by which White voters—and rural Whites most of all—retain electoral advantages at the national level. Those advantages are not as pronounced at the state level as they were prior to several landmark 1960s Supreme Court rulings, but gerrymandered U.S. House and state legislative districts likewise advantage rural voters and the modern

Republican Party that represents them. No group was ever dealt a better electoral hand than rural White Americans.

The inflated power of rural White voters confers upon them an unusual ability to force state and national governments to cater to their preferences and grievances. Herein lies the danger: Precisely because they wield inflated power, rural Whites' increasingly tenuous commitments to democratic norms and traditions are magnified across the U.S. political system in many of the same ways their preferences have been for two centuries.

THE RURAL SENATE

The malapportioned Senate assigns more power to smaller, more rural states, and this small-state tilt of malapportionment is greater now than when the U.S. Constitution was ratified. The population ratio between the largest and smallest states has ballooned from 13 to 1 in 1790 to 69 to 1 today. Even the ratio of the largest state to the mean population state has grown from 2.5 to 1 at the founding to 6 to 1 now. At the founding, a party could garner control of the Senate with 30 percent of the population, spread across the smaller half of the states. Today, that figure is down to just 17 percent, which means one-sixth of the country can theoretically use the Senate to block any legislation the other five-sixths support.[3] Residents of the District of Columbia—the jurisdiction with the highest African American population percentage and the highest Democratic vote share in presidential elections—have no senators at all.

County population disparities demonstrate how perverse Senate malapportionment has become. Los Angeles County has more people than any of the forty smallest states, but its 10 million residents must share two senators with nearly 30 million other Californians. There are a remarkable 120 U.S. counties that have more people than the entire state of Wyoming. Yet the Cowboy State's 581,000 citizens enjoy the same two votes in the Senate as the other forty-nine states do.[4]

These perversions of power will worsen in the decades ahead. By 2040, 70 percent of Americans will reside in the fifteen most-populous states and choose thirty of the one hundred U.S. senators. Concentrated in smaller and more rural states, the remaining 30 percent of the population will elect seventy senators.[5] No matter how distorted these population ratios become, each state is guaranteed its two senators—past, present, and forever.

Size and rurality are not identical. Nevada is one of the least rural states, featuring a small statewide populace, two-thirds of whom are packed into the Las Vegas metropolitan area. By contrast, North Carolina has the ninth-largest population, yet it ranks among the most rural states. But, in general, Senate malapportionment magnifies the power of states that are both small *and* rural. The U.S. population is 20 percent rural, but the median U.S. state is 30 percent rural, meaning more than half the American states are more rural than the nation overall; because each state has two senators, that means Senate representation is more rural than the nation overall, too.[6] And the Senate does not merely favor rural residents generally: It specifically assigns greater voting weight to rural Whites, especially rural Whites without college degrees, who are overconcentrated in smaller, more rural states. California is home to far more non-college-educated Whites than Wyoming, but Wyoming's non-college White voters exert way more power to elect their state's two U.S. senators than California's do.[7]

Given how rural Whites without college degrees vote, the rural skew of the malapportioned Senate favors the Republican Party. Following the 2020 election, among the eighteen states with rural populations at or above 30 percent, the three in New England—Maine, New Hampshire, and Vermont—boasted a mix of U.S. senators, with one Republican, three Democrats, and two independents who caucus with the Democrats. But these are partisan exceptions. In the remaining fifteen states, from Alaska through West Virginia, twenty-eight of the thirty senators were Republicans.[8]

Republicans have not always enjoyed an advantage among smaller, more rural states. When he examined this question in 2022, political scientist Lee Drutman of the think tank New America found no connection between state population size and partisanship during the first four decades of the twentieth century. Since 1940, however, the smaller states have steadily become more Republican. In fact, the size–partisanship correlation was stronger in 2020 than in any previous decade since World War II. By 2030, that correlation will almost certainly become stronger.

According to Drutman, at no time since 1950 has the Senate Republican caucus represented states containing the majority of Americans. Yet Senate Republicans wielded majorities for six years each in the 1980s and '90s, four years during the 2000s, and six more years in the 2010s. "Though the Senate has had a pro-Republican bias for many decades, the problem was not as pronounced when the Republican and Democratic parties had some meaningful overlap in their coalitions," Drutman explains. "But as cross-partisan compromise and ideological overlap has vanished from Congress, Republicans' small-state advantage has become much more consequential because partisan control of the chamber has become so much more consequential."[9]

Given current voting patterns, neither party will be able to obtain a comfortable majority in the Senate for the foreseeable future; the margins will continue to be tight, with each election potentially swinging control from one party to the other. But Senate Democrats represent far more Americans than do the Republicans. After the 2022 election, Democrats managed to obtain a 51–49 advantage in the Senate. Yet the 51 Democrats represented just under 193 million people, while the 49 Republicans represented fewer than 140 million, for a remarkable difference of 53 million.[10]

Senate malapportionment influences policy outcomes in all kinds of ways. For decades, bills proposed to expand healthcare coverage that passed the U.S. House have repeatedly died in the Senate.[11] Policy imbalances also strike at the very heart of U.S. national security: After the attacks of September 11, 2001, anti-terrorism funds were spent on states and areas regardless of threat assessment, which is why rural Wyoming received per capita funding seven times that of New York State, home to New York City's toppled Twin Towers.[12] Meanwhile, Congress has never hesitated to pass policies that directly benefit rural areas, including farm subsidies, rural postal services, and the Essential Air Service that subsidizes flights from rural airports.

But malapportionment delivers more than small-bore policy victories for rural America. When political scientists Richard Johnson and Lisa Miller in 2022 examined 804 key Senate votes between 1961 and 2019, they found that the outcomes clearly favored conservatives, Republicans, and rural Whites in particular. The reason, of course, is that small states have always had much higher shares of White and rural residents than the national average, favoring them in the Senate at the expense of racial minorities. "Whereas the Senate represents 'the minority' in one sense (i.e., those living in overwhelmingly white, rural states), it vastly underrepresents two underserved minority groups (i.e., Blacks and Hispanics), who tend to live in high-population states," Johnson and Miller write.[13]

And not only is the design of the Senate profoundly undemocratic, but the founders made it all but impossible to undo this via democratic means. They shielded only two constitutional provisions from amendment. The first of these so-called entrenched provisions was the twenty-year window, through 1808, during which the Constitution allowed new slaves to be imported. That provision expired more than two centuries ago, leaving the malapportioned Senate as the lone surviving entrenched provision. The last phrase of Article V's amendment process cements forever the two-senators-per-state design: "No state, without its consent, shall be deprived of its equal suffrage in the Senate."

That's right: Citizens would have to first amend the Constitution's amendment process and *then* propose and ratify another amendment to change the Senate composition.[14] The Senate as currently comprised is a forever institution that will always favor small, rural states and the White voters who live there.

REVENGE OF THE "SERFS"

The Republican Party and its rural White voter base also enjoy a pivotal advantage in presidential elections, which are decided by the Electoral College rather than by a national popular vote as is used in every other democracy in the world. Thanks to the inflated power that smaller states enjoy in the Electoral College, the past two Republican presidents entered the White House despite having lost the popular vote. It's not just possible but *likely* that yet another Republican in the near future will win the White House despite receiving fewer votes than their opponent.

According to *Cook Political Report* analyst Amy Walter, heading into the 2024 election the Republicans enjoy a two-point advantage in the Electoral College. The reason is that six swing states are currently at least two percentage points more Republican than the nation overall. This means the GOP can assemble an Electoral College majority even if the Republican nominee loses the national popular vote by as much as 2 percent—precisely what Donald Trump did in 2016. "That, however, is almost impossible for a Democrat to replicate," Walter writes.[15]

We can see how this plays out in practice by comparing the 2016 and 2020 election results. In 2020, Democrat Joe Biden amassed 306 electoral votes, 36 more than the 270 minimum needed to win, while winning the national popular vote by 4.4 percent. Four years earlier, despite losing the popular vote to Democrat Hillary Clinton by 2.1 percent, Republican Donald Trump also captured the same total of 306 electors. That's a net difference of 6.5 percent in the popular vote margins of consecutive winners, yet Trump and Biden won the exact same number of electors—a stunning indictment of how the Electoral College translates votes into victories.[16]

In recent presidential contests, small states Delaware, Hawai'i, Maine, Rhode Island, and Vermont have cast their 18 electors reliably for Democratic nominees. But the reliably Republican small states—Alaska, Arkansas, Idaho, Kansas, Mississippi, Montana, Nebraska, North Dakota, Oklahoma, South Dakota, West Virginia, and Wyoming—cast a combined 48 electors, more than twice as many. The GOP's advantage in rural states is indisputable: In 2020, Donald Trump won 98 of the 108 combined electoral votes cast by the eighteen most rural states.[17]

Small states wield greater per capita power in selecting presidents because of each state's two so-called Senate electors. To understand this effect, compare the populations of California and Wyoming, the largest and smallest states. There are sixty-nine Californians for every Wyomingite, but Californians' U.S. House representation ratio is only fifty-two to one because Wyoming is guaranteed its minimum one House member. Wyoming's lone House seat plus its two guaranteed senators thus yield the minimum 3 electoral votes, shrinking to eighteen to one the ratio between California's 54 electors and Wyoming's 3. Sixty-nine times the people, but only eighteen times the voting power—that's how malapportionment skews Electoral College power to smaller, more rural states over larger, more urbanized ones.

Defenders of the Electoral College offer no apologies for its rural, small-state tilt. To them, this bias is a feature, not a bug. In fact, too often defenders of the Electoral College justify its anti-democratic nature by, directly or indirectly, implying that the votes of rural voters *should* count more because those voters are somehow *better* than the rest of us.

Take a *USA Today* op-ed hyperbolically entitled "Rural Americans Would Be Serfs If We Abolished the Electoral College," by Trent England, director of Save Our States, an organization created in 2009 to oppose the national popular vote plan. If adopted by enough states, the NPV plan would trigger an interstate compact that would guarantee every national popular vote winner a 270-plus majority of electors because each state within the compact would agree to assign their electors to the national popular vote no matter how that candidate fared in their respective state. England argues that exaggerated rural power in the Electoral College is justified because rural America produces most of the nation's food and fossil fuel–based energy. Without Electoral College protections for rural citizens, he asserts, urban voters will exploit rural voters because "city dwellers have a nasty habit of taking advantage of their country cousins" in ways similar to the exploitation of feudal slaves or Russian serfs.[18]

England conveniently ignores the fact that cities produce far more of the nation's wealth and innovations than do rural communities. One can imagine how he would react if some coastal urbanite published an op-ed warning rural voters that they had better start voting "correctly" or else they might be deprived of the countless technologies the metropolises produce, from motion pictures to mobile phones, MRI machines to microchips. Not to mention the four hundred federal programs or the welfare benefits upon which rural voters increasingly rely, like the Child Tax Credit or the Earned Income Tax Credit—all of which are subsidized by the taxes paid by higher-income metropolitans from blue states whose votes are diluted by the Electoral College.

England is a former analyst for the conservative Heritage Foundation, and his organization is funded by the Bradley Impact Fund, which in turn is funded by the Lynde and Harry Bradley Foundation, one of the right's premier sources of money for ideological crusades.[19] Wealthy, conservative donors know that the current system assigns greater power to rural voters who, in turn, elect the conservative Republicans who shield the donors' fortunes from taxes and their businesses from regulation. This is why one can find spirited defenses of the Electoral College coming from all kinds of right-wing sources. The Heritage Foundation has an ebook called *The Essential Electoral College,* in which it writes that "large cities like New York City and Los Angeles should not get to unilaterally dictate policies that affect more rural states, like North Dakota and Indiana, which have very different needs."[20] It's apparently fine, however, for North Dakota and Indiana to "unilaterally dictate policies" that affect urban areas.

But it isn't only conservatives who defend the Electoral College's rural bias. In an otherwise thoughtful piece published by the Aspen Institute, rural policy advocates John Molinaro and Solveig Spjeldnes argue that "any people, when sufficiently disenfranchised and economically downtrodden, will eventually rebel." After invoking the January 6 domestic terrorist attacks, Molinari and Spjeldnes warn that "any concerted effort to eliminate the Electoral College now would backfire on those who support it." And then comes their kicker: "If done in the wake of the widely believed lies about the left 'stealing the election,' it would almost inevitably lead to additional violence."[21]

Molinari and Spjeldnes clearly intend to warn, not threaten. Yet they admit that rural voters who believe the "Big Lie" may commit violence to defend their outsize power to elect presidents, and worse, they offer this threat as a reason not to pursue the popular election of presidents.

Had anyone without Molinari and Spjeldnes's policy bona fides issued such a warning, however artfully phrased, their words would have been regarded as political blackmail.

Electoral College defenders also frequently resort to argumentative sleight-of-hand by pretending that the sheer number of counties a presidential nominee wins is an accurate reflection of the popular will, as though every county were the same. In a 2019 op-ed entitled "Only 'Sore Losers' Want to Abolish Electoral College," then-U.S. senator Jim Inhofe of Oklahoma wrote, "Consider this: Democratic presidential nominee Hillary Clinton may have prevailed in the popular vote in 2016, but she carried just 487 counties in the entire country. Compare that to President Donald Trump, who carried 2,626 counties and the Electoral College. You tell me which candidate better reflected the will of the entire country?"[22]

That's an easy one: It was Clinton, the candidate whom 2.9 million more voters preferred. If that 2.9-million-vote margin seems negligible, consider that it was larger than the number of Americans who voted that year in the rural Republican states of Alaska, Montana, Nebraska, North Dakota, South Dakota, West Virginia, and Wyoming *combined.* Clinton's margin of victory was twice the number of votes cast by all of Inhofe's fellow Oklahomans in 2016.

Perhaps most absurd of all, some Republicans have argued that when they win the Electoral College despite garnering fewer votes, the outcome is legitimate because they prevailed in counties covering a larger total acreage, as though we ought to assign power to land and not to citizens. This ludicrous claim has been made by Sen. Mitch McConnell, among others.[23]

The Electoral College—a selection method so flawed that the founders had to amend it just fourteen years after ratifying the Constitution—is also unpopular with Americans. The Pew Research Center periodically asks citizens how presidents should be elected. Since 2000, roughly 60 percent of Americans say they prefer to abolish the Electoral College in favor of a national popular vote, with only 35 percent supporting the current method. Although Democrats support a national popular vote at higher rates than Republicans, the share of Republicans who prefer a national popular vote rule grew steadily from 40 percent in 2000 to a 54 percent majority by 2016.[24]

Then Donald Trump was elected. What happened next? On cue, Republican support for electing presidents based on the national popular vote dropped by half, from 54 percent to 27 percent. Almost overnight, millions of Republicans abandoned their principles in favor of keeping an archaic and flawed method that elected Trump once and presumably would favor him for re-election in 2020—and did, despite his loss.[25] It favors him again in 2024, of course. By 2023, Republican support for the national popular vote had rebounded to 47 percent, yet it remains lower than it was during the pre-Trump era and continues to lag well behind the 82 percent support espoused among Democrats.[26]

In a rare moment of candor, three days before the January 6 domestic terrorist attacks, seven U.S. House Republicans acknowledged that the GOP enjoys a built-in Electoral College advantage. On behalf of his six House Republican colleagues, Kentucky's Thomas Massie issued a press release in which he worried about Trump's repeated attacks on the electoral certification process—*not* because Trump's incendiary language might lead to violence, as it did three days later, but because his attacks might undermine public support for the Electoral College. "From a purely partisan perspective, Republican presidential candidates have won the national popular vote only once in the last thirty-two years," Massie wrote. "They have therefore depended on the Electoral College for nearly all presidential victories in the last generation. If we perpetuate the notion that Congress may disregard certified electoral votes—based solely on its own assessment that one or more states mishandled the presidential election—we will be delegitimizing the very system that led Donald Trump to victory in 2016, and that could provide the only path to victory in 2024."[27] Of course, the operative words are "from a purely partisan perspective." But give Massie and his six co-signers credit for at least admitting that the Electoral College favors Republican presidential nominees.

Rural White citizens and the Republicans whom they overwhelmingly support benefit from malapportionment's effect on U.S. Senate representation and presidential elections. Short-term advantages can toggle between the parties, of course. If Democrats can mobilize new voters or persuade existing voters in small or rural states to support their party's candidates, they might eliminate or even reverse the GOP's current advantages. But if, in the near future, there is another "misfired election" in which the popular vote winner fails to win the Electoral College, expect the small, rural states to be instrumental in delivering the White House to the Republican nominee yet again.

BROOKLYN LOSES, THE DAKOTAS WIN

Malapportionment's rural-magnifying effect is not limited to the choice of elected officials. Of course, the consequences spiral out from there. It is particularly pronounced in confirming federal judges. The Senate wields sole power to confirm presidential appointments to the federal bench, something President Barack Obama and his 2016 Supreme Court nominee, Merrick Garland, understand all too well. Senate majority leader Mitch McConnell's decision to prevent Obama from filling the Supreme Court seat vacated upon the death of Justice Antonin Scalia is perhaps the most egregious recent example of minorities wielding Senate majority power. In fact, McConnell refused to confirm all but one of the Democratic president's appellate court appointees during Obama's final two years in the White House. Thanks to McConnell's dishonest and destructive intransigence, the total number of vacancies at all three levels of the federal judiciary when Donald Trump took office, 105, was more than twice the vacancies available for Joe Biden to fill upon his taking office four years later.[28] In effect, the last two years' worth of Obama's judicial vacancies were redistributed from Obama to Trump.

Consider the implications of McConnell's actions: A two-term Democratic president who won both election and re-election with national popular vote majorities filled six years' worth of judicial appointments, but so did a one-term Republican president who lost the popular vote. Adding policy insult to electoral injury, McConnell controlled the Supreme Court confirmation process even though the Republicans in his majority caucus represented fewer citizens than their Democratic counterparts. What applies to Supreme Court appointments likewise applies to other federal judges at the appellate and trial levels, too.

In the eight presidential elections from 1992 through 2020, Democratic nominees not only won the popular vote seven times but received 36 million more net votes than the eight Republican nominees. The three Democratic presidents—all of whom won the popular vote in their five victories and who have collectively won the White House for twenty years—appointed five justices to the Supreme Court. The two Republicans—in office for twelve combined years despite losing the popular vote in two of their three victories—also made five appointments. Simply put, the current Court's majority would not exist without the inflated voting power of rural White voters from small states to elect presidents and senators.

When the Court ruled in its landmark 1964 *Reynolds v. Sims* decision that state-level malapportionment was unconstitutional, Chief Justice Earl Warren explained the matter plainly enough that every citizen could understand: "Legislators represent people, not trees or acres," he wrote. "A citizen, a qualified voter, is no more nor no less so because he lives in the city or on the farm."[29] Yet the "one person, one vote" standard continues to be violated in both the U.S. Senate and the Electoral College. Extra trees and acreage continue to give rural citizens greater voting power than their urban counterparts.

Two days before the 2013 New York City mayoral election, President Barack Obama made a campaign stop at a Junior's Cheesecake in Brooklyn to support fellow Democrat Bill de Blasio's campaign for mayor. As the two politicians mingled with locals outside the bakery, a woman approached Obama and gave him a big hug. The reason? The recently enacted Affordable Care Act, informally known as Obamacare, had helped the woman's uninsured sister obtain healthcare coverage. Hoping to return the favor, the woman asked, "We love you—what can we do to support you?" Obama didn't miss a beat. "Move to North Dakota," he replied. "If I could just get about a million surplus votes in Brooklyn out to Nebraska, Wyoming."[30]

Obama was kidding, but only a little. A year later, he and the Democrats lost their Senate majority after Republicans flipped nine seats, including victories in the small, rural, and predominantly White states of Alaska, Montana, South Dakota, and West Virginia. Obama knows that Democratic Party power is significantly diluted by malapportionment, which assigns far more power to people from White, rural, Republican-leaning states like North Dakota, Nebraska, and Wyoming than it does to minorities and liberal Democrats who patronize Brooklyn pastry shops.

Malapportionment has always been that way. Barring either a second civil war or another constitutional convention, it always will be. And in years to come, the skew that favors White rural voters and the Republicans they elect will become only more pronounced.

RURAL GERRYMANDERS

The Supreme Court's landmark rulings in the 1960s eliminated malapportionment for the U.S. House of Representatives and state legislatures. But thanks to gerrymandering, rural voters continue to be overrepresented in the U.S. House and many state legislatures.

Gerrymandering, the strategic use of the redistricting process to maximize seats won per votes received, confers upon rural voters inflated power thanks to two interconnected phenomena. The first is that Democratic voters are more clustered than Republicans, a geographic reality that is the fault of neither party. The second is that Republicans exploit this clustering by packing urban and suburban Democrats into as few seats as possible in order to maximize the overall share of Republican-held seats.

U.S. House. Analyses conducted by *The Economist* prior to the 2018 midterms demonstrate the partisan impact of rural voting bias in U.S. House elections. That year, President Donald Trump's approval ratings were underwater everywhere except in rural America,[31] and Democrats led comfortably in the pre-election generic congressional polls. But when *The Economist* conducted ten thousand simulations of the expected House results, a shocking pattern emerged. Although Republicans won the popular vote in only one of every thousand simulated outcomes, the GOP maintained its House majority in 30 percent of those simulations.

Because partisan geography dilutes the voting power of urban and suburban Democrats to the advantage of rural Republicans, the Democrats potentially needed to win at least 53 percent of the House vote nationwide to build a House majority.[32] "The over-representation of rural America was not supposed to affect the House and the presidency. For most of the past 200 years, when rural, urban and suburban interests were scattered between the parties, it did not," *The Economist* explained, noting that the thirteen most densely populated states elected 121 Democratic House members and 73 Republican members, but in the remaining states the split was 163 Republicans to only 72 Democrats. "America has one party built on territory and another built on people."[33]

In the actual 2018 midterms, Democrats flipped enough seats to capture the House majority, returning Nancy Pelosi to the speakership she lost in 2010. Democrats fared a bit better than *The Economist* predicted, capturing 53 percent of the seats with 52 percent of House votes nationwide. They performed especially well in suburban areas where Republican mapmakers had overplayed their hand by creating Republican districts that were marginally safe but not safe enough to survive a Democratic wave. More than two-thirds of the Democrats' 41 net seat gains came in the suburbs.[34] Democrats flipped just one rural House seat, and that defeat of a Republican incumbent from Maine's Second Congressional District was decided by a ranked choice voting runoff.

However, Democratic gains were smaller than the same two-party share delivered to the Republicans six years earlier with the same maps, when the GOP won 54 percent of seats despite capturing only 48 percent of the national vote.[35] The rural-based Republicans successfully gerrymandered the House in a way that either produced GOP majorities despite minority support or mitigated their net seat losses in bad cycles like 2018.

How tilted in favor of rural citizens are House districts? Bloomberg's CityLab analyzed the geography of all 435 House districts created during the 2010 round of redistricting and classified them into six categories of increasing population density: "purely rural," "rural-suburban mix," "sparse suburban," "dense suburban," "suburban-urban mix," and "purely urban." For each of the six categories, the total number and share of all 435 districts, the share of each type of seat held by House Republicans, and its 2016 Trump voter share in those seats are presented in the following table.[36]

CITYLAB CLASSIFICATION OF U.S. HOUSE DISTRICT GEOGRAPHY				
	TOTAL NUMBER OF DISTRICTS (N = 435)	PERCENTAGE SHARE OF ALL DISTRICTS	PERCENTAGE SHARE HELD BY GOP	PERCENTAGE TRUMP VOTE SHARE
PURELY RURAL	70	16	84	63
RURAL-SUBURBAN MIX	114	26	82	56
SPARSE SUBURBAN	86	20	55	47
DENSE SUBURBAN	83	19	34	39
SUBURBAN-URBAN MIX	48	11	15	26
PURELY URBAN	34	8	6	14

Look at how the lopsided set of districts favors rural voters. Although more people live in cities than in rural areas, 42 percent of all districts, 184 in total, are either purely rural or rural-suburban in composition. Only 19 percent, 82 total, are either suburban-urban or purely urban. In a similar, four-category analysis, Suzanne Mettler and Trevor Brown reach the same conclusion.[37] Again, these perverse inequities result from the packing of urban minorities into as few urban-based districts as possible.

Estimates for the new maps after the 2020 redistricting show a slight uptick from 82 to 85 in purely urban or suburban-urban districts combined and a five-seat drop in purely rural and rural-suburban seats, to 179. That shift is due mostly to suburban gains: The number of purely rural districts increased by three, to 73, while purely urban districts held constant at 34.[38] Before and after 2020, the pattern is clear: Rural voters wield significant electoral influence in two-fifths of the 435 U.S. House districts, whereas the influence of more numerous urban voters extends across half that many. Rural power in the House is inflated.

This happens because in states where Republicans control redistricting, the GOP systematically maximizes the electoral power of rural areas at the expense of urban areas. In the most egregious case, Pennsylvania Republicans approved a map in 2011 that stuffed Democratic voters into five districts in the Pittsburgh and Philadelphia metro areas, leaving Democrats with just five out of eighteen seats, 28 percent of the delegation, in a state Barack Obama carried twice. Some called Pennsylvania's U.S. House map "the gerrymander of the decade." The eighteen House districts were so distorted in the GOP's favor that the Pennsylvania Supreme Court threw out the map in the middle of the decade and replaced it with a new one.[39]

In the 2020 round of redistricting, Republicans gerrymandered U.S. House districts in four states so grotesquely that judges ruled that the new maps violated federal law. GOP-led state legislatures in Alabama, Georgia, Louisiana, and Ohio—all states with significant rural populations—created maps that illegally diluted the voting power of urban minorities, yet the new districts were left untouched by the U.S. Supreme Court in the run-up to the 2022 midterm cycle. Why? Because state Republican officials intentionally delayed certifying their unfair maps until late into the 2022 election cycle, allowing the Supreme Court's conservative majority to leave them in place in deference to the so-called Purcell principle.

The Purcell principle is designed to prevent courts from issuing election-related rulings so close to Election Day that the decisions might confuse voters. In February 2022, the Supreme Court issued a stay against decisions by two federal judges who had ruled that House maps drawn by Republicans in Alabama and Louisiana illegally failed to create a majority-minority district that ostensibly would elect a Black

Democrat. A similar case in Georgia also stalled. The GOP's delaying tactics effectively denied House Democrats and the Congressional Black Caucus three seats. Despite a June 2023 U.S. Supreme Court decision ordering Alabama to redraw its U.S. House maps to create a second Black-majority district, state Republicans continued to resist for months, even requesting an emergency appeal with the Supreme Court; Republicans in Florida and Louisiana likewise pushed back against court edicts to compel them to redraw their maps to conform with the 1965 Voting Rights Act's protections for Black voters.[40]

Election expert David Wasserman estimates that the Supreme Court's refusal to intervene in the four state cases likely yielded five to seven extra Republican House seats in 2022. Meanwhile, judicial rulings in New York prevented Democrats in that blue state from the type of gerrymandering the Supreme Court had allowed in Alabama, Georgia, and Louisiana. Though neither of these two judicial outcomes alone would have been enough to prevent Republicans from flipping the House in 2022, together they may well have cost the Democrats their House majority.[41]

The courts may now intervene to redraw these maps. In fact, in early 2023, a federal court struck down South Carolina's House map as unconstitutional for its "racially discriminatory intent."[42] But if they remain untouched for the remainder of the decade, these illegal gerrymanders will persist for the four remaining House election cycles until the 2030 Census, diluting the power of minorities to the benefit of White voters, especially rural Whites. "We're seeing a revolution in courts' willingness to allow elections to go forward under illegal or unconstitutional rules," said Richard L. Hasen, UCLA law professor and director of the Safeguarding Democracy Project. "And that's creating a situation in which states are getting one free illegal election before they have to change their rules."[43]

Redistricting battles in Texas may have the widest implications, because the state is a vital outpost of Republican power, but one that is trending steadily in Democrats' direction. In the 2020 round of redistricting, Republicans there faced a problem: The state is rapidly diversifying, so much so that 95 percent of the growth during the prior decade came from non-White residents, especially Latinos. And yet the number of majority-Latino seats in the Texas House delegation actually *dropped* from six to five when Republicans were done drawing the lines. "It was clearly the intent to crack and pack and disenfranchise Latino and African American voters in Texas," Domingo Garcia, president of the League of United Latin American Citizens, told *Texas Monthly*.[44]

Rather than try to maximize the number of seats they held in Congress and the state legislature—which would have meant increasing the number of Republican-held seats where the GOP's advantage was marginal and therefore vulnerable—Republicans decided instead to solidify the advantage they already held. How did they do it? "The rural areas were used to neutralize the increasingly competitive suburbs," said Michael Li of the Brennan Center for Justice, an expert on Texas redistricting. "Historically, the suburbs are the Republican heartland," Li told us. "That's where the Republican rise to power in the South began, with people like Newt Gingrich and Tom DeLay. But in recent years, the suburbs have started getting more diverse," with people of color steadily moving into suburban areas.

"There are also political shifts among White voters, particularly college-educated White women. That has made the suburbs really dangerous territory for Republicans," Li said. So, they got creative: For instance, the Thirty-first Congressional District, which includes suburban areas north of Austin, was extremely competitive; Trump won it in 2020 by just two points. In redistricting, Republicans carved out the heavily minority city of Killeen from the Thirty-first and put it into the Eleventh District, which includes Llano, a place we'll visit later. This move gave them a cushion in the Thirty-first to keep it safely Republican but didn't hurt them in the Eleventh, as its rural residents are so overwhelmingly Republican that Trump won there by an 80–19 margin in 2020. If adding Killeen's 150,000 mostly Democratic residents to the Eleventh means that the next Republican nominee gets only 70 percent of the vote rather than 80, that's fine with the GOP.

But the key to the system is the assumption that no matter what happens, almost no rural Whites in Texas will vote for Democrats. "Rural voters are as Republican in Texas as Black voters are Democratic," Li said. He compared the situation to the 1980s and '90s in other parts of the South, where conservative Democrats still had control in many places even as the transition of Whites to the GOP was in process; during redistricting, those Democrats "used Black voters to prop up White Democrats. Right now, Republicans are using rural voters to prop up Republicans in suburban seats."[45]

In North Carolina, the U.S House delegation after the 2022 midterms was split evenly, with Democrats and Republicans each winning seven seats. This parity was achieved only because the state supreme court threw out the Republican-controlled legislature's proposed map. But in that same election, the GOP obtained a state supreme court majority. Democrats fear what's coming next. Asked if state Republicans would perhaps aim for a 9-to-5 or 10-to-4 favorable split now that they knew the court would likely uphold whatever map they drew, Democrat Kandie Smith expressed her unvarnished cynicism. "Fourteen to zero," the rookie African American state senator predicted when we interviewed her at Peaden's restaurant, her "district office" in Greenville. Smith smirked when we suggested that a 14–0 Republican seat map was impossible, but her purposeful exaggeration was not without warrant.[46]

Two hours later, in Tarboro, when we met her Democratic colleague, state representative Shelly Willingham, and posed the same question to him, the more reserved Willingham offered an equal dose of cynicism. "It's not going to be seven-to-seven when they finish," Willingham told us. He predicted that Democrats would be reduced to just two or three seats, similar to what they had in the late 2010s, when a gerrymander in operation between the 2014 and 2022 elections left the split at 10–3 in Republicans' favor.[47] (The state gained a fourteenth seat after the 2020 Census.)

Electoral rules and structures that favor rural areas may have made sense at the founding, a time when 95 percent of citizens lived in rural areas. But by 1920, a minority of Americans lived in rural areas.[48] Today, at most, 20 percent do, and that share declines with each new annual population estimate the U.S. Census Bureau releases. "If you're talking about a political system that skews rural, that's not as important if there isn't a major cleavage between rural and urban voting behavior," says political scientist Frances Lee. "But urban and rural voting behavior is so starkly different now so that this has major political consequences for who has power."[49]

State legislatures. The gerrymandering of state legislatures is arguably more advantageous to rural voters than that for the U.S. House. In his compelling 2019 book, *Why Cities Lose: The Deep Roots of the Urban-Rural Political Divide,* political scientist Jonathan Rodden proves that Republican-leaning rural voters enjoy inflated power in several state legislatures, especially in the Midwest. In recent decades, Republicans in Michigan, Minnesota, Ohio, Pennsylvania, Virginia, and Wisconsin wielded majorities in one or both state legislative chambers despite receiving fewer statewide votes than their Democratic opponents did. In Pennsylvania, the Republicans have controlled the state senate for four straight decades despite winning the popular vote statewide only about half that time. The Ohio GOP has controlled the state senate for thirty-five years even though Democrats have won about a third of statewide races for governor.

The factors that create rural overrepresentation in state legislatures are the same as for U.S. House gerrymandering: the natural clustering of Democrats in the cities and inner suburbs and the Republican exploitation of this geographic reality to maximize the number of GOP-held seats. The consequence of these tilted maps, says Rodden, is that they exacerbate urban-rural tensions. "This urban-rural polarization is a serious problem in its own right, but in many U.S. states, it has also created a geographic distribution of partisans that allows Republicans to win seat shares in excess of their share of the vote," he writes. "In turn, this asymmetry between votes and seats only further fans the flames of urban-rural sectionalism."[50]

Wisconsin is a particularly egregious case. Republicans there drew state legislative maps so shrewdly that in 2018, the GOP won 65 percent of Wisconsin House seats even though their candidates received only 46 percent of votes cast statewide, on the same day that Democrat Tony Evers won the governor's race by one point.[51] The GOP's legislative map deprived urban and suburban Wisconsin Democrats of their rightful legislative majority.

After Evers unseated three-term Republican incumbent Scott Walker, Wisconsin's Republican legislators responded to their defeat by voting in late 2018 to strip the governor's office of certain executive powers that Walker had exercised for twelve years but that Evers could not wield after he took office in January 2019. In effect, the GOP used its rural-inflated and gerrymandered legislative majority to dilute the power that Democrats had obtained by winning a governor's race the Republicans were powerless to rig because gubernatorial votes, aggregated statewide, are immune to mapmaking mischief.

Walker's loss so infuriated Wisconsin Republicans that they began saying the quiet part out loud—namely, that urban voters ought not to count as much as voters in the rest of the state. "If you took Madison and Milwaukee out of the state election formula, we would have a clear majority," said Wisconsin Republican House Speaker Robin Vos. "We would have all five constitutional officers and we would probably have many more seats in the legislature." His Republican counterpart, state senate majority leader Scott Fitzgerald, echoed this sentiment: "Citizens from every corner of Wisconsin deserve a strong legislative branch that stands on equal footing with an incoming administration that is based almost solely in Madison."[52]

Of course, if rural votes were removed from the equation, the Democrats would hold all five of those statewide offices, control both chambers of the state legislature, repeatedly elect two U.S. senators, and deliver the state's 10 electoral votes every four years to the Democratic presidential nominee. The difference is that urban Democrats in the Badger State are not suggesting that the votes of rural Wisconsinites be discounted or eliminated from the electoral equation. "In much of Wisconsin, 'Madison and Milwaukee' are code words (to some, dog whistles) for the parts of the state that are nonwhite, elite, different: The cities are where people don't have to work hard with their hands, because they're collecting welfare or public-sector paychecks," *New York Times* reporter Emily Badger wrote in 2018, as Republicans were stripping incoming governor Evers of his constitutional powers. "That stereotype updates a very old idea in American politics, one pervading Wisconsin's bitter Statehouse fights today and increasingly those in other states: Urban voters are an exception. If you discount them, you get a truer picture of the politics—and the will of voters—in a state."[53]

We asked Ben Wikler, the chair of the Wisconsin Democratic Party, what Democrats are up against in the state. Because of the rural gerrymander, he said, "urban areas send Democratic representatives who are essentially guaranteed to never serve as chairs of any committee, to never serve as the Speaker of the state assembly, and to never have the power to move a bill through the legislative process and into law."

The irony is that because there are so few competitive districts, rural voters don't get meaningful representation despite their influence at the ballot box. "The Republican representatives in rural Wisconsin only look over their right shoulder for primary opponents and face very little pressure to actually deliver for the broad majority of the residents in their districts. So, you wind up with a politics that serves the cultural far right and the economic elite, but where everyday concerns of rural Wisconsinites on things like Medicaid expansion are never addressed," Wikler added. There is, however, "an anti-urban agenda" aimed in particular at Milwaukee, the state's lone majority-non-White city. The legislature has sought to deprive the city of state spending, "which has led to a slow bleed of funding for things like first responders, for libraries, for basic services that people rely on." But that money isn't being redirected to rural areas; tax cuts are often the highest priority.[54]

Ohio is a similarly outrageous case of distorting the seats-won-per-votes-received calculus via shrewd mapmaking. Although Trump won Ohio by eight points in both 2016 and 2020, Obama narrowly carried the Buckeye State in 2008 and 2012. Ohio shades red, but not to the degree by which Republican state legislators wield their impervious supermajorities. Yet, with ruthless precision, Ohio Republicans gerrymandered for themselves a state legislative map that in the 2020 election gave them 64 percent of house seats and 76 percent of senate seats.

Emboldened by those majorities, Republicans in the Ohio legislature passed a number of policies that defy the majority will of Ohio's citizens. Abortion is a perfect example. With one of the nation's strictest anti-abortion laws, Ohio made national headlines in the weeks following the Supreme Court's 2022 *Dobbs* ruling when a ten-year-old rape victim had to travel to Indiana to get an abortion. As *The New Yorker*'s Jane Mayer explains, only 14 percent of Ohioans support a complete abortion ban without exceptions for rape or incest, and only 39 percent support a so-called heartbeat standard for obtaining legal abortions. Yet the Ohio Republicans who control both chambers of the state legislature need not worry that their views conflict with the citizenry at large, argues University of Cincinnati political scientist David Niven, who rates Ohio as the second-most gerrymandered state legislature in the nation. "Ohio has become the Hindenburg of democracy," Niven told Mayer in 2022.[55]

In his book *Laboratories of Autocracy,* former Ohio Democratic Party chair David Pepper describes how insulated from electoral consequences Ohio's Republican state legislators, secure in their gerrymandered districts, have become. After Gov. John Kasich and Republican state legislators passed a law in March 2011 restricting workers' collective bargaining rights, opponents vowed to repeal it, an effort that by state law required them to amass a minimum of 230,000 signatures in three months to put the repeal measure on that November's ballot. Labor activists collected *five times* that number, and the measure won by a 22 percent margin statewide. In a state where pro-labor Democrat Barack Obama carried only seventeen counties in his re-election bid a year later, majorities in a stunning eighty-three of Ohio's eighty-eight counties supported repeal.

Yet of the fifty-three state legislators who voted for the unpopular, now-repealed law, forty-one ran for re-election in 2012 and forty of them won, most by comfortable margins. "The popularity or lack of popularity of ideas is irrelevant. In fact, if an idea is not popular—if it defies the broad will of the people—the statehouses of this country are clearly the place to make it happen," Pepper writes. "The anonymity of statehouse members, and the gerrymandering that protects them, means they can take on unpopular causes without risk."[56]

Urban power dilutions are hardly new. Remember the study cited earlier in this chapter, in which an examination of 804 key U.S. Senate votes across a six-decade period showed that rural states and voters enjoyed a consistent advantage thanks to malapportionment? The same effect occurs at the state level. In a remarkable study of thirteen states over the 120-year period between 1880 and 2000, political scientists Gerald Gamm of the University of Rochester and Thad Kousser of the University of California, San Diego, determined that big-city delegations in state legislatures suffered far higher failure rates for their policy agendas.

In cases where state legislatures target cities for punitive or restrictive laws, racial dynamics are often at work. For example, Gamm and Kousser also found that between 1921 and 1961, six state legislatures systematically underfunded cities with higher shares of immigrant or non-White residents.[57] Two other political scientists, Baylor University's Patrick Flavin and University of Indianapolis's Gregory Shufeldt, examined how, since 2010, states have used pre-emption laws to restrict local governments. Because rural voters wield power at the statewide level they do not within cities, pre-emption laws are a way for rural Whites to restrict the authority of citizens from urban areas, who of course are more racially diverse, more liberal, and more Democratic. Flavin and Shufeldt found that "states where Republicans control both legislative chambers and the governorship, with more politically conservative citizens, a higher percentage of African Americans, and a stronger conservative interest group presence pass more laws that preempt local policymaking."[58]

Gerrymandered state legislative majorities also control the drawing of U.S. House districts. The inflated power of rural voters in state legislatures therefore gives Republican politicians in Columbus, Madison, and other state capitals the power to, in turn, inflate rural White influence in their U.S. House delegations. By one estimate, Republicans gained thirty-nine U.S. House seats between 2012 and 2016 thanks to

favorable congressional maps drawn by Republican-controlled state legislators.[59] Those thirty-nine seats are one-sixth the number needed to
build a House majority. None of this would be possible without the magnified power of rural voters.

Democrats in solidly blue states like Illinois, Maryland, Massachusetts, and New York practice partisan gerrymandering, too. But the
overall partisan tilt is clear. Ruralized gerrymandering helped Midwest
Republicans in states like Wisconsin and Ohio forge state legislative majorities despite receiving fewer of the votes cast. Consequently, in the
2020 round of redistricting, Republican state officials controlled the
mapmaking process for 187 U.S. House seats to just 75 in Democratic-
controlled states.[60]

Although the conventional wisdom is that gerrymandering exacerbates partisan polarization, experts disagree about how much. More rig-
orous analyses suggest that Americans have for decades been self-sorting
geographically into either bluer or redder communities and states, and
thus polarization would have occurred regardless of who drew the maps
for U.S. House and state legislative districts.[61] Gerrymandering, however, has had one clear and undisputed effect: Strategic mapmaking
magnifies the power of rural voters and the Republican Party at the expense of urban voters and the Democrats. "We are far and away the most
countermajoritarian democracy in the world," warns political scientist
Steven Levitsky, co-author of *How Democracies Die*.[62] This is a vital
piece of the context to understand: While there are tensions and conflicts between rural and urban people everywhere in the world, only in
the United States do so many elements of the political system give rural
citizens such outsize influence.

CALLS FOR SECESSION

Despite enjoying inflated voting power in so many states, rural voters
nevertheless complain that somehow they are the victims of structural
underrepresentation. Which explains why there are growing calls by
rural Whites for secession—just not the type of secession that comes to

mind when, say, one thinks about the circumstances that led to the Civil War.

Why are today's secessionist calls different? Because rather than demanding that states secede from the union, the modern secessionist movements are calling for rural counties to secede from blue states either to form new states or to become part of existing adjacent red states.

A decade ago, Whites in rural counties in Western Maryland agitated for secession to form a new fifty-first state. Currently, Oregon citizens are backing the "Greater Idaho" movement, which would redraw Idaho's borders to capture all the counties from the eastern half of Oregon and make them part of Idaho. Rural White California conservatives have repeatedly attempted to carve that blue state into pieces that they could, in turn, convert into new states. According to the Brookings Institution's Colby Galliher and Edison Forman, secessionist movements are gaining steam among rural red county advocates who are pushing a variety of ballot measures in blue states. "From the Mid-Atlantic to the Pacific Northwest, rural counties in blue states have taken steps to redraw state lines to subsume themselves under neighboring red states or to form new states of their own," they write. "In some cases, such exercises have drawn sizeable community support, leading to the placement of the secession question on local ballots and subsequent approval by voters."[63]

Moving rural, conservative, overwhelmingly Republican counties from a blue state into a neighboring red state could backfire, of course: After all, the state from which those counties secede would likely become more reliably liberal and Democratic, while the red state they join might only become more conservative and Republican. But a group of rural counties seceding to form a new state—complete with its guaranteed minimum of two U.S. senators, at least one U.S. House member, and three electoral votes—would immediately inflate rural voting power in Congress and in presidential elections beyond what it currently is.

Secessionist calls might be easily dismissed as just one more symptom of the polarization that increasingly divides red America from blue

America. But notice there are no calls from residents of, say, Philadelphia and Pittsburgh agitating to remove themselves from Pennsylvania
to form two new states so they can elect four new Democratic U.S. senators. And although the urban-rural split is not the only fault line creating
suspicion and tension in U.S. politics, it is now the key dividing line that
renders it more difficult for the nation to heal, move forward, and govern.

The United States nearly destroyed itself in a civil war that pitted
North against South. Our hope is that urban-rural splits do not lead to
another political crisis of that magnitude. Rural calls for counties to either secede from their states to join other states or form new states are a
nakedly hypocritical attempt to further inflate an already-inflated rural
power, and, worse, such calls exacerbate the growing animosity between
city and country.

A DEMOCRACY *AND* A REPUBLIC

When challenged about inequities created by malapportionment or
gerrymandering—in the Electoral College, the U.S. Congress, or state
legislatures—conservatives and Republicans offer a cheeky, one-excuse-
fits-all reply. *We're a republic, not a democracy,* they chirp.

This canard is false because the two concepts are not mutually exclusive. A democracy is a system in which the authority to govern derives
from the people. Republicanism is a representational form in which the
people exercise that authority by electing politicians to vote on their behalf rather than deciding policy via direct democracy votes on ballot
initiatives and referenda. The United States is a *democratic republic:*
both a democracy and a republic. Malapportionment is not a precondi-
tion for having a democratic republic.

The "republic, not a democracy" rhetoric is designed to excuse the
fact that our distorted system weights votes unequally, mostly to the benefit of rural Whites and at the expense of everyone else. Instead of simply
admitting that they have no regard for the "one person, one vote" principle, conservative Republicans and their rural supporters wrap them-

selves in phony defenses of small-*r* republicanism. They shrug as if they're helpless to do anything about it because that's just the hand the infallible Founders dealt us.

There is, of course, no other way to defend a system in which the party that lost the popular vote seven out of the past eight presidential elections has appointed as many justices to the Supreme Court as the party that won the popular vote in those seven elections, and now controls that Court by a 6–3 supermajority. There is no other way to justify why Senate majorities that represent fewer citizens or that were elected by a minority of voters during the previous six-year election cycle systematically favor rural voters over racial minorities. There's no other justification for one party wielding a state legislative chamber supermajority even though the other party received more votes statewide.

Rural voters are overrepresented in the United States. They always have been and—barring the highly unlikely termination of the U.S. Senate—always will be. For suburban and urban voters, the diluting of their votes is bad enough. Far worse are the apologists who try to gaslight the rest of the nation into believing that the inflated voting power of rural voters, especially rural Whites, is justified.

Still worse is how many of these same defenders of malapportionment point to blue-versus-red election maps to reinforce the false idea that sparsely populated rural communities are entitled to exaggerated power. Joe Biden and Donald Trump each carried twenty-five states in 2020, with Biden also winning the District of Columbia. But those sparsely populated, large-land-mass states appear to make Trump the winner.

County-level maps are more misleading. Even in solidly blue states, county results reveal small, densely packed islands of blue scattered amid vast seas of Republican red. In Michigan, Pennsylvania, and Wisconsin—the three key swing states that broke for Republican Donald Trump narrowly in 2016 but that Democrat Joe Biden flipped back four years later—Biden carried only 38 of 222 counties. County maps make these Biden statewide wins somehow look like dominant Trump victories.

After his 2016 win, Trump pointed to these lopsidedly red state and county maps to peddle the fiction that his was a landslide victory, even though he received fewer votes than Hillary Clinton. "He was taking advantage of the fact that large, rural areas with low populations are more visible than compact, heavily Democratic cities to suggest that his victory was broader than it actually was," writes *Washington Post* columnist Philip Bump. "In another sense, though, he was offering a judgment: That so much of the country was red was a reflection of how important those areas were. It was right to submerge the results in cities to those in rural areas since those rural areas voted correctly. Voted right."[64]

Harvard political scientist Theda Skocpol, a leading scholar on the conservative movement in the post–Tea Party era, summarized the daunting political-electoral realities succinctly. In many ways, the Tea Party's rise provided an early warning signal for the eventual rise of Trump's brand of White nationalism. Skocpol believes that Trump's 2016 presidential victory will be remembered as a turning point "toward a locking-in of minority rule along ethno-nationalist lines. The objective is to disenfranchise metro people, period. I see a real chance of a long-term federal takeover by forces that are determined to maintain a fiction of a White, Christian, Trumpist version of America."[65] This fiction relies upon rural Americans exercising an inflated electoral power no other demographic groups possess. Results from a 2022 Morning Consult poll show that 47 percent of Americans would support a candidate for Congress or the presidency who promised to "end partisan gerrymandering," but only 33 percent of rural respondents would.[66] Heartland citizens know that manipulative mapmaking favors them.

Imagine, for example, if liberals and Democrats started calling for stricter scrutiny of rural voters and voting results only in small, overwhelmingly White rural counties. Republicans and their conservative media allies would start howling—and they would be right to do so. Targeting the validity of some voters and not others based purely on the size or population density of their county is clearly discriminatory. But in Texas, Republicans are doing exactly that: In 2023, the Republican majority in the state legislature passed a bill, promoted by Governor Greg

Abbott, that gives the governor and state election officials authority to overturn the results in just one county: Harris, home to Houston and, not coincidentally, both the most populous and the most racially diverse of Texas's 254 counties.[67]

Taking electoral self-rule away from a single county—the biggest and most racially diverse county, at that—is nothing short of a naked power grab designed to intimidate Houston's voters and election officials. Imagine the fury that would spew from conservative talking heads on radio and TV if Democrats passed a bill in some state to usurp the authority of rural counties to control their election boards. You would literally have to imagine it because, again, power grabs of this nature emanate only from one side of the ideological-partisan divide.

The rural skew of elections also exacerbates the urban-rural fault lines that increasingly balkanize the nation. In his detailed analysis of what he calls America's widening "density divide," Niskanen Center analyst Will Wilkinson frets about the risks inherent in having an economically stagnant, politically recalcitrant, "monocultural" rural minority exert too much power over an increasingly vibrant, urbanized United States. "There is a great deal of wisdom embedded in America's constitutional scheme," Wilkinson writes. "However, in the context of the density divide, this system allowed Donald Trump and the party of the monocultural country—the party of urbanization's most tenacious holdouts—to seize total control of the American state with a minority of votes and a third of the economy. That's a recipe for disaster."[68] In other words, the antiquated U.S. electoral system allows rural White Americans to hold the rest of the nation hostage.

Directly or indirectly, the perversions of malapportionment and gerrymandering redound to the benefit of rural citizens, especially rural Whites. Taken together, Senate malapportionment and the gerrymandering of national and state legislative districts has so distorted policy outcomes that they defy public preferences. Rural Americans may not always get what they want, but thanks to their outsize power, they can far too often prevent the urban-suburban majorities from getting what *they* want. A representative democracy should reflect public preferences through policy. Those preferences may at times be too murky to discern.

But what is clear is the enduring and perverse distortion of those preferences to the benefit of rural citizens.

Rural White voters may not want to hear it, but their revanchist style of politics—magnified by their overrepresentation—is not some bulwark that protects the republic from ruin. Rather, their magnified power—in the Senate, in the Electoral College, and through strategic gerrymandering—now threatens the survival of American democracy.

CULTURES AT WAR

—

POLITICAL LEADERS HAVE BEEN HEAPING PRAISE UPON OUR RURAL CIT-
izens since the country's founding. In 1785, Thomas Jefferson wrote that
"cultivators of the earth are the most valuable citizens. They are the most
vigorous, the most independant, the most virtuous, and they are tied to
their country and wedded to it's liberty and interests by the most lasting
bands. As long therefore as they can find emploiment in this line, I would
not convert them into mariners, artisans, or any thing else."[1] Over the
decades, most of them were converted to other occupations, but the reverence for rural people and the places where they live has remained.

When politicians want to show they're authentic, sincere, and trust-
worthy, they often reach for a little rural cred, whether they come by it
honestly or not. Sen. Josh Hawley, son of a banker and a graduate of
prep school and then Stanford and Yale Law, looks into the camera and
says, "We've got two perfect little boys. Just ask their muhmuh." Mike
Pence steps out of a pickup truck and pretends to fill it up with gas to
show his concern over the cost of living; the ad for his 2024 presidential
run does not show him driving the truck back to his ten-thousand-
square-foot mansion in a tony Indianapolis suburb. George W. Bush,
who grew up summering at his family's Kennebunkport estate, buys a
"ranch" so he can clear brush for the cameras. This kind of signaling is
not just about saying to rural constituents, "I'm just like you," though it
is that. It's also about a web of values, traits, and beliefs that rurality rep-

resents. And while anger at what they have long perceived as condescension and disdain from coastal elites is close to the heart of the rural ethos, it's also true that in politics today, almost no group of Americans is catered to and lionized the way rural people are.

There are plenty of differences between the communities you'll encounter if you visit West Virginia coal country, the Nebraska Plains, or California's Central Valley. But there is also an identifiable set of ideas one can find thick on the ground in all those places, a philosophy and identity that run through rural America. These ideas have profound political consequences, shaping how rural people understand politics and how politicians appeal to rural people.

You don't have to be from a rural area to be familiar with the rural ethos as we've been taught to understand it. Rural people are supposedly independent, self-reliant, hardworking, competent, and capable—especially when it comes to the practicalities of everyday life. They're patriotic and devout, committed to family and community, and ready to lend a hand. The idea that rural people (or, more specifically, rural Whites) are the realest, best Americans is essential to the outsize power granted to the places where they live.

It's not always spoken aloud, but sometimes it is—as when Sarah Palin said on the campaign trail in 2008, "We believe that the best of America is in these small towns that we get to visit and in these wonderful little pockets of what I call the real America, being here with all of you hardworking, very patriotic, um, very, um, pro-America areas of this great nation."[2] Both Democrats and Republicans are prone to reassuring rural people that the places they come from are not just admirable and worthy of preservation but the truest America, where virtues like hard work and honesty practically bubble up from the soil. If you're looking for the heart of America, you're supposed to pass by the cities and the suburbs and head to where food is grown and you might not be able to see your neighbor's house from yours.[3]

Every candidate who can claim a small-town heritage will tout their "small-town values" as just what is needed in the state capital or Washington. When North Dakota governor Doug Burgum, a billionaire software magnate, launched his presidential campaign with a video proclaiming his "small-town values," one of us (Paul) wrote a column for *The Washington Post* suggesting that the things one learns growing up in a city—dealing with many different kinds of people, handling constant change—might be even more valuable to the presidency than what one learns in a small town. Burgum made the column the focus of a fundraising email, which was titled "They Hate Rural America." If you don't laud small towns as the source of the greatest wisdom and virtue, you're the enemy.

In much of the world, rural life has long been portrayed in almost Edenic terms, as a nearly lost idyll of beauty, honesty, and virtuous simplicity, a contrast with the harshness of modern urban existence.[4] Even if the real picture is more complicated and less perfectly idyllic, there's plenty of truth in those ideas about what rural life and rural people are like. Rural life has become an image, even a brand, one that exerts a powerful cultural pull. That brand is steeped in nostalgia, evoking an imagined time in the past when things were simpler and better, less tainted by modern life and its complexities.

The story of modernization, in America as everywhere else, is in no small part the story of people steadily leaving the farm and heading to cities. In the nation's early years, cities were tiny compared not only to what they are now but also to other world cities of the day. At the time of the first census, in 1790, when London's population neared 1 million, Boston contained 18,320 people, Philadelphia had 28,522, and New York was bursting at its seams with 33,131. Most Americans were farmers; it would not be until over a century later that the rural population would be in the minority.

Even those who didn't farm were embedded in the agricultural economy, but that steadily changed as well. When World War II ended, half the people living in rural America were farmers,[5] but their numbers dwindled rapidly as advances in technology required fewer people to farm, the agricultural economy was consolidated with the growth of massive agribusiness corporations, and the rest of the country grew faster. By 2019, only 7 percent of rural Americans were farmers.[6]

Nevertheless, the farm and the kind of person it creates are essential not just to the rural ethos but also to a contemporary vision of integrity and authenticity, one you can see all around you once you start to look. That myth is both pervasive and enduring, and it assigns exclusively to rural White citizens a special status: They are not only "real Americans" but are possessed of traits and abilities on which the rest of us are supposed to look with envious admiration. That status is vividly expressed in the vehicle we associate with rural America, no matter who's driving it: the pickup truck.

THE PICKUP TRUCK AND
EVERYTHING IT CARRIES

"A man will ask a lot of his truck," says the unmistakable rough-hewn voice of Sam Elliott in an ad for Ram pickups.[7] "Can it tow that? Haul this? Make it all the way over the top of that? Well, isn't it nice to know that the answer will always be *Hell yes.*"

There may be no consumer good more invested with identity than the vehicles we buy, and no more potent symbol of what "rural" is supposed to represent—both for rural Americans themselves and for the rest of us—than the pickup truck. If you drive through many rural areas, you'll find that pickup trucks dramatically outnumber cars on the road, and it's not because everyone *needs* them. In fact, most of them probably don't. What they've purchased is a luxury good—there are models of the Ford F-150 that start at around $85,000—that communicates some very important ideas about rural life and manhood. Like so many aspects of rural culture, the pickup is a symbol in communication with the past, and it helps us understand where that culture intersects with politics.

The pickup as we know it dates to 1917, when Henry Ford, reportedly having seen how farmers were putting their Model Ts to work hauling on their farms, produced the Model TT, a stronger platform made for more rugged work than motoring into town. Priced at $600 (an affordable $15,750 in today's dollars), it was the world's first production pickup truck.[8]

At the time, 30 percent of Americans lived on farms.[9] A hundred years later, in 2017, when that number had dwindled to around 1 percent, the three bestselling vehicles in the country were the Ford F-Series pickup, the Chevrolet Silverado pickup, and the Ram pickup. They were also the three bestselling vehicles in 2018, 2019, and every year since.

The majority of the men who buy pickups—and they are overwhelmingly men—does not need them to cart hay to the back forty. In fact, the remarkable thing about pickup sales is that they rose steadily as the number of people who needed the vehicle for work declined. As that evolution occurred, what the pickup represented changed dramatically. We chatted about pickups with a seventy-one-year-old man in Fredericksburg, Texas, who told us that when he was a kid, he hated having his father drop him off at school in his pickup, because it meant his dad was just a blue-collar worker, not someone of high status. Today, Fredericksburg is a thriving tourist town full of shops and restaurants, and its streets are filled with gleaming Rams and Silverados, not a speck of dirt on them.

Pickups symbolize a particular kind of masculinity rooted in the work rural people are supposed to do, and you can see it in ads like the ones Sam Elliott narrates, full of shots of trucks hauling and towing. The trucks communicate physical strength, ruggedness, capability, competence, and an indifference to people who might get in your way. And while there has been some media discussion about the increasingly absurd size of many pickups, it has mostly been about how they've gotten *taller* and more imposing, which makes it impossible to see what's in front of you if you're in the driver's seat. But what these discussions of size overlook is what has happened to the truck's back: The bed of the truck, the part used for work, has gotten shorter. Why? Because more room is needed for a large, comfortable backseat, which is what you'll want if you've spent a hundred thousand dollars on a truck. The bench seats are long gone, and the trucks are filled with infotainment systems and every other modern vehicular amenity you could want. While you can still buy a pickup with an eight-foot bed—which is what you need to haul full sheets of plywood—the demand for those models is dwarfed by that for the ones with either 5.5- or 6.5-foot beds; the latter is now referred to as "standard."

That's because most people who buy trucks aren't using them for the tasks for which the vehicles were originally designed. According to a 2019 report on the automotive website The Drive, industry data shows that the vast majority of pickup owners rarely if ever uses their trucks for towing or going off-road. Market research has shown that owners cite the desire to "present a tough image" and "have their car act as [an] extension of their personality" as reasons to own a pickup[10]—which the truck will do even if you never use it to haul anything more than your groceries home or your kids to soccer practice.

In the popular imagination (and much of popular culture), rural manhood is associated with physicality and strength, both in the work that rural men do and even in their preferred modes of recreation (hunting, fishing, four-wheeling). Unlike urban office workers, rural men spend their days both *in* nature and exercising their mastery *over* it, even if today that's true of some rural men more than others. So, these trucks have symbolic power both for rural people themselves and for people elsewhere who are capturing a bit of that rural conception of manhood by buying one. The burgeoning popularity of pickups coincided with the continued decline in the proportion of men whose work required physical strength, and if daily life offers limited opportunities to demonstrate one's manhood according to a traditional conception, driving a pickup can be a visible display of masculinity.

We spoke about this with Mark Metzler Sawin, a historian who—as far as we could tell—is one of the only scholars to have given serious thought to the meaning of pickup trucks. Conservative men in particular, he told us, have grown increasingly distressed as they watched the denigration of "everything that their grandpa did and was praised for," such as upholding traditional ideas and policing the borders of gender roles. "That's what they were supposed to do, and now they're doing exactly the same thing that their grandpa did, and now they're painted as the villain" by at least some in popular culture and social media, "and they're pissed." Every economic setback, strange new cultural trend, or renegotiation of traditional roles is a challenge to men's sense of manhood. This can be true for men in a variety of settings, but it's particularly true for rural men.

If you want to really understand the pickup's symbolism, you have to look at how it's marketed. For years, the automakers sold pickups by evoking their rural roots and power to do work; the typical ad might have told you what the truck could haul and how much it could tow, with images of strong men doing strong men's work. And while some of that work might have been on construction sites, the ads inevitably included scenes on farms.

And some ads were about *just* farms, at least on the surface. In one famous ad aired on the Super Bowl broadcast of 2013, Ram trucks are presented with a 1978 oration from conservative radio commentator Paul Harvey, called "So God Made a Farmer," in which Harvey extols farmers for their combination of capability and compassion, their hard work and family values. A scratchy recording of him delivering the piece in his powerful voice plays over a series of rural images (and a few shots of Ram trucks); the ad's tagline is "To the farmer in all of us." In other words, you are almost certainly not a farmer, and you may not even live in a rural area, but you have some ember of the American farmer and all his virtues glowing within you, which you can keep alight by buying a pickup.

More recent truck marketing has worked to build an emotional bridge between the rural and everyone else, using rural imagery to evoke masculine virtues that you can capture no matter who you are, where you reside, or what you do for a living. One fascinating 2019 commercial features a diverse cast of people singing "Thank God I'm a Country Boy," most of them in *urban* settings, most notably a young Black woman singing it as she rides a subway.

That woman has no need for a pickup. With the ad's multicultural cast, the main target may be urban and suburban liberals who feel the urge to buy a truck but who need to be convinced that it can be integrated with their existing worldview. It's a kind of double bank shot, from the rural imagery of the song; to the racially diverse group of people singing it; to the liberals, many of them White, who could provide a vast new market for the vehicles.

For a time, Sawin told us, pickup manufacturers focused on rural customers who "were moving from occupations that did need a truck to occupations that don't need a truck, but maintaining the truck let you maintain feeling masculine." But "they saturated that market within ten years or so, and they still needed to sell more trucks. So they really start to turn to targeting the suburban White man."[11]

The target of the marketing isn't always the people who are shown onscreen, at least not all of them. You don't have to feel alienated when shots of people driving to the grocery store are intermixed in these ads with shots of other people hauling hay; the point is that even in your suburban life, you can capture a bit of that rural masculine spirit.

Consider one more Super Bowl ad, this one for Chevy. It begins with the words "Can a truck make you more handsome? More dependable? More rugged?" It then shows focus group participants presented with twin pictures of the same man photoshopped standing in front of a small sedan and a giant pickup. When asked about him, the group describes the version standing in front of the truck as more handsome, capable, sexy, and cool, protecting his children and helping a friend in need. The potential buyers are a group of youngish-to-middle-aged men, one of whom says that the man in front of the sedan is merely "existing," while the man with the truck is "living." The end of this bit of meta-marketing is the tagline "You know you want a truck."

The raw physicality of the pickup truck—its size, the power in its engine, the ridiculous amount of gas it requires—lies at the heart of its attraction, particularly for men who are uncertain about their place in a changing world. Many of those men are also targeted by right-wing po-litical opportunists claiming that they face a "crisis of manhood," one in which the fact that most jobs no longer require a great deal of upper-body strength has left them wondering how long they'll stay atop soci-ety's hierarchy. It's why a politician like Josh Hawley writes a book called *Manhood* in which he purports to tell the reader how to be a man, and why former Fox News host Tucker Carlson, a doughy boarding school grad, buys a house in rural Maine, creates a streaming show taped in a wood-paneled studio that looks more like a tree house, and advises men to skip college, get a blue-collar job, and restore their testosterone levels by tanning their testicles.[12]

The story of pickup trucks and their spectacular popularity demon-strates how even today, rural iconography and ideas about what "rural" means continue to have a powerful place in our culture. At their heart is a contradiction: As much as rural people are convinced (not always without reason) that they are looked down upon, the lionization of them and rural culture is an equally powerful force. And alongside the idea of rural people as uniquely virtuous is the contention that they are uniquely beleaguered and attacked by cultural, political, and economic forces emanating from cities and the coasts.

UNPACKING THE CULTURE WAR

"Are you a racist? Do you hate Mexicans?" These are the arresting first words of a 2022 campaign ad aired by J. D. Vance in his bid to be the Republican nominee for Senate in Ohio. Vance became famous for his 2016 book *Hillbilly Elegy,* which unsparingly chronicles the struggles of his dysfunctional working-class White rural family. In it, he is especially candid about the sufferings of his mother, Bev, who hopscotched from one abusive partner to the next on her eventual path to opioid addiction.

But by 2022, Vance had reinvented himself as a Trump-loving culture warrior, stabbing away at the resentments of downscale voters and blaming their troubles on liberals. "The media calls us racist for wanting to build Trump's wall. They censor us, but it doesn't change the truth," he went on. "Joe Biden's open border is killing Ohioans, with more illegal drugs and more Democrat voters pouring into this country."[13]

Gone was the tough love of his book; the man who had written "You can walk through a town where 30 percent of the young men work fewer than twenty hours a week and find not a single person aware of his own laziness"[14] was nowhere to be found. Now Vance was acting as though he were seething with bitterness at distant elites who were not just looking down their noses at small-town folk but literally trying to murder them. In one interview with a popular far-right conspiracy theorist, Vance accused President Biden of intentionally flooding rural America with fentanyl to kill conservative voters. "If you wanted to kill a bunch of MAGA voters in the middle of the heartland, how better than to target them and their kids with this deadly fentanyl?" he said. "It does look intentional. It's like Joe Biden wants to punish the people who didn't vote for him."[15] Rep. Tim Ryan, Vance's Democratic opponent, tried to portray Vance as a dishonest climber who had abandoned Ohio to pursue a Silicon Valley fortune, but it didn't work. With Donald Trump's endorsement in hand, Vance won the election by six points.

As he revised his own history, Vance cast off the critiques he had made of his own people. After mentioning illegal drugs coming across "Joe Biden's open border," Vance says in the ad, "This issue is personal: I nearly lost my mother to the poison coming across our border." But in his book, Vance says his mother was addicted to *prescription* narcotics, which don't come over the border.[16] As most of the country now knows, it was domestic drugmakers and distributors who were guilty of addicting millions of people like Vance's mother. The Connecticut-based drug company Purdue Pharma, owned by the billionaire Sackler family, targeted sales of its OxyContin pain pills to poor, rural White citizens who worked in physically demanding, injury-prone occupations like mining. Perhaps better than most, Vance understands this history, because he worked for a law firm whose lobbying arm was paid to defend Purdue Pharma.[17] That's right: Indirectly, Vance profited from the miseries wrought upon rural Americans by the now-bankrupt and discredited drugmaker.[18] Commenting on Vance's transformation, Sen. Mitt Romney told his biographer, "I don't know that I can disrespect someone more than J. D. Vance."[19]

In those few words that begin his ad—"Are you a racist? Do you hate Mexicans?"—Vance encapsulated so much about how the culture war operates. Race is inescapable, not just in liberal accusations of racism but also in conservatives' insistence that liberals are constantly accusing them of racism, always unfairly. This idea rests inside the larger belief that people in small towns and rural areas are forever demeaned and degraded by snooty liberals seeking to destroy the way of life enjoyed by *real* Americans.

What distinguishes the culture war from the ordinary contest for political power is the centrality of identity. The culture war is not a competition (let alone a negotiation) between ideas or ideologies, but an existential battle between clearly demarcated groups of people whose worldviews are utterly incompatible. In rural America, the culture war vibrates with a particular intensity, as elite Republicans know well—and they use it to keep their voters in a state of constant agitation. They use it to divert attention from the places where their agenda is unpopular even among their own supporters. They use it to make sure that those supporters won't even *consider* voting for a Democrat ever again.

The more the culture war becomes the focus of GOP politics, the higher the stakes seem—and the more the rural voters who are the linchpin of Republican power come to see democracy itself as a threat. Their inability to affect what comes out of Hollywood or New York makes them only more eager to use their political power to make sure the liberals they despise can't win elections, no matter what the majority of voters thinks.

The term *culture war* was popularized by sociologist James Davison Hunter in his 1991 book *Culture Wars: The Struggle to Define America*, but the actual American culture war has existed throughout our nation's history, not to mention that of many other countries. Sometimes it has been a conflict between religions (the *Kulturkampf* between Protestants and Catholics in late-nineteenth-century Germany), while at others, it has manifested as a struggle between religiosity and secularism. Different issues may define it at any time—racial integration, the teaching of evolution, access to abortion, equality for women, LGBTQ+ rights—but it's always about drawing lines of identity that define who is *us* and who is *them.*

And in the current American conservative version, it's also about victimization, both present and future. Conservatives are told over and over that they are encircled by hostile forces bent on subverting their way of life and destroying everything they value. Unfortunately, victim-based anger is ripe for exploitation by conservative Republican politicians. As Thomas Frank argued two decades ago in *What's the Matter with Kansas?*, those politicians push victimization themes during the election cycle and then, after they win, promptly turn their attention to what matters most to their rich and corporate benefactors: cutting taxes, deregulating business, and allowing companies to consolidate and monopolize their respective industries.[20]

The policy outcomes are often barely noticed, and politicians don't

have to work too hard to convince rural constituents that identity matters and that they should look with suspicion on those who live in different, unfamiliar places. Rural people understand perfectly well the long
arc of economic and social history and how the center of American life
has moved from the farm to the city to the suburbs. They feel the
disdain—or, nearly as bad, the disregard—that cosmopolitan urban liberals have for them; according to one 2018 Pew Research Center poll,
70 percent of rural residents said people who live in other kinds of communities don't understand their problems.[21]

Whatever non-rural people may or may not understand about rural
life, however, they feel a strong attraction to it. In a 2020 Gallup poll,
48 percent of Americans said they'd like to live in a small town or rural
area, despite the fact that a far smaller number actually does. The 31 percent who specifically said they'd prefer to live in a rural area was almost
three times as many as the 11 percent who cited a big city as their preferred home. Not surprisingly, the responses varied by party: Only
16 percent of Democrats said they wanted to live in a rural area, compared with 47 percent of Republicans.[22] Similarly, the Pew Research
Center found in 2021 that 35 percent of Americans said they'd like to live
in a rural area, compared with 21 percent who expressed a preference for
the city. (The suburbs were more popular than both.) And rural residents were the *least* likely to say they'd like to live elsewhere: Only
25 percent expressed a desire to move to a different community, compared with 43 percent of urban residents, even though, as we discussed
previously, so many of them do in fact advise young people to leave.[23]

What's most interesting about these results, however, is the fact that
they contradict the actual choices people have made. They are in direct
contrast to what economists call "revealed preferences"—not what people *say* they want but what their behavior reveals. It suggests that there
are millions of people who have an attraction to rural life, just not a
strong enough one to pick up and actually go there.

Of course, not everyone has the ability to move even if their desire to
do so is sincere; we can be held where we are by family ties or economics, even if we'd rather go elsewhere. But it may also be the case that
many people who live in the suburbs and cities are attracted to an idyllic

view of rural life, one they associate with something akin to retirement. It's one thing to picture yourself sitting on a porch drinking sweet tea while watching the sun set over rolling hills and quite another to have to drive an hour to get to the supermarket or the nearest hospital in an emergency, realities about which it's doubtful suburbanites and people in cities who express a yearning for rural life are thinking. This disconnect may help explain why the many utopian experiments Americans have undertaken have usually planted themselves in the country, not only because land could be acquired cheaply but also because the projects usually included some kind of agrarian ideal, an ideological belief that the small community would achieve its perfection at least in part through a recaptured connection to the land. That connection is something we all had once but most of us no longer do.

The ideas Americans hold in their heads about rural America are complex and not always coherent; alongside the idealization of the rural are the stereotypes of rural residents as uneducated, uncultured people with boring lives and limited views of the world. Just think of all the insulting terms we have to refer to rural folk: *hayseed, bumpkin, yokel, hick, rube, hillbilly, redneck.* The insult *White trash* might sound contemporary, but it first became common in the 1850s.[24] The contempt between rural and urban people may have always been mutual, but the economic and cultural power enjoyed by urbanites meant that those on the rural side would wind up feeling insulted and resentful.

There are good reasons for this asymmetry. It's possible for urbanites to all but forget that rural people exist, whereas even if rural people construct and maintain their own culture, they live within a broader culture created largely in cities. The movies they see, the TV they watch, the music they listen to, the sports they follow—all or at least most of it comes from cities. What's different today is that the subset of that broader culture cultivating that anti-urban hostility is stronger than ever, feeding a resentment that is simultaneously organic and sincere on the one hand and encouraged from above on the other. In an ironic twist, even the effort to maintain rural resentment comes largely from cities. Nashville, the heart of country music that supplies endless encomia to the superiority of rural life, is a blue enclave in a sea of red. (Joe Biden beat Donald Trump in 2020 in the city by a two-to-one margin.) Fox News is headquartered in New York, from where it pumps out a steady stream of horror stories about urban decay and condescending liberal "elites" who want nothing more than to destroy all the things rural people value.

The message is clear: *Those liberals are coming for you and your family. Though you are the truest Americans, they hate you and everything you stand for. They call you a racist and a redneck. They want to force their perverted ideas about sex and family on you. And the best way to fight back is to vote Republican—and forget about those democratic principles you learned in school. This is a war, and there's no time to play fair.*

The belief that rural Americans are losing the culture war over the long term only intensifies the feeling of victimization, making them an ever-more-attractive target for culture war appeals. And they are losing, without question. Despite the occasional victory—the overturning of *Roe v. Wade,* the passage of state laws preventing children from being taught too much about racism—the big picture is that every day, the United States grows more secular and racially diverse. Liberal values on gender equality and parenting may not be universally accepted, but they are now the norm; if you loudly proclaim that women should stay in the home or that children need to have their behavior regulated with the periodic application of physical violence (i.e., corporal punishment), you won't be alone, but in many quarters, you will be challenged, even scorned.

And while there is still an enormous amount of homophobia that the right encourages and capitalizes on, America's views about sexuality have grown more liberal with astonishing speed. Those over fifty may not have had a single out gay classmate in high school, but now their kids probably have peers who are gay or nonbinary, and maybe even one or two who are trans. And though they may be able to participate in the furious political backlash against trans kids that Republicans have engineered if they're so inclined, they probably know that over the long term, this is a battle they'll lose just like they lost the others.

The culture war may be present in every corner of America, but it has a particular shape in rural places, where it isn't just about those broad social trends against which people react but rather a long tradition of hostility toward cities and the people who inhabit them. Rural folks have long been disrespected by the typical media portrayal of people like them; for every *Andy Griffith Show* portraying small-town life as friendly and caring, there were many more portrayals of rural people as ignorant bumpkins, or movies like *Deliverance* and *The Texas Chainsaw Massacre,* which presented rural areas as places of terror. Those narratives have never disappeared, especially on reality TV, with regular programs encouraging viewers to gawk at the backwardness of rural people and their ways. Rural residents are rightly offended by these depictions.[25]

Nevertheless, Hollywood also paints rural America in more dignified colors, even in the ways rural people see themselves and their communities. In one familiar plotline, an arrogant city slicker finds himself in the country, only to discover that the rural people he initially dismissed are possessed of extraordinary common sense, folk wisdom, and practical competence, while the city dweller can barely tie his own shoes.[26] In the immensely popular *Hunger Games* books and films, the good people of the countryside are starved and oppressed by the government on behalf of a decadent and immoral city-dwelling elite. The extremely popular Hallmark and Lifetime Christmas movies, of which there seem to be hundreds churned out every year, often feature a young woman from the city who finds herself stuck in a small town through some accident of fortune, whereupon she learns the value of a simpler life and often dumps her no-good boyfriend back in the city in favor of the hunky small-town man she meets early in the movie.[27]

Even so, many more cultural offerings are found in cities—including nearly all the cop shows, lawyer shows, and doctor shows that dominate television—which can make rural people feel as though the culture usually overlooks them. Then they are told by conservative media that whatever their identity—as a conservative, as a White person, as a man, as a Christian—the liberals who allegedly run the country hate them for that identity and will hound them merely for being who they are. As scholar Anthony Nadler noted after conducting extensive conversations with conservatives, "Some talked about personal experiences of feeling slighted or castigated by liberals—especially on social media. But even more frequently, and often more passionately, they told me about stories demonstrating liberals' disdain for conservatives that they had encountered through conservative news."[28]

This perception isn't just about a general us-versus-them conflict. Shame is a key component: fending it off, arguing against it, and being angry at liberals and urbanites for allegedly wanting conservatives and rural people to feel it. As Nadler concluded, for many conservatives, political life is "a constant battle against liberals and leftists driven by a goal of shaming and humiliating conservatives and their communities."

So, in media spaces like Fox News and conservative talk radio, the same kinds of grievances rural people have nurtured for generations—about being looked down upon, dismissed, and shamed for who they are—are extrapolated to the wider conflict between right and left. More than anyone, Rush Limbaugh mastered this narrative when he emerged in the 1980s, and every outpost of conservative media today follows his template in some way, whether it is national outlets such as Fox News or the smallest, most local radio station. Even if you live in a rural area where there isn't a liberal for miles around, the story about liberals trying to shame conservatives resonates, because you already know that those liberals have nothing but contempt for people like you.

It may seem strange to think that a person in rural Nebraska or Oklahoma could be instructed by a pundit from Washington, D.C., on a TV network owned by an Australian media magnate, on how to understand their own identity. But all of us are influenced by what we see in the media, and we integrate it with our own experiences to form a picture of the world and of our place in it. And conservative media are particularly focused on identity, both in fortifying connections between different kinds of conservatives through their mutual victimization by the left and in constructing walls so that their audience won't consider any liberal as someone with whom they could share anything at all.

It isn't just the conservative media; these kinds of messages are reinforced even by mainstream outlets that the right considers liberal. For all the insistence that rural life is mocked and maligned, the belief that small towns and rural areas are "authentic" is shared by the residents of those places and, ironically, elite journalists. Political reporters are forever explaining how out-of-touch Democrats can't possibly relate to the good folks of the heartland, who can supposedly see right through their phony personas and insincere appeals.

In their conception of authenticity, journalists have internalized the criticisms the right makes of them. Overwhelmingly middle or upper class, amply educated, and residents of coastal cities like Washington and New York, journalists characterize the authentic as rural (not urban), downscale (not upscale), and Midwestern or Southern (not Northeastern).

What the media really value, however, is not actual authenticity but the deftest *performance* of authenticity. One of their favorite rituals involves the brutal takedown of a presidential candidate who eats some regional delicacy in an improper way. When John Kerry didn't order his cheesesteak the way that a regular South Philly guy would (he asked for Swiss cheese, the most elitist of all cheeses!), or when Kirsten Gillibrand briefly took a fork and a knife to her fried chicken in South Carolina, the judgment from campaign reporters was swift and harsh: *Look how inauthentic they are.* In the inverse case, a rural person struggling to understand the ways of the city—parallel parking, say, or ordering at a hip downtown restaurant—might be presented as unsophisticated, but no one would call them a phony.

In its repetition (especially at campaign time), this double standard reinforces the disturbing conclusions about rural White power we have been exploring. If a small-town, blue-collar man is the most authentic American, then the fact that his vote counts for more than that of a Black urban lawyer or a Latino suburban government worker won't arouse the outrage and demand for change that it might were he not so valorized.

DANGEROUS IDEAS, COMING FROM YOUR LOCAL LIBRARY

The sense that alien and morally degraded liberal cultural ideas are encroaching has produced a backlash on the right, one that is newly aggressive and willing to use government power to restore what people perceive they have lost. In many rural areas, this has meant conservatives trying to seize control of a place where people believe their values have been particularly undermined: the local library.

It's been said that liberals have cultural power but wish they had political power, while conservatives have political power but wish they had cultural power. At libraries all over the country, conservatives are using their political power to attempt a takeover of this one area of the culture. One such battle began with *I Need a New Butt!* The 2012 book by Dawn McMillan and Ross Kinnaird is recommended for children ages six to ten, and if you've ever had such a child, you know they find this kind of humor absolutely hilarious; it's why the *Captain Underpants* books have sold more than eighty million copies. But when some folks in the Hill Country town of Llano (known as "the deer capital of Texas" for the area's hunting opportunities, and where a statue of a Confederate soldier stands in the middle of town) found out in the summer of 2021 that *I Need a New Butt!* and other titles like it were in their local library, they mobilized.

A woman named Bonnie Wallace sent an email to a local official in Llano with the heading "Pornographic Filth at the Llano Public Libraries." She attached a spreadsheet with a list of sixty books she objected to, many with LGBTQ+ themes and some—like Ta-Nehisi Coates's *Between the World and Me*—that concerned racism. Books were moved, one librarian was fired and another quit, a lawsuit was filed by liberals opposed to censorship, and a brief round of national news coverage ensued.[29]

When we visited Llano nearly a year later, many people told us that the fight had made relations in town uncomfortably political. The conservatives, however, were eager to explain that *they* were the moderate ones; they just wanted to have books in the library be age appropriate. And they were very conscious of how the other side perceived them. " 'Oh, they're trying to ban books, and it's a bunch of Christians.' That's what people said here in town, making fun of us," one woman who had spoken at town meetings about the books told us.[30] They didn't want the books banned, she said, just moved to where little kids couldn't see them. She described parents being shocked at what their kids were reading in school libraries, and said, "Well, send your kids to a government training facility, enjoy." She homeschools her own children.

The controversy in Llano dragged on for months. When the judge in the lawsuit ordered in April 2023 that a group of books that had been taken off the shelves be put back, the county commission met to consider closing down the libraries entirely until the lawsuit was concluded. During the time for citizens' comments, Bonnie Wallace and two of her allies took their turns to read sex scenes from young adult novels. "I am for closing the library until we get this filth off the shelves," one concluded.[31]

Llano's was just one of many such controversies around the country. Recent years have seen a growing number of efforts to ban books from schools and municipal libraries; PEN America reported that in the 2021/22 school year, there were attempts to ban books in 138 school districts in thirty-two states.[32] The American Library Association tracked 1,269 efforts to ban books in libraries in 2022.[33]

Many of these efforts occurred in rural areas, where libraries have become a target of controversy over books with LGBTQ+ themes or discussions of racism. Just a few examples: In Craighead County, Arkansas, residents voted to cut their tax contribution to the library in half in the 2022 election after a controversy involving LGBTQ+ displays.[34] In Maury County, Tennessee, the library director resigned after being "targeted and bullied as part of a right-wing pressure campaign" over a Pride Month display.[35] In Boundary County, Idaho, the head librarian resigned amid threats and harassment over LGBTQ+ books, especially *Gender Queer: A Memoir*, a book the library didn't even own.[36] In rural Jamestown, Michigan, the librarians were accused of being "groomers," i.e., people trying to prepare children for sexual abuse, before voters chose to defund their only library.[37]

These controversies aren't exactly new, but they're growing more frequent and more intense, driven by national right-wing groups such as Moms for Liberty and saturated with the latest incendiary rhetoric. Listen to local conservatives talk about books they find objectionable, and it won't be long before they say the books are meant for "grooming."

"There are some major scary things going on in rural America," said Kathy Zappitello,[38] executive director of the Conneaut Public Library in rural Ashtabula County, Ohio. It's a place Barack Obama won handily in both 2008 and 2012, but that then swung hard to Donald Trump, who beat Hillary Clinton in Ashtabula by nineteen points and then beat Joe Biden there by twenty-three. Zappitello has a unique perspective: Not only did she serve as president of the Association for Rural and Small Libraries, but she also ran for state representative in 2022, jumping into the race late, after the Democratic nominee was gerrymandered out of her district and Democrats scrambled to find a candidate.

Zappitello was motivated to run because the incumbent, Sarah Fowler Arthur—who proudly notes that she is the first homeschool graduate to serve on the state board of education—had sponsored a bill aimed at banishing "divisive concepts" from Ohio classrooms, which Zappitello and many others considered a book-banning bill. "It's the beginning of the end for Ohio libraries if that bill gets passed," Zappitello told us.

Asked why so many of these library controversies are happening in rural areas, Zappitello said, "This stuff is ugly and not very fun to talk about. And I'm talking about my friends and neighbors." While she said she was well aware of controversies affecting rural libraries around the country, they hadn't come to her library in any significant way—until she ran for office. But in running against Arthur and her bill, Zappitello told us, "and by talking about that in my community, and then losing, I inadvertently beat the bushes" and soon found far-right activists investigating libraries and schools in her area to look for objectionable material.

In her twenty years as a librarian, she said, the library had changed in people's minds from a place to find information to a locus of ominous social developments, a place that, to many, is part of the outside forces threatening the rural way of life. Zappitello's experience running for office was a shock, and not in a good way. The Democratic Party in her area was all but absent. "There's no help. There's no coordinated effort. All I got was 'Where's your people, Kathy, we need you to go knock on doors.' It's like, where are *your* people, Democratic Party? I need *you* to go knock on doors." She wound up losing by over twenty points.

Zappitello did meet liberals on the campaign trail—but many of them weren't open about how they actually felt. "I had so many people that whispered to me and held my hand real quick and tight and said, 'Oh my god, thank you,' and whispered and kept walking." She choked up as she described going to meetings that were pleasant enough "until you talk to the woman who is asking you for help and doesn't know what to do, who's in a horrible situation and saw that there's a political meet-and-greet and decided to come and seek help because her son had just committed suicide, and [she] didn't know where else to go. And now she's standing in front of me, and I have her name, and I have her phone number, for what? How am I ever going to help her? What am I going to tell these neighbors in Geauga County, the county below Ashtabula, who came up to me in a parking lot and said, 'Kathy, I can't take one of your signs, because I'm so afraid of my neighbors. I can't even talk to anybody, but you have my one vote, and I promise you that.'"

Zappitello isn't sure if she'll continue to be involved in politics, or even what the future holds for her as a librarian in her town. "I tried," she told us with a resigned laugh. "Put that on my tombstone. 'I tried.'"

Not every committed librarian in rural areas will be intimidated, be fired, or find themselves so discouraged that they leave town, though some already have. Nor are these controversies limited to rural areas. But this is clearly a way rural conservatives have found to fight back against a wider culture they see as opposed to them and their beliefs. And they seem eager to keep that fight going.

Book bans and fights over local curricula are not limited to rural communities. But rural citizens may feel unusual pressure to bend to state and national standards they find overwhelming, even oppressive. In that sense, these seemingly small-time, localized fights are symptomatic of resistance emanating from rural communities against what they perceive as predations against not merely home rule but also their self-professed traditional values.

THE CULTURE WAR CONDUIT

Conservative media may not have created the culture war grievances like those driving book-banning efforts out of whole cloth, but they are the engine that drives such efforts forward, elevating certain issues at certain times and telling people what they should be angry about: immigration one day, critical race theory the next, trans kids playing sports the day after that—all contextualized within a broader cultural conflict. Those messages from conservative media are poured into an informational eco-system in which rural people have fewer and fewer options for news that exists outside the liberal-conservative conflict. In 2008, 71,000 people were employed in newspaper newsrooms across the country—reporters, editors, photographers, and so on. By 2020, that number had plunged to under 31,000.[39] Between 2005 and 2022, 2,500 American newspapers went out of business, a fourth of all the papers in the country.[40] These closures have happened for multiple reasons, including the disappear-ance of vital classified ad revenue, as those ads migrated to places like Craigslist and Facebook, and the predations of media conglomerates that buy up local newspapers, strip out the local reporting, and often consolidate the papers into weak collections of wire stories.

The decline of local news is a particular problem in rural areas, where newspapers were already vulnerable and thinly staffed. As a result, many rural areas turned into local news deserts over this period. As Nancy Gibbs of Harvard's Shorenstein Center points out, some of the places with the most disproportionate political power are without any local newspapers. She gives one striking example: "With all that added clout for shaping the composition of Congress and, less directly, the Supreme Court and the White House, the voters in about half of South Dakota's 66 counties have only a single weekly newspaper. Seven counties have no newspaper at all."[41]

The disappearance of local reporting isn't just unfortunate, it's a cri-sis for democracy itself. When no one is reporting on city hall or the county council, corruption flourishes. Voter turnout often declines, as does people's understanding of politics and government.[42] Citizens have no idea what their leaders are doing or whether they are actually representing their constituents.

This void leaves people in these areas unaware of what's happening close to home, but they can tune in to national news, where they see a politics that is confrontational and polarized. And for a great many of them, national news means *conservative* news, especially Fox and talk radio. That's not to mention the multitude of local conservative radio stations spread across rural America that echo the same ideas in between their locally focused content. Many people in rural areas have the radio on for hours every day—in farmers' tractor cabs, in their cars if they're driving long distances, in the places where they work. A team of researchers at the University of Wisconsin counted eighty-one conservative talk stations delivering hundreds of hours of right-wing talk around the state every day.[43]

The relative lack of competing news sources in rural areas makes radio even more powerful. It takes the news of the day, as well as a steady stream of liberal outrages, and contextualizes them within a few key themes that are hammered home again and again: *Democrats hate you, liberal elites are immoral and dishonest, and we are engaged in an apocalyptic struggle against those who want to destroy us and our way of life, which if the liberals succeed will leave America a depraved and desiccated husk of what it once was.*

Those who consume conservative media are also given a constant reinforcement of political boundaries. They learn all about the sins of the left, but they're also instructed in the common cause of conservatives from different places who might have different interests. And few unifying forces are more powerful than the idea that all "real" and "regular" Americans, whether they're from the suburbs or the country or even the city, are scorned and targeted by powerful elitist liberals. In this telling, those liberal elitists have *personal* contempt for the real Americans precisely because of their virtues, such as patriotism and piety.

Because they have lots of airtime to fill, radio hosts can unpack and explain events to contextualize them for their audience. As scholar Scott Ellison notes, the hosts often do "deep readings" of news items from mainstream media, to "work through the text, often line-by-line, and re-interpret it so as to . . . situate the news piece within the grand narratives of contemporary American conservatism."[44] They explain not only what listeners should believe but also how they should go about understanding the news—which makes talk radio a daily instruction in what to think, what to think about, and how to think.

This work is done every day by the hundreds of mini-Limbaughs spread around the country on conservative talk radio, many of whom are popular in rural areas. They take policy disputes and turn them into irreconcilable identity issues, so, whether the topic of the day is immigration or healthcare or inflation, it's an opportunity to draw a line separating *us* from *them*. When pundits claim that the resentment of small-town Republicans is driven not by increasing diversity or the propaganda efforts of the conservative elite but by their own circumstances and the excesses of "political correctness," we would respond that no two of those factors are mutually exclusive. White, rural, religious Americans are reacting to their very real decline as a proportion of the U.S. population and to the attendant risk to their status, but they're also reacting to what they're told in the media every day.

Cable news and the internet work together to show people who are afraid of change just how much change is occurring, which reinforces their sense of fear and resentment. We may grasp the fact that increasing demographic diversity is often understood by rural Whites as a threat to their way of life, but increasing cultural diversity may be just as important. It can be hard to remember just how narrow our perception of the outside world was before the internet and, in particular, social media gave us a view of so many different kinds of people and ideas. If there were aspects to the cultural life of a big city that a rural person found unnerving, it didn't matter much, given that they had little opportunity to learn about those aspects, and even when they did, they seemed like something far away that couldn't possibly come to their community. But now, everything is right in everyone's face, and it's not hard to move from shock to repulsion to fear and anger, especially when there are media figures on trusted outlets like Fox News telling you that fear and anger are precisely what you should feel. And of course, social media is an unceasing engine of outrage and disgust, amplifying every conflict and elevating trivial incidents into national awareness.

It's no accident that many of the most prominent and admired Republicans in Congress are little more than Fox News personalities with side gigs as legislators. Few of them have ever written a law of any significance, not only because they aren't particularly interested in the work of governing but also because governing undermines their larger project of delegitimizing government. Among them is a bevy of elite, Ivy-educated lawyers like the senators Ted Cruz, Tom Cotton, and Josh Hawley, who are more likely to indulge in moral panic and cringe-worthy "My pronouns are 'Kiss my ass'!" performative politics than to offer a thoughtful policy critique.

So, the politicians and the media figures cooperate to create a permanent backlash politics in which rage at social change is their primary political tool. Politics has no goal more important than lashing out at your enemies and making dramatic gestures like removing books from libraries or firing gay teachers, gestures that won't do anything to reverse the actual societal changes people find so threatening, but that will make those people feel a little more powerful, at least for a moment.

The trouble is that this feeling of empowerment is fleeting, and change continues—which is where the real danger of the culture war may emerge. When people realize that they'll continue to get older, that America will continue to get more diverse, that "traditional" values on sexuality will continue to evolve, and that the people they hate will not disappear, what will happen? There is no easy way to predict, but authoritarian and radical right-wing movements have always found many of their adherents among those who felt they once had power and status and were losing it.

"Try to see America through their eyes," read a November 2022 Associated Press report about people in rural Wisconsin who are increasingly convinced that dark conspiracies are bent on destroying everything they believe in and are gathering weapons in case a civil war comes.[45] This instruction—you, reader, must make an effort to understand the perspective not just of people in rural areas but of the most politically radical and the most disconnected from reality among them—is one that news consumers have been given for years. We're encouraged to sympa-thize with even extremely dangerous people who are literally stockpiling weapons, but only if they come from the places where the "essential mi-nority" resides. There are no articles about radical Black nationalists preparing for civil war that begin, "Try to see America through their eyes." But rural Whites are given greater moral latitude. Their excesses may not quite be excused, but we're called upon to understand these people—the implication being that whatever dangers they may present, it's only because the rest of us haven't given them the consideration they deserve.

THE DARK AND DANGEROUS CITY

The increasing geographic polarization between the parties has become a regular topic for national news outlets, yet stories about Republicans' inability to win in cities are far rarer than stories about Democratic struggles among rural voters. There's an implicit judgment at work, one that says that Democrats' failure to win over rural voters is a kind of *moral* failing, one that can only be bred of insensitivity or contempt. Republicans' struggles in cities, however, are seldom examined and less often judged; it's just how things are.

This double standard is reinforced by the fact that journalists are al-ways ready to amplify those few cases in which a Democrat says some-thing dismissive about rural areas and the people who live there. But try to imagine a Democratic state legislator saying that the rural areas where 20 percent of his state's population lives are a "hellhole" and sponsoring a bill calling for those areas to be spun off into their own state so the rest of the state can be rid of them. Now imagine the Democratic Party mak-ing that legislator their nominee for governor.

That's what happened in 2022 in Illinois, but with the parties re-versed: Republicans nominated state senator Darren Bailey, who had repeatedly called Chicago a "hellhole" and who introduced a resolution to make it its own state. During the campaign, he temporarily moved to a luxury high-rise in the city, telling reporters he wanted to "immerse myself in the culture." What did he find? "Chicago is living The Purge, when criminals ravage at will, and the cops stand down," he said, referring to the horror movie franchise in which all crimes become legal one night a year.[46] Somehow Bailey managed to avoid being killed during his time there, but the people of Chicago were skeptical that he had any sympathy for their problems; he got just 16 percent of the vote in the city and was easily beaten in the state overall, losing to incumbent Democrat J. B. Pritzker by twelve points.

Bailey's view of big cities is shared by many conservatives, even some who live in those cities but who see political advantage in encouraging people to fear them. And few people have fed conservative contempt, and myths, about cities more than native New Yorker Donald Trump. "We have a situation where we have our inner cities, African-Americans, Hispanics are living in hell because it's so dangerous," Trump said in a 2016 debate with Hillary Clinton, at a time when crime was the lowest it had been in decades. "You walk down the street, you get shot."[47] This was a regular theme of Trump's over the course of his presidency; he would paint a picture that seemed frozen in the 1970s New York of Charles Bronson's movie *Death Wish,* in which vicious gangs roving grimy streets terrorized a (White) middle class.

Denigrating cities and the people who live in them doesn't come just from Trump. The supposed depravity and danger of American cities is hammered home again and again on conservative media, frequently with the implication that the more Black people a city contains, the more dangerous that city must be. (Breitbart, the popular right-wing news site formerly run by Trump adviser Steve Bannon, for a time had a "Black crime" tag so all its stories about Black people committing crimes could be located in one place.) Republicans across the country were convinced by Fox News that during the protests following George Floyd's murder in 2020, entire American cities literally burned to the ground, that if you went to Portland or Seattle today, it would be little more than a pile of rubble.

The drumbeat on conservative media then seeps into mainstream media—a dynamic that has always been an essential part of the strategy under which those conservative media outlets were created. In the 2022 midterm elections, for instance, Fox News pounded day after day on the supposed crime wave in "Democrat cities"; in the week before the election, they aired 193 separate segments about crime (the weekly number plunged to 71 once the election took place).[48] Mainstream news outlets ran plenty of similar stories, which may have featured slightly less inflammatory rhetoric but still reinforced the idea that cities run by Democrats were engulfed in crime. "Democrats are embracing the police, but can that distract from crime in their cities?" asked one NPR story at the time.[49]

Crime continues to be portrayed as an almost exclusively urban phenomenon. When crime rates spiked during the Covid-19 pandemic in 2020, it led to a wave of media coverage that, in both mainstream and conservative media, focused on cities such as San Francisco and Chicago, both supposed to be bastions of liberal values and nightmares of crime. What wasn't a topic of extended discussion in the media was the fact that at the same time, there was a dramatic crime increase in rural areas, where violent crimes rose 25 percent in 2020.[50]

This narrative of the dangerous (blue) city and the safe (red) rural area has been a staple of conservative rhetoric for so long that it encourages Republican politicians to ignore or dismiss the violence suffered by their own constituents, as Oklahoma's governor Kevin Stitt proved during his 2022 re-election bid. In a remarkable moment during a televised debate, Stitt literally scoffed when his opponent, Democratic nominee Joy Hofmeister, pointed out that the Sooner State's violent crime rate is higher than New York's or California's. Stitt peered out at the in-person audience, laughed, and said with a huge grin, as if he couldn't believe his opponent was so dumb, "Oklahomans, do you believe we have higher crime than New York or California? That's what she just said!" But Hofmeister was right: According to the CDC, the homicide rate in Oklahoma at the time was 9 per 100,000 people, while in California it was 6.1, and in New York it was 4.7. And Oklahoma's violent crime rate has been higher than either New York or California *for two decades*.[51]

Stitt found the mere suggestion that his White, rural, conservative heartland state—Trump carried every single Oklahoma county in 2016 and 2020—could possibly suffer a higher crime rate than two racially diverse, coastal, urban states preposterous. When the audience chuckled along with him, Stitt seemed convinced he was right. Or maybe he knew the truth about crime rates but took comfort in a more useful truth about truth itself: It no longer matters. His supporters no doubt found the idea that Oklahoma could be more dangerous than New York or California simply too absurd to believe. A month later, Stitt cruised to re-election by thirteen points.

Egged on by conservative media, Republican politicians around the country reinforce these myths about which parts of America are safe and which are unsafe. As U.S. Senate candidate Blake Masters, a Republican from Arizona, said in 2022, "We do have a gun violence problem in this country, and it's gang violence. It's gangs. It's people in Chicago, St. Louis shooting each other. Very often, you know, Black people, frankly. And the Democrats don't want to do anything about that."[52]

This dark vision of the supposed miseries of urban life comes up again and again. In 2022, Sen. Tom Cotton of Arkansas warned on Fox News that Democrats who want to address climate change "want to make us all poor. They want to make you live in downtown areas, and high-rise buildings, and walk to work, or take the subway."[53] People pay huge amounts of money for the ability to walk to work in a downtown area full of accessible public transportation, entertainment, and restaurants, which is why rent and the prices for goods in so many cities have been driven so high. But Cotton sought to convince rural Americans that urban life is some kind of dystopian hell of endless suffering to which liberals want to condemn rural people.

Contrast those statements with Barack Obama's memorable 2008 comment about people in small towns clinging to guns and religion. His then-opponent Hillary Clinton attacked him for it, the news media eagerly turned it into a big story, and for years afterward, Republicans held it up as proof of the contempt with which Obama and, by extension, all liberals regard regular White Americans.

But what really matters about that incident is how *right* Obama was.

In fact, he offered an insightful analysis of how the events of recent decades had altered the nature of political identity among Whites in rural
areas and small towns. Here's what he actually said:

> You go into these small towns in Pennsylvania and, like a lot of
> small towns in the Midwest, the jobs have been gone now for 25
> years and nothing's replaced them. And they fell through the
> Clinton administration, and the Bush administration, and each
> successive administration has said that somehow these communi-
> ties are gonna regenerate and they have not. And it's not surpris-
> ing then they get bitter, they cling to guns or religion or antipathy
> to people who aren't like them or anti-immigrant sentiment or
> anti-trade sentiment as a way to explain their frustrations.[54]

What Obama was describing was essentially the culture war displac-
ing material arguments as the main focus of politics. He indicted both
Republican and Democratic administrations for not helping these communities through the process of deindustrialization that was fed by trade
agreements made in the 1990s and for making promises of economic
revitalization that never came to pass. He argued that the response of
those communities was essentially to give up hope that either party
could help them economically and to focus their political attentions on
issues such as guns, religion, and immigration.

Though there are policy choices involving these issues, Obama
wasn't talking about debates on whether we should have universal background checks or increase the number of agricultural guest workers we
allow into the United States. Guns, religion, and immigration, as he pos-
ited them, are storehouses of *identity*, solidifying political attachments
to the Republican Party that are extremely difficult for Democrats to
uncouple.

This episode amplifies something scholars have been talking about
for some time: the "post-materialist values" theory associated with political scientist Ronald Inglehart. Beginning in the 1970s,[55] Inglehart argued that as Western societies became more prosperous, their politics
became more focused on noneconomic issues such as individual rights

(e.g., the feminist and later gay rights movements) and environmental-ism. Arguments over economics didn't disappear, but the relative pros-perity experienced by post–World War II generations enabled them to shift their concerns toward social issues.

Obama was arguing that economics had departed the political pur-view of people in small towns not because those people were prosper-ing, but because they had given up on either party's being able to solve their material problems. If both Democrats and Republicans seemed to be supporting the same neoliberal economics that left rural people poorer and with fewer opportunities, they might as well vote for whom-ever they agreed with on guns or same-sex marriage.

Of course, Obama himself—just like any partisan—would argue that in fact there is plenty that separates the two parties on economics and that his party would do more for the people in small towns. We happen to agree with him on this, but it doesn't mean that the conclusion of those who put economics aside is necessarily foolish.

Rural people are not necessarily being hoodwinked into voting Re-publican. Post-materialist issues are meaningful and have practical con-sequences in people's lives. Still, the resignation Obama was describing is an enormous gift to Republicans, who, even as they win elections, re-main the targets of well-earned suspicion from poor and working-class voters around the country (not just in rural areas) over whether they have those voters' economic interests at heart. If Republicans don't need to convince those voters that conservative economics works for them, but can merely say that Democrats are indifferent to their plight, the GOP's work is almost complete.

The reaction to Obama's comments about what people in small towns and rural areas think about when they think about politics has become familiar. A Democratic politician says something that can be in-terpreted as insulting to rural people. Umbrage is loudly expressed. Re-porters leap to remind everyone that Democrats look down on rural people and must change their ways. And the idea that the most essential Americans are scorned by the urban liberal elite is reinforced anew.

This story and the resentments it produces are nothing new. In 1896, William Jennings Bryan thundered in his "Cross of Gold" speech at the

Democratic National Convention, "I tell you that the great cities rest upon these broad and fertile prairies. Burn down your cities and leave our farms, and your cities will spring up again as if by magic. But destroy our farms and the grass will grow in the streets of every city in the country." The fact that cities depend on the resources mined or grown or gathered in rural areas only increases the perception that in addition to their other sins, city dwellers are insufficiently appreciative of what rural people give to them.

WHAT "RURAL" MEANS

Despite the diversity both within particular rural communities and among them, if you were asked what "rural culture" means in America today, you'd have a pretty clear picture in your head. Some of it would have to do with admirable values and the pleasingly pastoral lifestyle, but it would also involve a series of habits and signifiers displayed with a kind of defiance, even some that long ago passed into cliché. One can even argue that rural areas around the country have lost their distinctiveness, merging together into an entity with a single cultural terroir, one with southern intonations no matter how far from the Mason-Dixon Line you might be. One can find Confederate flags flying in rural areas in every corner of the country, all the way to the Canadian border.[56]

This process of cultural homogenization was undoubtedly fed by cable TV or, more broadly, the spread of a nationalized and multiplied media with many more sources of information and entertainment than our parents and grandparents had access to. Fifty years ago, everyone might have seen the same movies and network television shows, but today we see everything everywhere at once, which, among other things, shows us both the people we hate and the people with whom we share something. So, two people watching TV or scrolling through social media in rural Montana and rural Mississippi can see themselves in each other's uncertain circumstances and find a kind of kinship.

This communal effect could be the seed of a genuine rural political movement, but as of yet, it hasn't been, and this is one of the central tragedies of rural American politics: Rural people across the country may feel a sense of connection with one another, and they share some of the same antipathies, but they haven't been offered meaningful paths to political engagement beyond giving their votes to the same candidates they've been supporting for years. What they're left with is a profound sense of precarity and loss, and all the resentment that comes with them, which can be easily turned into rage by cynical politicians and media figures looking to profit from their material and emotional distress. And while rural Whites may not have the firmest partisan loyalties, the kind that will make someone vote for literally anyone on their party's ticket, they do have a stack of ideas, beliefs, and relationships that push them away from Democrats and toward Republicans. Every now and then, an extraordinary event like the 2008 economic crisis—which was so traumatic that voters were eager to vote for change in almost any form it would have been offered—can come along and topple this stack, but that's what it takes: a cataclysm of circumstance. What won't do it? A well-thought-out rural development plan on a Democrat's campaign website, or a smartly written speech, or a powerful TV ad.

Plenty of Democratic candidates come from rural areas, speak rural people's language, and understand rural people's concerns. They tell voters how they were raised on farms and live in small towns, and they're informed and earnest about the challenges of rural life. Both in who they are and in how they campaign, they're doing exactly what their party's critics, from the right and among journalists, have told them innumerable times they must do to appeal to rural voters. And most of the time, they still lose.

Like their Republican counterparts, they sing the praises of places that are small and rural, assuring voters that their communities are where the life lessons are true, the people are good, and character is forged. Many in both parties will leave out the part about how, in order to achieve their ambitions, they left. In order to demonstrate their authenticity, they'll claim to be small-town boys, no matter where life took them, and will put a little extra drawl in their accent. But the Republicans in particular know that when they really need those votes, the best way to get them is to amp up the culture war, telling voters that the next election—indeed, the fate of the country—is all about *us* and *them*.

There will be no final battle in the culture war: Should we come to a consensus on one controversy, another will quickly emerge, and the war will continue forever. But rural Americans know that when they enter those battles, they come with a status that will always be given special consideration by the political world. They may sometimes lose, but when they do, that loss will become one more grievance other Americans will be called to respect.

Rural Whites have thus become the recipients of a benefit that echoes what W.E.B. Du Bois identified nearly a century ago as "a sort of public and psychological wage" offered to White laborers by virtue of their race during the period of Reconstruction, even if they were poor. "The police were drawn from their ranks, and the courts, dependent on their votes, treated them with such leniency as to encourage lawlessness," Du Bois wrote. "Their vote selected public officials, and while this had small effect upon the economic situation, it had great effect upon their personal treatment and the deference shown them."[57] Today, rural White Americans receive a special kind of deference, not necessarily from the legal system but from the political and cultural systems, one enjoyed by no one else.

THE UNLIKELY KING
OF RURAL AMERICA

—

A S THE 2016 ELECTION APPROACHED, WALLY MASLOWSKY, A RETIREE
in rural Lapeer County, Michigan, decided he just had to express his
affection for his favorite candidate. So, he took out some graph paper,
did a little drafting, then went out on his riding mower and cut into his
lawn the word *TRUMP* in perfect 176-foot-tall letters.[1]

Not to be outdone, Doug Koehn, a rancher from eastern Colorado,
went out to his fields, paced off that same talismanic name, got on his
tractor, and carved it into the soil—in letters 800 feet high, stretching for
an entire mile. The name would be visible only from high above, but
who knows, Doug thought, maybe Trump would fly out of the Denver
airport, see his sign, and stop in to say hi. "I'll buy him a beer. I'd love to
shake his hand," Doug said, perhaps unaware that Donald Trump's
many vices do not include alcohol.[2]

Maslowsky and Koehn were not alone in their grand ambitions, even
if their Trump signs were among the biggest. If you've driven through
rural parts of the United States in the last few years, you've probably
seen them: not just Trump signs, but absolutely *massive* Trump signs, as
though with their sheer size, they could cry out over the miles to the man
himself and attract his notice as he jets back and forth between New
York and Florida. On the side of barns, staked in the ground, built out of
hay bales, and flying from flagpoles, they reach ten, twenty, thirty feet
high and more, each one a tribute to their maker's boundless love for a

president who was as far removed from their lives and experiences as anyone could be.

Long after the campaign ended, those signs stayed up, testifying to the power of Trump's movement and the bitter divisions it had made so much worse. Never before in American politics has a single syllable carried so much symbolic weight. "TRUMP" is thrust at liberals, chanted at high school games when the opposing team contains a lot of non-White kids, shouted in the air, and scrawled on the sidewalk, carrying boundless aggression in its percussive simplicity. It says *I'm mad* and *We're winning* and *Screw you* all at the same time.

How do we explain how a man from Queens with soft hands, one whose greatest life ambition was to be accepted by elite Manhattan society, became the hero of rural America? It's a complicated story, but one that makes perfect sense in retrospect. And Trump is not alone; other Republican politicians whose claims to represent rural America range from tenuous to nonexistent have pulled off versions of the same trick, albeit not quite so spectacularly.

Whether Trump succeeds in returning to the White House in 2024, his curious appeal to rural Americans is the most important rural political story in decades. Whatever the future holds for Trump, he has left an indelible mark on rural America and, in the process, revealed fundamental truths about the people who find him so compelling.

Whenever someone asks what candidates need to do to appeal to rural voters, the answers are always the same: In rural America, we're told, people want to know you understand their lives. You know what they go through, what they've experienced, how they speak, what they do on Saturday night and Sunday morning. It's best if you've lived it yourself, but at a minimum, you have to demonstrate that you *get it*. You have to take your time and listen, and show respect.

That's why we see presidential candidates troop to rural areas—especially in Iowa, where the first caucuses have loomed over the primary race since the 1972 election[3]—to show voters they understand rural lives and the rural lifestyle. They put on casual clothes and tramp across fields. They tour a granary and nod knowingly while being told about recent trends in agricultural commodity prices. And they definitely head to the state fair to wolf down whatever food-on-a-stick is popular that year.

Donald Trump did none of those things. When he came to the Iowa State Fair in 2015, he didn't try to convince anyone he was "in touch" with rural folks in any concrete way. He made a dramatic entrance in a helicopter with his name emblazoned on the side, attracting extra attention and blowing people's hats off. The message was not *I get you;* it was, as ever, *Look at me!*

This was of a piece with Trump's entire approach to rural America. He didn't grasp for "authenticity," which is always about performing the most convincing simulacrum of the real. He wouldn't, like George W. Bush, buy a "ranch," don a cowboy hat, and clear brush for the cameras. He was not going to try his hand at milking a cow; the only reason Donald Trump will bend over is to retrieve a golf ball.

His opponent, for her part, believed naïvely that she could compete for rural votes with a more traditional, substantive appeal. Hillary Clinton had a plan to invest in rural America; she unveiled it in Iowa in August 2015. "America's rural communities lie at the heart of what makes this country great," she said, but "despite their critical role in our economy, too many rural communities are not sharing in our nation's economic gains." So, she proposed a suite of initiatives to change this, including loan guarantees, education for beginning farmers, and public-private partnerships to create investments in rural areas.[4]

How much credit did she get for it? Zilch. "A lot of us in rural areas, our ears are tuned to intonation," said Dee Davis, founder of the Center for Rural Strategies. "We think people are talking down to us. What ends up happening is that we don't focus on the policy—we focus on the tones, the references, the culture."[5] This becomes an all-purpose excuse that has almost nothing to do with reality; Clinton could have gotten down on her knees to beg, and they still would have accused her of having the wrong "tone." But Trump, who couldn't tell a combine from a corn dog? Does anyone actually think he's tuned in to "the references, the culture"? Of course not.

This is the reality Trump exposed: White rural voters don't actually demand that candidates be like them, come from where they come from, have a deep appreciation for their lives and their concerns, or sincerely want to help them. All that doesn't hurt, but it isn't enough, and you may not need it at all if you can offer something else—even something dark and ugly—that they'll respond to.

Not only was Donald Trump not the kind of person who could relate to rural folks, but you couldn't imagine any candidate *less* capable of relating to them. A lifelong New Yorker, Trump is a walking repudiation of every value rural Americans claim to hold. They say they prize integrity and straight talk; he's the most corrupt president in American history and can barely open his mouth without lying. They say they pull together and care for one another; he's the embodiment of selfish narcissism. The only thing rural folks say they put ahead of country and even family is God; asked on TV to name his favorite Bible passage, Trump couldn't come up with one.[6]

He's never worked with his hands. He brags about his penthouse apartment. His professions of piety are laughably phony. He cheated on all his wives and seems to barely know his kids, except the daughter he talks about with a profoundly disturbing sexual interest. He wears makeup and spends hours on his hair. Neither he nor anyone in his family served in uniform.

And yet, rural voters don't just like him, they *worship* him.

This devotion can be traced to some key features of Trump's personality, which we'll address in a moment. But Trump also had a message for those who felt the world was leaving them behind. First, he told them they were right: *American society is rigged against you by people who aren't like you and who wish you ill.* Second, he let them know that the appropriate reaction to social changes that made them uncomfortable is rage—not quiet acquiescence, not accommodation, not an attempt to understand others' point of view, but rage. And best of all, they should take that rage and shove it right in the liberals' goddamn faces.

This is what rural people mean when they say that Trump "speaks our language," something we were told more than once during our travels. It's not that he understands their culture in any substantive way; instead, it's more visceral. Trump stroked people's darkest impulses and said: *You deserve to feel this way. You have been wronged and cheated and mocked. Now I will be your wrath. Look at everyone you hate—those over-educated liberals and Hollywood elites and arrogant city people and social justice warriors trying to make you feel bad for being White and being a man and being American. They despise me just as much as they despise you. Let's show them who this country really belongs to.*

And so, they did. And in 2024, it is entirely possible that Donald Trump will win back the presidency, due in no small part to the support he gets from rural Americans who could not be more different from him, but who love him all the same.

TURNING TOWARD TRUMP

As he took over the Republican Party, Trump taught a cadre of other politicians how they could appeal to rural Whites and that authenticity was beside the point. Perhaps no one's transformation makes this clearer than that of Elise Stefanik, whose rapid rise in Trump's remade Republican Party shows just how far a politician can go by applying Trump's lessons to the new rural political landscape.

To run for the U.S. House of Representatives in 2014 from New York's most rural and sparsely populated district, Stefanik established residency in Willsboro, Essex County, in the Adirondack North Country, which we visited in Chapter 1. But she did not grow up there: Willsboro is where her parents bought their summer home. Stefanik grew up in the suburbs of Albany, where she attended elite Albany Academy prep school. From there, she went to Harvard, the crown jewel of the Ivy League and a place conservatives and Republicans routinely mock as a breeding ground for out-of-touch elitists.

Stefanik has no stories to tell about milking cows or baling hay; she spent her career in politics and government. After college, she worked in President George W. Bush's administration, staffed some political campaigns, and then began preparing her first run for Congress. A liberal Democrat with Stefanik's bio who ran for her seat would have been pilloried as a privileged, inauthentic, carpetbagging poseur.

Stefanik presented herself to Adirondack voters as a fresh-faced, likable moderate who would keep her head down and get things done. She pledged to protect the environment and gay rights, and her pitch worked. Despite her outsider status, and thanks to eight hundred thousand dollars from the Koch brothers and the backing of former Bush adviser Karl Rove,[7] Stefanik won the 2014 Republican primary by twenty points. That November, she won the general election in the Twenty-first District, which includes Essex and other rural counties reaching westward to the St. Lawrence Seaway. Her victory made her the youngest woman to that point ever elected to the House of Representatives.

Running for re-election in 2016, Stefanik initially distanced herself from Trump and continued to portray herself as a results-oriented centrist, which may not be surprising given that in 2008 and again in 2012, Democrat Barack Obama carried several counties in her district, including her adopted Essex County. Besides, she insisted, Trump would never win the Republican nomination for president. Stefanik cruised to re-election by more than thirty points.

But Trump won the nomination and the election, and carried her district. Voters there flipped from Obama to Trump at some of the highest rates not only in New York but nationally. In fact, eighteen counties in the state voted twice for Obama but flipped to Trump in 2016. Six of those—Essex, Franklin, Saratoga, St. Lawrence, Warren, and Washington—are counties partly or wholly contained in Stefanik's district.

Stefanik quickly seemed to realize she did not fully understand or even recognize the dark underbelly of her own constituency. Nor did her mentors within mainstream Republican circles, Tim Pawlenty and Paul Ryan, both of whom were vocal Trump critics. "Voters made their voices heard very strongly," Stefanik said. "They wanted someone who's not traditional, who's going to break up the status quo."[8]

If that's what they wanted, then Stefanik was ready to give it to them, and by the end of Trump's term, her transformation was complete. During Trump's second impeachment, the new Elise stood alongside Rep. Jim Jordan complaining that the president and his supporters were the real victims of the January 6 attacks. The new Elise refuses to dispute the so-called Big Lie that the 2020 election was stolen. And two days after the mass murder of African American grocery shoppers in her own state, the new Elise issued a tweet echoing "great replacement" theory, warning that "Democrats desperately want wide open borders and mass amnesty for illegals allowing them to vote."[9] The new Elise is a vocal, aggressive populist who fits what Essex County never used to be but may soon become: a hotbed for angry White voters whose devotion to Trump supersedes their commitment to democratic values.

Not all her constituents appreciate Stefanik's transformation. Karen Edwards is a professor of math education nearing retirement at Paul Smith's College in Franklin County. But she isn't a liberal transplant who parachuted into the Adirondacks to teach at a liberal arts college. She grew up on Keese Mills Road, a few miles from the college, and attended a two-room elementary school where she was one of just three kids in her grade. Her family made ends meet by boarding and feeding out-of-town hunters every autumn, and in summers her mother took in laundry from the nearby exclusive lodges that catered to rich visitors. (She remembers her mom having pillowcases sent back because her ironing didn't meet one local lodge's exacting standards.)

Edwards knows which of the county's vast forested tracts are or were owned by the Du Ponts, Rockefellers, Marjorie Merriweather Post, or, more recently, by Alibaba billionaire Jack Ma or Texas real estate baron and Clarence Thomas benefactor Harlan Crow, whose huge spread in Keese Mill is a stone's throw from Edwards's childhood home. "We had all these rich people, so I suppose I was exposed to inequity early on," she admits. "I saw that kind of stuff as a kid, and you don't know what you're internalizing, but you are." Edwards was infuriated when Stefanik justified the behavior of the January 6 insurrectionists. "Locals here will say, 'Elise backs the blue, and we back Elise,'" Edwards told us. "But police officers were killed [on January 6]. She doesn't back the blue. She just says she does."[10]

Judging by election results, this opinion is a minority one among Stefanik's constituents. After seeing which way her party and her district were moving, Stefanik successfully morphed into a Republican who opposes not only big-*D* Democrats but small-*d* democrats, too. Trump has few more vigorous defenders in Congress, and with each step she took down into the dark heart of authoritarian politics, Stefanik's stock rose with the GOP. When Rep. Liz Cheney turned against Trump over the January 6 insurrection, House Republicans replaced her as conference chair, the third-ranking position in party leadership, with Stefanik. And Stefanik got a prime-time speaking slot at Trump's 2020 convention. People began suggesting that she could be Trump's running mate in 2024. "Man, is she moving fast. That means at this rate she'll be President in about six years," Trump himself said about her at a 2022 fundraiser. "She goes to Washington as a young beautiful woman who took over and all of a sudden she becomes a rocket ship, she's the boss."[11]

Elise Stefanik's story shows the reach of Trumpism in rural areas, and she is hardly alone. Politicians are attuned to nothing so much as their own fortunes, and if you have a White rural constituency, survival means standing behind Trump. Do it with enough skill and enthusiasm, and you might thrive.

THE RURAL GEOGRAPHY OF TRUMPISM

To understand Donald Trump, you have to start with Barack Obama. Trump's successful candidacy would not have been possible in the wake of any other presidency; it was the backlash against America's first Black president that pushed Trump into the White House. As Ta-Nehisi Coates wrote in 2017, Trump was "the first president whose entire political existence hinges on the fact of a black president,"[12] and no successful presidential candidate had made Whiteness so central to their campaign. It's no accident that during the 2016 campaign, at times the only liberal commentators who seemed to take seriously the idea that Trump could win were Blacks and feminists, both of whom had an intimate understanding of the politics of backlash and who knew what it was like to be on its receiving end.

After the election was over, the results revealed something remarkable: 206 counties around the country that had voted for Obama in both 2008 and 2012 swung to Trump in 2016. While they included some more urban and suburban counties—Suffolk County on Long Island, Macomb County in Michigan—most of them were exurban and rural counties. Of the 206 counties, 137 are classified by the census as "nonmetro," places like Quitman County in Georgia, Traverse County in Minnesota, and Sargent County in North Dakota.[13]

These weren't just swing counties going with whoever was the ultimate victor. In 2020, only 25 of the 206 swung back to Joe Biden, despite all that had happened in the prior four years. In other words, these aren't swing counties flipping back and forth from election to election. Most of them turned Republican and will probably stay that way for a long time to come.

It is puzzling to see these kinds of places vote for the nation's first Black president and then turn around and vote for someone running a nakedly bigoted campaign in the way Donald Trump did. But it makes more sense when you consider how unique both of Obama's campaigns were. In 2008, he ran at a moment of economic cataclysm piled on top of an unpopular war and the departure of an incredibly unpopular Republican president. Many Americans were eager for any kind of change, no matter how radical it might have struck them to elect someone like Obama.

Four years later, Democrats ran a ruthlessly effective campaign against Mitt Romney that played on many of the themes that would be effective for Trump. Romney was a living caricature of the wealthy capitalist who was responsible for moving jobs out of small towns and rural areas across the country. You could see it in his history, his manner, and his approach to politics and policy. And it was how Democrats successfully portrayed him; one brutal ad aired by a pro-Obama PAC featured a man named Mike Earnest recounting how his bosses had him and his co-workers at a paper factory in Marion, Indiana, build a makeshift stage and how, days later, a group of men climbed that stage and told them that Bain Capital, Romney's company, was shutting the plant and that they were all fired. "Turns out that when we built that stage, it was like building my own coffin," the man says.[14] But Obama won reelection by half his margin of victory from four years earlier, and in 2012 rural turnout rates dropped more than twelve points, from 67.2 percent in 2008 to just 54.9 percent in 2012.[15]

Angst over the effects of late-stage capitalism remained a powerful theme in 2016, but now it was the Republican nominee arguing that the places where deindustrialization had hit hardest had been exploited by an "establishment" that included both parties. But Trump's election wasn't just a reversion after the two unique elections that preceded it. In many places, 2016 marked White rural voters' final break with the Democratic Party.

The capsule history goes like this: After the Civil War, Abraham Lincoln's Republican Party was the enemy of White southerners for a century, which meant that in many places in the South, every White voter was a Democrat, whether they were liberal or conservative. For decades, the Democratic Party suppressed its more liberal impulses on race in order to keep together a coalition that included southern segregationists, but the civil rights movement of the 1950s and '60s changed that for good. Southern conservative Whites began fleeing to the Republican Party; many of the most prominent archconservatives of later years, including such figures as Strom Thurmond and Jesse Helms, had started their careers as Democrats.

This process, which political scientists call "realignment," took a few decades to play out completely, and in some places, particularly where union membership had been strong, it took longer than in others. It can be seen most vividly in West Virginia, which is politically unique in many ways; like much of the South, it retained an affection for the Democratic Party as a legacy of the Civil War era, but unlike other southern states, it is almost entirely White and native born. According to the census, West Virginia was 91 percent non-Hispanic White in 2021, compared to 59 percent for the country as a whole. And while 13.5 percent of American residents were foreign-born that year, in West Virginia the figure was just 1.6 percent, smaller than that of any other state in the union. On those measures, Mingo County is West Virginia, but even more so: In 2021, the county was 95.7 percent non-Hispanic White and 0.3 percent foreign-born.

The long hold of the Democratic Party in West Virginia is also a function of its (formerly) high union representation. But as unionization faded—today, fewer than one in ten West Virginia workers is a union member—so did the Democratic Party's fortunes. It happened in Mingo County even more starkly than in the state as a whole. Although Bill

Clinton in 1996 was the last Democratic presidential candidate to take
the state, Democrats kept winning Mingo County until 2004, when John
Kerry beat George W. Bush there by thirteen points. But with every elec-
tion since, the Republican margin of victory has grown, and just twelve
years after Kerry's comfortable win, Donald Trump beat Joe Biden in
Mingo by a remarkable sixty-nine-point margin, 83–14. Out of fifty-five
West Virginia counties, Kerry's third-best performance in 2004 came in
Mingo; just twelve short years later, it was Trump's third-best.

How much did West Virginians and residents of Mingo County hate
Barack Obama? In 2012, a man named Keith Judd paid the $2,500 filing
fee to appear on the West Virginia Democratic primary ballot, despite
his residing at the time in a Texas prison, where he was serving a 210-
month sentence for extortion. Judd beat Barack Obama in Mingo by
60–40, even better than his 41 percent showing statewide.[16]

The swing from Democratic to Republican victories wasn't as dramatic elsewhere in the country, and in many rural areas, the immediate
reaction against Obama was tempered by the unique circumstances of
his two elections. But when one looks at many of those Obama-Trump
counties, one is tempted to ask, "What took them so long?" The answer
seems to be that they were waiting for someone like Trump to redefine
politics for them in all the ways he did—but especially when it came to
race. And it helped that as much as there was racist rhetoric swirling
through the political ether in 2008 and 2012, both McCain and Romney
took pains to keep it at arm's length, making it difficult for anyone to see
them as the vehicle for a reassertion of White identity. Trump did just
the opposite.

When one looks to the places where Trump's support was most intense, again and again one arrives in majority-White rural areas. Consider the one hundred counties where Trump's vote margins were
widest in 2016. Almost all of them are rural counties, where Trump got
anywhere from 85 percent of the vote (in Clinton County, Kentucky) to
95 percent (in Roberts County, Texas).

Trump's support was most intense in some of the least-populated
counties in the country. At the smallest end, there's Loving County,
Texas, which in 2020 had a population of 64, according to the census.

Most of the rest have populations measured in four figures; only three of these top one hundred Trump counties have a population over 50,000. The largest is Cullman County, Alabama (population 88,000), whose county seat was a notorious "sundown town" during Jim Crow, where Blacks were not allowed to linger after sundown lest they risk being lynched. While Cullman County contains a small Black enclave called Colony, in the 2020 Census it remained 89 percent White, down from 94 percent ten years before.

To repeat, Cullman is the largest county on Trump's 2016 Top One Hundred list. The rest are more sparsely populated, many significantly so. After four years of watching Trump in action—including all the scandals, the coronavirus pandemic, the collapse of the economy in 2020— what happened? The affection for Trump among people in these places, at least as expressed in their votes, only *deepened.*

In fact, in a year in which Trump lost to Joe Biden by 7 million votes in the country as a whole, Trump gained ground in these Trumpiest of counties. In a remarkable ninety-one out of those one hundred counties, he improved his vote percentage from 2016 to 2020. And in the nine remaining counties, his percentage declined by only a tiny bit (in seven of the nine, it went down by less than one percentage point). Raw vote totals are even starker: In ninety-eight of his one hundred top-performing counties in 2016, Trump got more total votes in 2020 than he did four years before.[17]

You can find these places of near-unanimous Trump support dotted across the country, places like King County, Texas (where Trump got 95 percent of the vote in 2020), Garfield County, Montana (94 percent), Wallace County, Kansas (93 percent), and Grant County, Nebraska (93 percent). All are rural, none had more than a thousand voters, and in every one, Trump did better in 2020 than he had in 2016. The smaller the community you lived in, the more likely you were to vote for Trump.[18] The smallest places are the backbone of "Trump Country."

In these places, voters weren't carefully judging Trump's performance in office and then voting accordingly—or, if they were, it was only if we think of "performance" not as a matter of improving the practical circumstances of their lives or those of the country but as providing the

THE UNLIKELY KING OF RURAL AMERICA

"psychological wage" W.E.B. Du Bois wrote about. He may not have done much to help them, but he provided them an emotional benefit few other politicians had.

WHAT MAGA MEANS

By most traditional measures, Donald Trump is not a smart man. (People who are actually smart don't go around saying, "I have a very good brain."[19]) But he does have an instinct for marketing, and like any good comedian or performer, he spent a good deal of time trying out material on his audiences, which helped him understand what appealed to them. And when he hit upon the slogan "Make America Great Again," he struck gold, especially with a certain kind of voter.

The most effective campaign slogans synopsize for voters what the problem is, what the solution is, and why the candidate is the only one who can get us from the first to the second. "Make America Great Again" does that. The problem is that America was once great but is great no longer, and Trump, the champion of everything loud, large, and covered in gold leaf, is the person to make it great again.

The slogan's most important word is *Again,* because it emphasizes a past greatness that could be regained. This is a three-part story, beginning with a lost time of glory, followed by the fall, and ending with the restoration. It's a very different story from the one liberals tell, especially Trump's predecessor. Through his most important speeches, Barack Obama built a narrative of inexorable progress, of an America always heading in the direction of its noble ideals and becoming better all the time.[20]

That is not Trump's story, nor is it the story that most rural Americans tell. The rural mythos is saturated with nostalgia, the idea that in an earlier time things were better than they are now. And sometimes, this is true: If someone in a small town walks down Main Street and sees boarded-up stores, they know that at one time those stores were open.

The GOP has long been the party of backlash: It takes whatever recent social change is most salient, tells voters to cultivate resentment and a sense of alienation about it, and then offers empty promises that all that unsettling progress can be reversed. Rural Whites are a particularly fertile audience for this kind of appeal because so much of their identity is infused with nostalgia. There are people everywhere who believe that things were better in the old days, but in rural America, one's entire environment may be an embodiment of "the old days," an environment that in its idealized form is fragile, if not doomed.

As political theorist Corey Robin wrote in his book *The Reactionary Mind,* from its beginnings, conservatism was at its heart about "the felt experience of having power, seeing it threatened, and trying to win it back."[21] As much as Republicans worried in 2016 that he might not be a "real" conservative, in this sense Trump was the truest conservative of them all. He promised a restoration, a rollback, a reversion to a prior age, when the right people were atop society's hierarchy and everyone else knew their place.

Trump never specified when this lost period of American greatness was. Some might have said the 1950s, but for many, the time of greatness came down to "when I was younger." That's when the world was simple, when things made sense, when you felt like anything was possible and you were the hero of your story. If you're a middle-aged man who lacks the economic security you feel you deserve, and the country is changing and you feel alienated from popular culture, the idea that America might revert to the time when you were at your peak sounds awfully appealing.

For those men, watching liberals celebrate all the social changes that caused them distress was particularly galling. Then along came Trump, who said that nothing in America worked anymore, that we had been made into a bunch of losers, that we were living in an absolute hellhole, and that the only way to drag ourselves out was to turn back the clock.

This included a promise of restored dignity through dominance, an idea that could be found in one of Trump's core promises: to build a wall on the southern border to keep out immigrants. Trump didn't just promise to build a wall, he promised to build a wall *and make Mexico pay for it.* It became a call-and-response at his rallies, whenever he brought up the wall. "And who's going to pay for it?" he'd say to the crowd, to which they'd respond, "Mexico!"

To understand where Trump was coming from, you have to remember that his worldview is built on the ideas of domination and submission. As far as he is concerned, nearly every human interaction is a zero-sum contest, and if you aren't the winner, then you're a loser. Because of this, Trump understood at a visceral level the way many people, especially men, felt, that in the decline of their communities something beyond income had been taken from them. They had lost some of their dignity, their status, and their manhood. So, he found ways to promise that if he were president, they could regain it.

Making Mexico pay for the wall was not about money; we have far more money than Mexico does. It was about domination, like Michael Corleone in *Godfather II* telling Senator Geary he expected him to pay the fee for the Corleones' gaming license personally. The point was that Mexico would have to kneel before us, take out their thin wallets, and hand over the money to fund their own humiliation. And humiliation was precisely the point: By forcing them to submit, we would regain our own dignity.

Just after taking office, Trump had a phone conversation with Mexican president Enrique Peña Nieto in which he begged Peña Nieto not to say publicly that Mexico would never pay for the wall. "You cannot say anymore that the United States is going to pay for the wall. I am just going to say that we are working it out," Trump said, to which Peña Nieto replied, "This is an issue related to the dignity of Mexico and goes to the national pride of my country." Which, of course, was precisely the point.[22]

While Trump eventually stopped talking about Mexico's paying for the wall, the notion did its job during the campaign, thrilling his supporters with the dream. They surely knew it was never going to happen, but just the idea was enough to make them laugh and cheer. Trump offered this kind of wish fulfillment again and again, his campaign an exercise in fantasy that allowed his supporters to indulge their desires.

It's hard to know how many rural Whites, especially men, knew how false his promises were. Trump couldn't make all the immigrants disappear or force China to give us back our jobs; nor could he undo decades of social advancement for women, racial minorities, and LGBTQ+ Americans. At the end of his time in office, no fewer people were speak-

ing Spanish down at your local grocery store than had been before he
was elected, kids today were no less infuriating and inscrutable, and the
societal hierarchies that had once put certain people in an advantageous
position had not been reinforced. The clock did not turn back. But there
was no evidence that his rural supporters held him responsible or
blamed him for these failures. The fact that he had given voice to their
anger was enough. Trump's messages were not intended solely for rural
Whites, but they resonated strongest in the heartland.

WHAT THE TRUMP VOTE WAS
REALLY ABOUT

As soon as the 2016 votes were counted, a vigorous debate began on
what could have produced the swell of Trump votes among the White
working class and in rural areas. Was it "economic anxiety," as so many
in the news media declared? Or was it racism, as many liberals alleged?
The real answer is: It's complicated.

One thing we can say is that on an individual level, economic hardship alone did not seem to push people toward voting for Trump. Instead, his voters were motivated by wider concerns, many of which were
not about them personally but about how they saw their communities
and their country. What mattered more than whether you had lost your
job were things like the perception that in today's world, traditionally
dominant groups were threatened.[23] This was as true for rural residents
as for anyone else, if not more so; one study found that a sense that rural
people's way of life was disrespected was a particularly strong predictor
of Trump support, even when variables such as party identification were
held constant.[24]

This didn't mean that support for Trump had nothing to do with
economic decline, but there is a subtle distinction between what you
personally experience and what you see around you. There are plenty of
people who are doing okay financially but whose communities are struggling. And it was in many of these places where Trump not only got the
most support but increased his party's vote compared to what Mitt
Romney had garnered four years before.

As a further layer of complication, it was places that had seen a *decline* in fortunes where Trump's candidacy was often most compelling; they may not always have been in desperate straits, but they are now, and people there still remember what it was like when things were better. As one group of researchers wrote, the places where Trump made the greatest gains compared to Mitt Romney's performance of four years before "are not all among the poorest places in America (though Appalachia certainly holds that distinction), but they are places that are generally worse off today than they were a generation or two ago."[25]

But it didn't play out the same way everywhere. One study of Iowa's shift to the right in 2016 found that economic distress *didn't* affect whether a county moved toward Trump; what mattered was how rural, White, and educated the county was (fewer college graduates translated to more Trump votes).[26] Researchers also found that hostility toward Blacks, Hispanics, and LGBTQ+ people was a powerful predictor of support for Trump—but not of support for other Republicans or for the party as a whole, suggesting that Trump's bigotry was uniquely appealing to some voters.[27]

All this means that if we ask whether Trump's appeal to rural voters was "really" about economics or cultural resentments, we're posing the wrong question. Both were true: His critique of a "rigged" system resonated with people who believed both parties had failed their communities in building prosperity, and his poisonous cultural politics resonated with people who had been waiting for someone to express their own dark feelings in the way he did. As political scientists John Sides, Michael Tesler, and Lynn Vavreck found, "economic sentiments were refracted through group identities." What mattered was less whether a voter thought they might lose their job than whether they thought their group—that is, White people—was losing ground to immigrants and minorities.[28]

As the literature on rural resentment makes clear, these forces were present before Trump, just waiting for the right candidate to exploit them. And though these sentiments aren't all about race, race was the inescapable backdrop to Trump's campaigns. Strange as it is to say, the two campaigns involving America's first Black president turned out to have been *less* determined by race than the two campaigns that followed, both of which featured two White candidates.

Race mattered less in 2008 and 2012 in large part because neither John McCain nor Mitt Romney ran campaigns based on White identity. There were certainly other Republicans who did so—and who, during Obama's first term, did everything they could to race-bait—but when it came to Election Day, White voters were not able to cast their votes for an avatar of Whiteness in the way they would be able to in 2016. In fact, polling showed that a substantial proportion of Whites who voted for Obama in 2012 held views that were dismissive of racism and unsympathetic toward Black Americans' struggles.[29] Those voters obviously had other reasons to support Obama, but what they didn't have was a Republican candidate working to elevate the salience of their White identity. That candidate arrived four years later.

The same effect is evident on the related issue of immigration. When Mitt Romney said in the primary campaign that immigration policy should be geared toward "self-deportation" (i.e., making life for undocumented immigrants unpleasant enough that they returned to their countries of origin voluntarily), it created enormous controversy, and Romney was roundly criticized for being cruel and unfeeling. He responded by arguing that his position was more humane than he was being given credit for, repeatedly saying that "we're not going to round people up."[30] When Obama challenged Romney in their second debate on his stated support for a controversial anti-immigrant law in Arizona, the former Bain Capital executive insisted that he supported only the part of the law that required employers to verify the citizenship status of their workers.

The net effect was to communicate to voters that Romney was *kind of* anti-immigrant, or at least opposed to illegal immigration, but he certainly was not crusading to re-Whiten the country. Four years later, Trump was unequivocal in portraying immigration as a source of nothing but cultural infiltration, economic misery, and horrific crime. He told a lie about Muslim Americans in New Jersey celebrating the September 11 attacks. He proposed banning Muslims from entering the United States. He told a series of lurid stories about "beautiful" White women—it was always very important to stress that the women were physically attractive—being murdered by undocumented immigrants. He said an American-born judge with Mexican heritage presiding over a case in which Trump was being sued for fraud couldn't be fair to him because "He's a Mexican."[31] When his supporters set upon a Black Lives Matter protester with punches and kicks at one of his rallies, he responded with "Maybe he should have been roughed up,"[32] just one of many times Trump encouraged his supporters to engage in mob violence.[33]

For many years, it was assumed that successful racial appeals had to be offered subtly, to provide voters a kind of internal plausible deniability, so that they could tell themselves they weren't being racist when they responded to such appeals. By the time 2016 came around, this was no longer true.[34] White identity had become important enough that Trump could succeed by wearing his bigotry on his sleeve.

So, not only were both economic and identity appeals effective in the aggregate, but in many cases they were doubtlessly present in the same individuals. There's nothing about being upset at the decline of manufacturing that prevents you from also being upset about immigrants or the changing ideas about gender. The point is that questions of circumstance and questions of identity combined in intricate ways to make rural America the most fertile ground for Trumpism to grow. In the end, even the Trump campaign itself was surprised by how much support it got from rural voters. "Trump supporters are more rural than even average Republicans," said the campaign's digital director after the 2016 race ended. "What we saw on Election Day is that they're even more rural than we thought."[35]

THE ELITE AND THEIR VICTIMS

Right-wing populism has always combined resentment toward an "elite" with anger at immigrants or racial minorities, painting a picture in which the supposedly truest citizens are assaulted from both above and below. Both halves of this appeal resonate in rural areas, the first because it's largely true (rural areas really have been screwed over by rapacious capitalists) and the second because it activates the distrust of outsiders and fears of racial diversification common in places that were homogeneous for so long.

In earlier elections, Republicans had trouble fully exploiting resentment toward the elite, because Republicans so obviously *were* the elite, both personally and in their economic agenda. While they tried to encourage this resentment in various ways, especially by working to define the elite in noneconomic terms as college professors and Hollywood celebrities rather than CEOs and venture capitalists, it was always a complicated argument to make.

Like no Republican in memory, Trump offered the entire right-wing populist argument with no hedging and no weasel words. Immigrants, he said, were rapists and murderers. The economic powers that be stole your jobs and sold them to China. His contempt for intellectuals was unapologetic, and he gloried in their contempt for him, which was highly appealing to his rural supporters. As one study found, those with a strong rural identity are more anti-intellectual than the larger group of people who just happen to live in a rural area but who may or may not see rurality as central to who they are. Intellectuals may be seen by strong rural identifiers as both inherently urban (and therefore alien) and threatening to rural people.[36]

There were some false notes in Trump's rhetoric, few more jarring than those arising from his desperate desire for acceptance into the sphere of the very elite upon whom he heaped scorn. His whole life, Trump wanted nothing more than to be welcomed by the Manhattan brahmins who saw him as a vulgar Queens climber, and he was as apt to whine about their personal affront to him as the hardship they had imposed on the working classes. "I always hate when they say, well the elite decided not to go to something I'm doing, right, the elite," he told the crowd at a rally in Charleston, West Virginia. "I have a lot more money than they do. I have a much better education than they have. I'm smarter than they are. I have many much more beautiful homes than they do. I have a better apartment at the top of Fifth Avenue. Why the hell are they the elite? Tell me."[37]

One might have expected the audience of West Virginians listening to this riff to be puzzled at this expression of Trump's personal resentment, but if they were, it didn't last. And critically, Trump never suggested any kind of systemic change to correct the predations of the elite; his solution to everything was he himself. If trade agreements had decimated manufacturing in the heartland, it was because they were "bad deals" agreed to by people who lacked his brilliant negotiating skills; he'd fix everything by negotiating "great deals" instead. "Draining the swamp" turned out to mean not eliminating corruption and influence peddling but replacing the existing set of corrupt influence peddlers with his own collection of crooks and cronies. "I alone can fix it," he promised at his 2016 convention speech, and if he didn't get around to fixing it . . . well, too bad.

From the beginning of the primary campaign, Trump offered a vivid contrast to the rest of the field, in ways that were bound to appeal to people naturally suspicious of existing power structures and everything we put under the broad heading of "the establishment." He had never held public office; he didn't speak in the careful and practiced cadences of a politician; for all his dishonesty, he often displayed a shocking brand of candor (as when he happily admitted to getting politicians to give him favors by donating to their campaigns); and he was contemptuous of everything about politics.

His candidacy thus exposed a profound division between the Republican Party and the base of voters upon whom it relied, making clear that the base and the elite are different people with different priorities. This division can be seen in any number of ways, but one vital way is the personal comfort most Republican elites have with the kind of social changes they themselves exploit for votes. A group of researchers used surveys of Michigan voters and insiders around the state government in Lansing to demonstrate that "aversion to social change is strongly predictive of support for Trump at the mass level, but not among political elites."[38] The study showed not just that elite Republicans supported Trump regardless of whether they were resistant to social change, but that they as a whole were not nearly as resistant to change as Republican voters were.

As people in Washington know, plenty of elite Republicans attended

Ivy League schools, have gay friends, and are eager to hire Black or Latino conservatives, yet craft messages and campaigns that are saturated
with anti-intellectualism, race-baiting, homophobia, xenophobia, and a
rhetoric of anger over supposedly lost American greatness. Those elites
are giving the base what they think it wants, and while they're usually
not wrong, it's hard to avoid the conclusion that much of the GOP elite
views its base as a bunch of easily manipulated rubes.

WHY TRUMP WAS THE PERFECT
RURAL CANDIDATE

Across the country, people looked at Trump's personality and either
loved or hated what they found there. But what was not so apparent in
2016 was that so much of what liberals hated about Trump actually en-
deared him to rural Whites.

Whenever we spoke to liberals in rural areas, they'd tell us that something changed in 2016. Before then, while it may not have been particularly comfortable to be outnumbered, politics didn't have the kind of
hard edge it took on once Trump came to dominate the political environment. Afterward, these liberals felt threatened in a way they hadn't
been before, as a new anger came bubbling to the surface, directed at
them. Trump's presence, and eventually his election victory, gave rural
Whites permission to let out the sentiments they had formerly suppressed either under pressure from a culture they resented or in the demand of simple civility. It was a demand they no longer felt obligated to
respect.

We were hardly the only ones who noticed. One researcher found a
secret group of Hillary Clinton supporters in rural Texas that formed
just after the 2016 election, whom she described as "women so afraid to
speak openly with their community that they met by nightfall." One of
them described a friend visiting from out of town who "was run off the
road by some guys in a truck pointing at the Obama sticker on her wind-
shield. And then other people have had their stickers pulled off their car
and vandalized. You know, it's pretty hostile."[39]

Black Democrats we interviewed in Eastern North Carolina shared similar stories. State senator Kandie Smith told us about how hard she works to visit as many of her constituents as she can, but when she knocks on doors in the rural parts of her district, "I have to be very careful. Because where have I seen the most Confederate flags or more Trump stickers? In the rural areas. More so than you see it in the other areas, because [some people in suburbs or cities] believe it, but they don't want their neighbors to see it. . . . But you go to the rural areas? Man, everywhere. And you got to be careful." Smith emphasized that it wasn't all the White people in rural areas, but enough of them. "I've been out there. I've had some have been very nice, and some will listen to me. And then some, I know I need to get off their land before I get shot."[40]

Geneva Riddick-Faulkner, a county commissioner in Northampton County, told us that on multiple occasions she has received envelopes mailed to her home containing blank pieces of paper; she believes White Republicans are sending them in the hope that the letters will be returned to the post office as undeliverable and that they can then use this to say that she doesn't actually live at her address as a pretext for removing her from office. This technique has roots in Republican attempts to purge voter rolls of Democrats. "How many letters are you going to send with a blank piece of paper in it? I live in my house," Riddick-Faulkner told us with a barely perceptible hint of anger under a resigned laugh. "And there are people who still have Confederate flags flying and Trump 2020 flags flying." Riddick-Faulker and many of her constituents are just as rural as their White neighbors. But the bonds of shared rural identities are too often broken by the divisions of race. "That became the new Confederate flag here," she went on. "The ones who didn't want to put that up, they put the Trump flags up."[41]

The Trump flag represents far more than a statement of intention to vote for a candidate; it's an expression of a worldview and a personal identification with the man. It's not just belligerent; it's aggrieved, a way of saying, *The world has done us wrong, and this is our response.* And no one, despite all he has been given, thinks the world has done him wrong more than Donald Trump.

While all presidents fume at their opponents and believe the media are unfair to them, never in American history did a president spend as much time whining and complaining about his alleged victimization as Trump did. "Over the course of your life, you will find that things are not always fair. You will find that things happen to you that you do not deserve and that are not always warranted," he told Coast Guard cadets at their commencement from the U.S. Coast Guard Academy in 2017. "Look at the way I've been treated lately, especially by the media. No politician in history—and I say this with great surety—has been treated worse or more unfairly."[42] In his speech announcing his 2024 campaign, he said, "I'm a victim. I will tell you I'm a victim."[43]

To most people, this complaint probably seemed utterly preposterous. Who could have *less* claim to victimhood than Trump, a man born into wealth who spent a lifetime breaking rules and probably laws, skittering away from his debts, and conning people out of their life savings without ever experiencing a moment of accountability?

But to many rural Whites, that's only another reason to love him. They can see in him an exaggerated embodiment of their own sense of victimhood, even if they, unlike him, may have actual reasons to believe they've gotten the short end of the stick. If he can claim that status, surely they can, too. One study published in 2022 found that people who believed they had been victimized by getting less than they deserved were more likely to support Trump, even when controlling for a range of other variables, including party identification and political ideology.[44]

And just like him, they've been looked down upon and laughed at by those snooty, self-satisfied elites. Even before the 2016 primaries were over, *The Washington Post* tallied over one hundred times that Trump said someone—China, OPEC, Mexico, the entire world—was laughing at America.[45] The irony was that Trump, who was so desperate not to be laughed at, wound up being laughed at more than any other human being on earth. Those who feel denigrated and disrespected by popular culture could relate.

If you were looking for someone to say what others only implied, Trump was your man. He was hardly the only culture warrior in the GOP, but what distinguished him was how explicit he was about everything. He didn't bother pretending to be concerned about abstractions like "equality" or "religious liberty," or to favor legal immigration but not illegal immigration. He'd come right out and say that White people and Christians are being oppressed, and we shouldn't let in anyone from "shithole countries." He made himself the face of the racist "birther" conspiracy theory when other politicians only danced around it in an attempt to encourage it while retaining some plausible deniability.

Everywhere you look, you can find character flaws in Trump that, if understood the right way, might resonate with rural people whose experiences are radically different from his. For instance, people in rural areas, particularly in the rural South, are no doubt aware of in their daily lives what scholars call the "culture of honor," the idea that interpersonal slights must be answered quickly and decisively, even with violence, lest one lose social standing. This culture of honor has been suggested as an explanation for high rates of homicide in the South and elevated levels of violence in rural areas.[46] While there is some scholarly disagreement about its sources and effects—for instance, some argue that it operates more strongly where structures of authority, including police, are more distant[47]—at the very least it's something with which people are quite familiar.

Trump enacts his own, very visible version of the culture of honor, in which every slight he encounters, no matter how trivial or from whom, is met with venomous retaliation. Other politicians, celebrities, random citizens on Twitter—if they said something mean about him, he was going to strike back no matter how petty and shallow it made him look. As he said in one of his books, "If you do not get even you are just a schmuck! . . . When you are wronged, go after those people, because it is a good feeling, and because other people will see you doing it."[48] One pair of scholars studying different working-class communities found that for many people, Trump's obsession with those he believes have wronged him is a sign of strength.[49]

Even the common, and perfectly accurate, criticism that Trump doesn't practice what he preaches likely resonates in rural areas, where you often find a strong moral code that is regularly violated by many of the people who live there. The fact that rural areas have plenty of infidelity and teen parenthood (which occurs at significantly higher rates among rural Americans than city dwellers[50]) doesn't necessarily make people reject traditional "family values"; it can make them cling to those values all the more fervently, as they consider them under constant, visible threat. Seeing someone like Trump mouth the words of propriety and piety with obvious insincerity made him, if nothing else, deeply recognizable.

Trump's view of the world as one made up of winners and losers, where only suckers play by the rules, is also one that can appeal to even those who in their own lives mostly follow the rules. Trump does not offer paeans to the timeless truth of the American dream, which people in rural areas know well is so often a lie. They see all around them people who work plenty hard but who continue to struggle. Even if they assign a strong moral value to the willingness to work hard, they know it is anything but a guarantee of success and prosperity. Trump tells them that to succeed, you do need to work hard, but you also need to be shrewd and ruthless, willing to exploit others and destroy your enemies. Even if they aren't living his brand of amoral ambition in their own lives, one can see why many would decide he's right.

THE BIG LIE AND RURAL ELECTIONS

After the 2020 election, some rural places became epicenters of the looniest manifestations of the Big Lie, the belief held by Trump's supporters that the election was stolen from him. In a number of counties, the shenanigans featured local officials allowing Trumpist conspiracy theorists to come into their offices and copy confidential data for the purposes of uncovering phantom voter fraud. In rural Mesa County, Colorado, the county clerk, Tina Peters, was indicted on ten counts related to her allegedly allowing pro-Trump "consultants" to copy data from official computers as part of their wild goose chase in search of voter fraud.[51] Peters then ran for secretary of state, attempting to become the chief elections official for all of Colorado; she lost in the Republican primary.

In Coffee County, Georgia, surveillance video that became public in September 2022 showed a group of "consultants" hired by the unhinged

Trumpist attorney Sidney Powell arriving at the county election office on January 7, 2021, being met and brought inside by a Republican official, and then not leaving until 2.5 hours after the office's closing time. Though Trump won Coffee County by forty points, the election supervisor there said she allowed the men in because she did not trust Joe Biden's win in Georgia and hoped they could prove "that this election was not done true and correct."[52]

As shocking as those incidents were, more often it was rural election officials trying to do their jobs and run fair and efficient elections who were being hounded by residents convinced of dark conspiracies to steal the election from Trump. And the most fervid election conspiracies flourish in rural areas, even when the results are exactly what the conservatives who live there hope for. To take just one example, in rural Nye County, Nevada, the county commission voted in 2022 to ditch all its voting machines and count ballots only by hand, after hearing paranoid testimony about counting machines switching votes—even though Trump had beaten Joe Biden in Nye by over forty points. "It just made me feel helpless," said the county clerk, a Republican who had administered elections there for two decades. She resigned.[53]

Asked why it seemed to happen so much in rural areas, election law expert Richard Hasen of UCLA told us, "Because this is where these folks can have the most impact. They live there and can pressure and in some cases vote out of office these officials. They can show up and dominate local meetings."[54] A lot of devoted public servants in rural areas are left wondering whether safeguarding democracy is worth the aggravation.

Election denialism isn't just about the acceptance of bizarre conspiracy theories. It's rooted in something Trump says often: that your political opponents are not just wrong, they are so evil as to be almost inhuman. ("Our biggest threat remains the sick, sinister, and evil people from within our own country," he said at one speech in 2022. "This nation does not belong to them. This nation belongs to you."[55]) Once you accept this, you must also accept that they cannot possibly hold power legitimately. Any election they win is fraudulent by definition, and therefore, you should have no loyalty to the processes of democracy, as they are merely tools of your own destruction. Abandoning democracy isn't just something unfortunate you might have to consider; at times, it becomes something you *must* do in order to preserve your family, your community, and your way of life.

TRUMP, NOW AND FOREVER

In a speech in early 2023, Trump told a conservative audience, "In 2016, I declared I am your voice. Today, I add: I am your warrior. I am your justice. And for those who have been wronged and betrayed, I am your retribution."[56] It was an apt distillation of what he had always been about, a bitter sauce of resentment reduced to its viscous essence.

What is retribution, after all? Nothing but the opportunity to see those you feel have wronged you suffer in equal proportion. You will get nothing material from retribution; your struggles will not be lessened, your pain will not be eased, your children will not be granted the things of which you have been deprived. But you will get the momentary satisfaction of watching the distress of someone you despise.

This kind of validation of their resentments was what Trump always offered rural people. Yes, he made a bunch of transparently bogus promises about how he'd turn their communities into a paradise. But the real promise—and the one on which he delivered—was the opportunity to give a giant middle finger to everyone they felt looked down on them, the liberals and the urbanites and the establishment.

Political developments often seem obvious and predictable in retrospect. So, with the phenomenon of Trump's appeal to rural America, it's tempting to ask why nobody saw it coming. Why couldn't Democrats speak to that same sense of anger over lost opportunities and community decline? Maybe they could have, with different candidates and different policy choices. Bernie Sanders blamed NAFTA for shuttered factories just as Trump did, and who knows? Maybe Sanders could have pulled more rural votes than Hillary Clinton or Joe Biden did.

But Trump's peculiar combination of character flaws and venomous impulses is unique, and uniquely suited to the disappointments and resentment so many White rural Americans feel. When Trump supporters are asked what it is about him that they love, they often say, "He tells it like it is." This means not that he speaks verifiable truths—no politician in American, if not world, history, lies so promiscuously—but that he says things they want to hear, in a way they want to hear them. He does not hedge or shade or speak with care, especially not when he is being vulgar and hateful. He says what he and they believe, without regard to who might scold him for it. Places where tribalism exerts a powerful hold found a hero in the most tribalist of presidents, someone who is forever drawing lines of race, nationality, and belief, with his people on one side and the despicable vermin on the other.

That is what heartland folks find so intoxicating about him. That's what leads you not just to vote for a man but to paint his name on the side of your barn.

Even if Trump fails in 2024 and becomes nothing more than the laughable two-bit grifter he always has been at heart, his effect on the politics of rural America will be felt for a generation, if not more. He showed every Republican what rural Whites, and the GOP base more broadly, really want and how to give it to them. The result is a politics saturated in bitterness and bile, and a party whose most loyal voters don't expect their leaders to offer them anything but the ugliest kind of emotional satisfaction. Even when Trump is gone, in rural America he will still be king. And the rest of the country will suffer for it.

CONDITIONAL PATRIOTS

—

THE FOUR-MAN SPLINTER GROUP FROM KANSAS WITH VIOLENT URGES AND a loose connection to White nationalists called themselves "the Crusaders." Lest there be any doubt what the group's name implied, Patrick Stein, their unofficial leader, explained his beliefs in conversations with his three confederates. "There's only one good kind of Muslim, and that's a dead motherfucker, straight up," Stein chirped. "If you're a Muslim, I'm going to enjoy shooting you in the head." The group's preferred nickname for Muslim immigrants? *Cockroaches.*[1]

Stein and his buddies wanted to do more than vent their anti-Muslim anger. They began plotting to kill Somali immigrants in Garden City, one of three small, rural meatpacking towns that form the so-called Meat Triangle in the southwest corner of Kansas. Meatpacking is a dangerous industry, one where fast-moving conveyors and sharp blades cause repetitive-motion injuries and occasionally claim an employee's finger or more. With long hours, meager pay, few benefits, and a high burnout rate, meatpacking jobs are the kind that most Americans refuse to perform. Which is why profit-hungry agribusiness executives fill their factories with recent immigrants from Latin America, Africa, and Asia who have limited employment prospects.

Garden City is the seat of rural Finney County, which Donald Trump carried by thirty points in the 2016 election. Raised in a farming family,

Patrick Stein was thrilled by the campaign promises Trump made that year, especially the Republican nominee's pledge to ban Muslim immigrants. Each one a White, middle-aged conservative who owned guns and adored Trump, Stein and his buddies regarded themselves as "sovereign citizens."[2]

According to the Southern Poverty Law Center, the sovereign citizen movement is "based on a decades-old conspiracy theory . . . that the American government set up by the founding fathers, under a common-law legal system, was secretly replaced" with a shadow government based on admiralty law, either after the Civil War or in 1933, when the United States abandoned the gold standard. Founded by John Birch Society member William Potter Gale, the movement claims that "U.S. judges and lawyers, who they believe are foreign agents, know about this hidden government takeover" but cover it up.[3] Stein's sovereign Crusaders was a splinter group of the Kansas Security Forces militia, itself an offshoot of the White nationalist Three Percenter movement. Stein and his fellow Crusaders likely knew and perhaps chanted aloud the Three Percenters' militant, anti-government motto that bastardizes the meaning of Thomas Jefferson's warning, "When tyranny becomes law, rebellion becomes duty."

By the summer of 2016, conversations among Stein and his three friends morphed into plans for a lethal terrorist bombing. The four men amassed three hundred pounds of urea nitrate fertilizer. They chose as their target a brick apartment complex that houses hundreds of Somalis. They researched how to make a blasting cap detonator. They even picked a date: the day after the upcoming U.S. presidential election. Any earlier, the four men worried, and they might provide Democratic nominee Hillary Clinton with a campaign talking point.

What Patrick Stein did not know was that only two of his confederates, Curtis Allen and Gavin Wright, were as hell-bent on blowing up innocent immigrants as he was. The fourth "Crusader," Daniel Day, was working as a paid FBI informant. Once the group moved from loose, angry talk to concrete plans, the FBI asked Day to introduce the plotters to "Brian," an undercover FBI agent posing as a black-market bomb maker.[4] Soon thereafter, the FBI arrested the three would-be terrorists. They were each convicted and sentenced to more than twenty years in federal prison.

THE FOURFOLD THREAT

Episodes like the Garden City terrorist plot often fail to make the news because law enforcement officials foil many of these plots. The FBI and other law enforcement agencies at any given moment are tracking hundreds of potentially violent plans to harm or kill civilians. Increasingly, successful or would-be terrorists also target government agencies, buildings, and employees. Whether well planned like the 1995 Oklahoma City and 1996 Olympic bombings or spur-of-the-moment like the 2017 Charlottesville car attack, violent White supremacists, radicalized militia groups, or Christian nationalists have murdered hundreds of innocent people.

The perpetrators of these crimes are often White men, some but surely not all of whom hail from small towns or who organize in remote, rural locales. Often, their victims are non-Whites, non-Christians, immigrants, LGBTQ+ people, or agents of the state or federal government whom the perpetrators believe are acting on behalf of these out-groups.[5] During the Trump presidency, the FBI and the Department of Homeland Security issued similar reports that identified White supremacist groups as America's biggest domestic terrorist threat.[6]

Violent or not, anti-democratic sentiments and behaviors come in many forms and emerge from all over the nation. But rural Whites pose a unique threat. Heartland citizens may salute the flag and proclaim how much they love America and cherish its ideals. They may promise to fight to the death to defend those ideals. The uncomfortable truth, however, is that the patriotism of millions of rural White Americans seems conditioned on the expectation that U.S. democracy serve *them* primarily, if not exclusively.

Specifically, rural Whites pose four interconnected threats to the republic:

First, in a nation experiencing rapid demographic change, rural

Whites are uniquely xenophobic toward Americans who look, speak, act, or pray differently from them. Their animus toward racial and religious minorities, and immigrants especially, is unmatched. More than any other demographic group, rural Whites reject cultural diversity and bristle at the idea of a pluralist, inclusive society. A striking share of them believes Whites are the real victims of racism. Millions of rural White Americans also harbor deep-seated, place-based resentments toward people of any race or citizenship status who live in cities.

Second, the views of rural White citizens are least tethered to reality. Rural Whites are most likely to believe the 2020 presidential election was rigged and that former president Donald Trump would be returned to the White House months after Joe Biden had already taken office. Rural Whites are also most likely to subscribe to fantastical QAnon conspiracies about Democrats running secret pedophile rings, or that a coming "storm" will overthrow and imprison nefarious "deep state" elites. With fatal consequences, rural Whites were more likely to dismiss the Covid-19 pandemic as a hoax and to refuse lifesaving vaccines. Rural Whites also seized upon the birther controversy that gave life to Trump's political career, and they did so *before* Trump in 2011 began questioning President Barack Obama's citizenship.

Third, rural White citizens are less supportive of democratic principles like free speech, a free press, the separation of church and state, and the value of constitutional checks and balances. Rural White Americans are more likely than other demographic groups to support efforts to limit ballot access and less likely to accept the legitimacy of election results. Many are enthralled by either White supremacist or White Christian nationalist messages and movements. Locally, a growing number of rural county sheriffs—almost all of whom are White men—falsely claim their authority supersedes state and national law.

Fourth and finally, rural Whites are more inclined to justify the use of force, even violence, as an appropriate means for solving political disputes. They are more likely than other Americans to excuse or legitimize the domestic terrorist attacks of January 6, 2021, and not only to support the extralegal reinstallation of Trump in the Oval Office but to believe it ought to be done by force.

———

THESE THREATS ARE NOT just serious, they're interconnected: Attitudes or behaviors of one type often lead to or bleed into others. For example, a person with a heightened fear of immigrants is more susceptible to conspiratorial claims about immigrants voting illegally. From there, it becomes easier for that person to question the legitimacy of elections, to back undemocratic efforts to restrict ballot access, and perhaps to pester election boards with frivolous Freedom of Information Act requests designed to hamstring election officials. From there, it becomes easier for that person to support or even participate in efforts to intimidate, harass, or even harm those officials.

The would-be Garden City bombers exhibited all four threats. They targeted a racial and religious minority group. They believed in wild conspiracies and affiliated themselves with a group founded upon absurd conspiracies. They harbored undemocratic or anti-democratic attitudes, including hatred toward government and public officials. And they intended to use violence to carry out their political agenda—the very definition of domestic terrorism in the federal code.[7]

Rural White Americans assert a deep reverence for the Constitution and America's democratic principles. Millions of them demonstrate this reverence daily. But the democratic commitments of too many rural Whites are weak, limited, or quickly abandoned. Poll after poll confirms that rural Whites are the vanguard for the xenophobic, reality-defying, undemocratic, and increasingly violent movements that currently threaten to undermine the world's oldest constitutional democracy and the pluralist society that democracy protects.

The attitude of too many rural Whites may best be described as "I love *my* country, but not *our* country." Their brand of exclusive patriotism appears conditioned upon maintaining or remaking the U.S. political system to their advantage at the expense of equality and opportunities for Americans different from them. If these conditions are unmet, millions of rural Whites appear willing to abandon the nation's most sacred constitutional norms and principles in favor of reactionary, even violent alternatives. Because rural Whites often brag about how much they love the United States, we call this phenomenon the *patriotic paradox of rural America.*

Given the position they hold, rural Whites ought to be the role models for democratic citizenship. They ought to have the highest voter turnout, the best-run elections, the most participatory local government, and the most passionate commitment to binding American ideals. Instead it's the opposite.

Dozens of surveys and academic studies confirm that a disproportionately high share of rural Whites harbor unusually xenophobic, conspiracist, anti-democratic, and even dangerous attitudes. We recognize that these attitudes are often (but not always) expressed by a minority of rural Whites, but we emphasize that rural White support exceeds that not only of their rural minority neighbors but also of White Americans who reside in cities and suburbs. What follows is detailed, empirical evidence of rural Whites' opinions and beliefs as they relate to the four threats.

THE FIRST THREAT:
RACISM AND XENOPHOBIA TOWARD OUT-GROUPS

Rural and urban Americans recognize each other as different. This makes sense: Cultural traditions and lifestyles in the city and the country diverge in notable, if mostly harmless, ways. Questioning the values of fellow citizens, however, can turn superficial differences into chasmic civic divides.

How differently do urban and rural citizens see each other? According to a 2017 *Washington Post*/Kaiser Family Foundation poll, 48 percent of urbanites describe rural Americans as having values "different from them," with 18 percent describing the values of rural citizens as "very different." Whether viewed as skepticism or scorn, that degree of perceived difference may seem high. Yet skepticism runs much deeper in the opposite direction: Fully 68 percent of rural residents say urban Americans exhibit "different" values, and 41 percent describe urban values as "very different." Both groups recognize the chasm, but a much higher share of rural citizens views urbanites as having different values than the other way around.[8]

Racial antipathy and rural resentment. Part of rural citizens' judgments are coded forms of *racial antipathy,* the too-polite term pollsters use to describe racist attitudes. Surveys repeatedly confirm that citizens from rural communities—the Whitest part of the United States—express deep resentments toward their racially diverse counterparts in cities.

In 2020, political scientist Kal Munis published results from his study of "place resentment." Raised in a rural Montana town of nine hundred people, Munis examined whether Americans resent people from other parts of the country for getting benefits they believe their in-group does not. If the enmity between country folk and city folk is mutual, resentments should exist across the board.

But place-based enmities are not symmetrical. Munis identified five characteristics that predict place-based resentment: Those who are young, male, live in rural areas, hold strong place-based identities, or who score high on racial antipathy measures exhibited significant resentment toward those outside their communities.[9] With his colleague Nicholas Jacobs, Munis also determined that rural resentment had a powerful, independent effect on Republican voting in both the 2018 midterm and 2020 presidential elections. "Place resentment, or rural resentment more specifically, appears to be a powerful explanatory factor in understanding the urban-rural divide that now so strikingly characterizes American politics, beyond the fact that rural areas are simply whiter, older, and more likely to have Republican partisans," they conclude.[10] The root of these antagonisms, they say, is the belief among rural residents that they suffer from "geographic inequity" in the form of less government attention and more cultural scorn. "Without these beliefs, the urban-rural political divide would not be as vast as it is today."[11]

Rural citizens also exhibit unusual hostility to the prospect of an inclusive and diverse society. Fully 65 percent of urban Americans say they are comfortable with a changing and diversifying America, nearly double the rate of the 38 percent of rural residents who express comfort.[12] According to a 2018 Pew Research survey, only 46 percent of rural White citizens say they value diversity in their communities—the lowest share of any geographic subgroup. Rural America is also the only place where a majority of citizens disagrees with the statement "White Americans benefit from advantages blacks do not have."[13] Support for Donald Trump's Muslim travel ban ran about 15 percentage points higher among nonmetro residents than Americans who live in metropolitan areas.[14] Rural majorities also believe it is either "very" or "somewhat" bad for society to recognize gay marriages,[15] and rural Whites rate gays and lesbians thirteen points lower on one-hundred-point feeling thermometers than urban Whites do.[16] According to the Trevor Project, 49 percent of rural LGBTQ+ youth describe their communities as "unaccepting" of LGBTQ+ people, nearly twice the 26 percent of suburban and urban youth who say so.[17]

Not surprisingly, the rural-urban divide is evident in White attitudes toward the Black Lives Matter movement. The 2020 American National Election Study (ANES) asked respondents to assign a one-hundred-point feeling thermometer score to various groups, including unions, corporations, the police, and the National Rifle Association, with one hundred indicating the highest approval score for a group. The twenty-four-point gap between rural Whites' average thermometer score of thirty for BLM and the fifty-four score among urban Whites was the widest for any group about whom the survey tested respondents' feelings.[18]

Some scholars stress that rural Whites' views about race may not be explicitly racist because those attitudes stem from broader beliefs about class, work, and government dependency. Law professor and rural Arkansas native Lisa Pruitt stresses that rural Whites distinguish between the "settled" members of their communities who may struggle yet who work hard and live right and their "hard-living" White neighbors who lack the proper work ethic, tend to rely upon government support, and tend to engage in transgressive behaviors like drug use and petty criminal activities.

Settled rural Whites, Pruitt argues, should be regarded differently for two reasons. First, they reject overtly racist language or stereotypes and shun White supremacists who embrace them. Second, they lump hard-living folks of all races together in a way that evinces a class-based, race-neutral disdain for people who fail to carry their societal weight.[19]

But after spending eight years interviewing small-town Americans in all fifty states, Princeton sociologist Robert Wuthnow concluded that race and rural resentments are inextricably bound. He acknowledges that attitudes toward government help explain rural Whites' hostility toward cities and the minorities who live there. But Wuthnow found race to be the key factor driving rural resentment. "I'm not sure that Washington is doing anything to harm these [rural] communities. To be honest, a lot of it is just scapegoating," he says. "And that's why you see more xenophobia and racism in these communities. There's a sense that things are going badly, and the impulse is to blame 'others.'"[20]

In her 2016 book *The Politics of Resentment,* Katherine Cramer argues that it can be difficult to precisely determine when rural resentments are based in race and when they aren't, even if "the urban-versus-rural divide is undoubtedly in part about race."[21] But when we interviewed her, she told us, "The social welfare programs of the sixties, the civil rights movement of the sixties, the changes just demographically in the country, all of that has kind of been a slow burn in rural communities as in other communities, and yes, I think that's part of the reason Donald Trump was able to use racism as a tool."[22]

Combining survey data with interviews of rural Wisconsinites, social scientists Matthew Nelsen and Christopher Petsko also found rural consciousness to be specifically linked to negative, racialized attitudes that rural citizens express toward urbanites. "The words rural Americans use to describe city dwellers as well as the mental representations they call to mind seriously challenge the idea that rural consciousness exists independently from racial resentment. While rural consciousness may not be reducible to simply racism, as scholars of rural America suggest, it appears at least in these data to play a central role," they write. Nelsen and Petsko found that the higher degree of rural consciousness Wisconsinites expressed, the more racialized their attitudes were toward residents of Milwaukee, home to the state's largest population of African Americans.[23]

Race- and place-based resentments also influence rural citizens' eval-
uations of the two major political parties. In 2021, Rural Objective PAC
surveyed two thousand rural Americans in nine battleground states to
find out whether they associated nineteen principles or attributes with
either, both, or neither of the two major parties. The items included
ideas or phrases like "honesty," "getting money out of politics," and
"fighting for the underdogs." What's remarkable is how similar the eval-
uations of the two parties are for many items, in some cases a difference
of only a few points. In the eyes of rural voters, the Republicans' biggest
net advantage, twenty-two points, was being perceived as "pro-small
businesses." For Democrats, it was their seventeen-point edge on "working for affordable health care."

The most stunning split—third largest in magnitude among the nineteen items—was how rural respondents rated the two parties on the
phrase "pandering to racists." The partisan gap was sixteen points, 46
percent to 30 percent, but rural Americans described *Democrats* as more
pandering.[24] That's right: The same rural Whites who exhibit high rates
of racial antipathy and who routinely sneer at "woke" Democrats for
supporting greater diversity nevertheless believe the Democrats pander
more to racists because, to them, the real racists are liberals and minorities who play identity politics and criticize others for being racially in-
sensitive.

Anti-immigrant xenophobia. Nowhere does rural anger run deeper
than the xenophobic opposition to immigrants. Rural Whites we met
while reporting this book repeatedly insisted that they harbor no ill will
toward legal immigrants and that they are angered only by those who
arrive in the United States "illegally." We take them at their word—but
they must be outliers, because polls repeatedly show that rural Americans are the demographic cohort most fearful of, and furious about, immigrants.

In a 2017 *Washington Post*/Kaiser Family Foundation poll, 62 percent
of suburbanites and 71 percent of city dwellers agreed with the statement
"Immigrants today strengthen our country because of their hard work
and talents." Only a 49 percent plurality of rural citizens agreed—and
that's despite the likely influence of what researchers call "social desir-

ability bias," the tendency of survey respondents to shade their true feelings in order to adhere to perceived social norms.[25] In a similar finding a year later by the Pew Research Center, 57 percent of rural respondents said that the "growing number of newcomers from other countries threatens traditional American customs and values."[26] Notice that the wording in those polls explicitly uses *immigrants* or *newcomers* without indicating how these immigrants/newcomers arrived in the United States, nor their citizenship status. In other words, these results reflect rural citizens' attitudes toward *all* immigrants, not just those who are undocumented.

At a Llano County Tea Party chapter event in November 2022, we saw how frustrated many Texans are about immigration policy. The guest speaker that night, Sheena Rodriguez of the Alliance for a Safe Texas, came to Llano to promote her organization's effort to have the state's border situation declared an "invasion." Rodriguez circulated a two-page resolution that cites Article IV, Section 4, of the U.S. Constitution, which mandates that the federal government "shall protect each [state] against Invasion." During her lecture, entitled "The Lie: Immigration Is a Federal Issue," she assured attendees that she is "not against legal immigrants—and there's nothing racist about opposing illegal immigration or wanting safe communities." Rodriguez shared experiences from her visits to the Rio Grande Valley. She told harrowing stories about "coyotes" (human smugglers) who use color-coded bracelets to traffic people across the border; about dead immigrants found in the farms and yards of citizens who live close to the border; about how immigrants seeking to enter the United States outnumber border patrol agents by sixty to one; and about a conversation with one border agent who told her, "I need help; we're being invaded." Her ambition, as stated at the end of the resolution, is to persuade Llano and the state's other 253 counties to "recognize our southern Texas border is under invasion."[27] The Tea Partiers in Llano nodded along with her presentation, then gave her a rousing round of applause.

What Rodriguez and those who follow her fail to mention is that anti-immigrant sentiments fuel radical ideas and leaders. Citizens whose anti-immigrant feelings lurk near the surface need little inducement from politicians to summon their dormant xenophobia. It's bad enough that Donald Trump referred to certain immigrants as coming from "shithole countries." Worse was his telling four U.S. House Democrats—all of them minority women and U.S. citizens, three of them born in the United States—to "go back" to the countries they came from. Platoons of talk radio hosts and media figures like Tucker Carlson echo these attacks daily with paranoid rants about border caravans and "replacement theory."

Not surprisingly, 60 percent of rural Americans support building a wall between the United States and Mexico, a share significantly higher than the 46 percent of suburbanites and 34 percent of city dwellers who do.[28] Anyone who thinks that rural anti-immigrant sentiments are a recent phenomenon triggered by the election of the first Black U.S. president or his openly anti-immigrant successor should think again. According to results from a national phone survey conducted back in 2004, on twelve of thirteen immigration-related questions posed, rural Americans expressed greater anti-immigrant sentiments than suburban or urban residents did.[29]

The pattern is clear: Rural xenophobia toward immigrants arrived at the station long before the "Trump Train" did. If non-White rural voters were eliminated from the survey results that lump rural citizens together, support for immigrants among only rural Whites would be even lower.

Backlash driven by a fear of immigrants is hardly unique to the United States: A study of Western democracies found that once the foreign-born population reaches about 22 percent nationally, the share of right-wing populists tends to breach 50 percent.[30] And the actual size of out-groups need not be large if they're *perceived* to be so. Polls consistently show that people vastly overestimate the size of minority populations; for instance, in a 2022 YouGov poll, Americans asked to estimate the size of various groups said on average that 41 percent of Americans are Black (the actual number is 12 percent), 39 percent are Hispanic (it's 17 percent), and 27 percent are Muslim (it's 1 percent).[31] Political scientist Ashley Jardina refers to this phenomenon of overestimating the size and power of racial or religious minorities as the "myth of the white minority."[32]

To be sure, America's White majority *is* shrinking as a proportion of the population. Yet Whites continue to wield disproportionate power and will do so even after relinquishing their numerical majority. White legislators are overrepresented in both chambers of Congress and in all fifty state legislatures.[33] The overrepresentation of White executives in corporate C-suites is even more profound; in 2021, 93 percent of the CEOs of Fortune 500 companies were White, and 86 percent were White men.[34] "Demographic changes in which whites' relative share of the population continues to decrease may lead whites to feel that their relative power as a group has waned considerably," writes Jardina, and they may eventually "come to believe that their group is actually racially disadvantaged."[35] Clearly, millions of rural Whites already believe this.

Hostility toward out-groups. Social isolation magnifies rural White fears of the "other." Isolated and homogeneous rural communities are infertile laboratories for understanding, much less accepting, people who are different. Forty-two percent of rural Americans live in the community in which they grew up, a rate higher than for either suburban or urban residents.[36] Rural Americans are most likely to say they have few if any friends of a different race.[37] Rural citizens and people who reside in less racially diverse U.S. states are also less likely to hold a U.S. passport or use it to travel abroad.[38]

Missouri state representative Ian Mackey understands these sentiments all too well. Growing up gay in rural Hickory County—home to 8,600 residents, 96 percent of whom are White—Mackey always felt out of sorts. In a floor speech confronting colleague Chuck Basye, a Republican co-sponsor of an anti-trans bill, Mackey delivered the type of passionate remarks rarely heard in the well of any state legislative chamber. "I couldn't wait to move out. I couldn't wait to move to a part of our state that would reject this stuff in a minute," Mackey said of his home county. "Thank god I made it out, and I think every day of the kids who are still there who haven't made it out—who haven't escaped—from this kind of bigotry."[39]

Self-sorting does more than create cultural silos and fuel prejudices. In his fascinating "density divide" study, Niskanen Center analyst Will Wilkinson explains how rural and urban parts of the United States increasingly differ beyond characteristics like race, ideology, or even partisanship. In fact, so great is this density divide that rural and urban Americans now diverge on some of what psychologists have identified as five core personality traits, especially the "openness to experience" trait.

According to Wilkinson, citizens who score high on the openness trait are more likely "to make an in-state move, and nearly twice as likely to move to a new state. Which is to say, people with close-minded dispositions are less likely to move. This difference in propensity to migrate between individuals with liberal-skewing and conservative-skewing temperaments is exactly what we'd expect to find if the density divide is a result of liberal self-selection out of lower density areas."[40] Unfortunately, once the citizens more open to experience—the Ian Mackeys—leave rural communities, a higher share of close-minded rural residents remains, exacerbating personality divides between city and country.

Plenty of city folk are equally uninterested in bridging the urban-rural divide. But rural Americans' combination of isolation and incuriousness increasingly separates them—not merely geographically but dispositionally—from the rest of the nation. "Travel is fatal to prejudice, bigotry, and narrow-mindedness, and many of our people need it sorely on these accounts," Mark Twain famously quipped. "Broad, wholesome, charitable views of men and things cannot be acquired by vegetating in one little corner of the earth all one's lifetime."

Rural isolation would not matter much in a stable democracy with low levels of partisan or geographic polarization. That was the state of affairs in America during the immediate postwar years, when the partisan differences among rural, suburban, and urban citizens were small compared with today's chasmic geographic divides.

That America no longer exists. The civil rights, feminist, and gay rights revolutions of the 1960s and '70s were quickly followed by a major immigration reform act—passed in 1986 by a Republican U.S. Senate and signed into law by Republican president Ronald Reagan—that created a massive new wave of citizens by offering amnesty to anyone who had immigrated to the United States prior to 1982. A new and very different-looking nation promptly began taking shape. Fast-forward to today, and the United States is diversifying rapidly and becoming increasingly polarized and more politically unstable. As political columnist Ezra Klein argues in his book *Why We're Polarized,* the single biggest driver of polarization in the United States is rapid demographic change.[41] Demographic changes are impactful and perhaps unsettling to millions of Americans living in all parts of the country. Yet these effects may be felt most acutely by rural Whites, which is ironic given that demographic changes are smaller and arrived later (if at all) to most rural communities.

Place-based resentments exist everywhere and arise among citizens of varying backgrounds. But politicians and the media who cite tensions on both sides of the rural-urban divide are peddling the false equivalency that resentments operate in both directions and in equal measure. They do not. The truth is that rural Whites are the nation's most resentful demographic group, especially on matters of race, place, religion, and sexual identity. Their higher levels of racism and xenophobia exacerbate America's cultural divide and foment political instability.

Wherever they take root, racist, xenophobic, and place-based resentments are born from a desire to turn back the clock on history—which is why *again* is the key word in Donald Trump's campaign slogan "Make America Great Again." For many rural Whites, Trump's slogan recalls an exclusive, more familiar American era, during which members of what we call the nation's essential rural minority faced little competition in business, educational, and social circles from people who looked, thought, or prayed differently from them. Not surprisingly, studies show that White Trump supporters exhibit unusual animus toward minority groups.[42] "Trump's campaign promise of a return to the imaginary past was largely a promise to transport Americans to a time when racism, misogyny, and xenophobia were mainstream attitudes," writes Masha Gessen, author of *Surviving Autocracy.* "More than that: it was the promise of a new history in which a greater inclusivity not only had not happened but would never happen."[43]

The nation's demography is changing rapidly, but the United States cannot be magically transported to some imaginary past—nor should it be. Sadly, millions of rural White Americans are triggered by these

changes and are lashing out accordingly, imperiling the nation's transformation into a more pluralist and inclusive society.

THE SECOND THREAT:
BELIEF IN CONSPIRACIES

On Sunday, December 4, 2016, Edgar Maddison Welch was driving
northbound on Interstate 95 from North Carolina to Washington, D.C.
He pulled out his cell phone, stared into its camera, and hit the Record
button, to save for posterity and his daughters some final thoughts in
case a fatal martyrdom awaited him. "I can't let you grow up in a world
that's so corrupted by evil," a bearded Welch, in a black winter cap,
promised his daughters in that recorded message. "I have to at least
stand up for you and for other children just like you."

Welch was on a mission. From his hometown in Salisbury, North
Carolina—he called it "Smallsbury"—the twenty-eight-year-old father
of two young daughters was determined to investigate what he believed
was a dungeon where Hillary Clinton, her longtime Democratic adviser
John Podesta, and their satanic network of allies molested children they
had kidnapped. With his trunk full of firearms, Welch intended to save
those helpless kids.

Welch was a walking contradiction. A divorced but devoted father
and volunteer firefighter, he worked twelve-hour shifts at the local Food
Lion supermarket to provide for his daughters. He had two Bible verses
tattooed on his back and had traveled with his church group to Haiti to
help earthquake victims. That was Welch's public persona.

Privately, he was unraveling. Painful memories of losing his older
brother twenty years earlier in a fatal car accident may have been revived
by a more recent tragedy: Two months prior to his messianic mission,
Welch accidentally hit with his car and wounded a thirteen-year-old boy.
(The boy survived.) Welch's parents, who live in the rural outskirts of
Salisbury, had no idea their son had fallen down an online rabbit hole
where he listened to conspiracy theorist Alex Jones and read QAnon
articles about a child abduction ring that top Democrats allegedly ran

out of the basement of a Washington pizza parlor called Comet Ping Pong.[44]

That afternoon, Welch learned the truth about the "Pizzagate" conspiracy he had read so much about online. He brought a loaded AR-15 assault rifle and a revolver into the pizza parlor. As traumatized customers cowered in fear, Welch ordered an employee to show him Comet Ping Pong's basement. He fired his gun into the lock of a closet door. A few minutes later, a confused Welch surrendered to police upon realizing the building *had no basement.* He was convicted of transporting a firearm and assault with a dangerous weapon and sentenced to four years in prison.[45]

Conspiracy theories attract women and men, people of every race and religion, and the young and old alike. Although those who espouse either far-left or far-right views tend to be more conspiratorial, there's scant evidence that conspiracists fall along one side of the ideological divide or the other.[46] However, conspiracy scholars have identified a few demographic and psychological traits that make people more inclined to believe conspiracies. Conspiracists tend to be less educated. They often feel a loss of control in their lives. They are less politically active or likely to vote. They tend to have generally prejudiced personalities and are more likely to commit petty crimes, evince populist or Manichean worldviews, and condone violence as a way of solving problems.[47] In the United States, conspiracy theories also flourish in rural communities.

QAnon. Let's start with QAnon. In 2021, the Public Religion Research Institute (PRRI) surveyed Americans to determine who subscribes to one of the three major QAnon conspiracies. The language for each statement and the nationwide share of Americans who agreed with it were as follows:

- **Pedophile network, 15 percent:** "The government, media, and financial worlds in the United States are controlled by a group of Satan-worshipping pedophiles who run a global child sex trafficking operation."
- **Storm coming, 20 percent:** "There is a storm coming that will

sweep away the elites in power and restore the rightful leaders."

- **Justified violence, 15 percent:** "Because things have gotten so far off track, true American patriots may have to resort to violence in order to save our country."

PRRI discovered that 85 percent of what it calls "QAnon believers" also say the Covid-19 virus was human-made in a foreign lab, 73 percent claim the 2020 election was stolen from Donald Trump, and 39 percent believe the Covid-19 vaccine "contains a surveillance microchip that is the sign of the beast in biblical prophecy."[48] The conspiratorial mind contains multitudes.

Republican partisanship and conservative media consumption are major drivers of QAnon conspiracism. But PRRI found rurality also to have a powerful, independent effect: QAnon believers are one and a half times more likely to live in rural than in urban areas.[49] According to an Ipsos poll taken two weeks before the January 6 domestic terrorist attack, QAnon followers tend to be "largely male, non-college educated, Republican, and primarily from the South and Midwest regions . . . and largely from rural and suburban areas." The same poll found that 49 percent of rural Americans—ten points higher than the national average—believed the QAnon theory that a "deep state" network of officials is "working to undermine" Donald Trump.[50] "It's one thing to say that most Americans laugh off these outlandish beliefs, but when you take into consideration that these beliefs are linked to a kind of apocalyptic thinking and violence, then it becomes something quite different," PRRI director Robert Jones says of QAnon adherents.[51]

Rurality also fosters anti-intellectualism, which in turn helps conspiracy theories flourish. Political scientist Kristin Lunz Trujillo discovered that citizens who express a strong rural self-identity are unusually anti-intellectual. Her findings help explain the skepticism that rural Americans, especially rural conservatives, express toward professors, scientists, and experts generally.[52] Scientific skepticism proved especially lethal when rural Whites—the citizens most dubious of pandemic experts—refused safe Covid-19 vaccines at rates higher than urban and suburban citizens. That skepticism proved fatal for more rural Americans than would have died had heartland vaccination rates mirrored those nationwide percentages.

Election denialism. Rural citizens are also more likely to believe that the 2020 presidential election was stolen from Donald Trump and to doubt the legitimacy of elections generally. PRRI's 2021 "Competing Visions of America" poll found that 47 percent of rural Americans either "completely" or "mostly" agree that the 2020 presidential election was stolen. The comparable combined shares for those who live in the suburbs and cities, 30 percent and 22 percent, respectively, are significantly lower.[53] Were non-Whites removed from these results, the share of election deniers among rural Whites alone would be higher.

Given rural Americans' higher electoral support for Trump—who continues to repeat the "Big Lie" and other bogus claims about election fraud—these differences make perfect sense. Prior to both his 2016 and 2020 campaigns, Trump cast doubt on whether any election he lost could be legitimate. Never mind that he paid two firms $1.3 million to investigate supposed voter fraud in 2020 and then quietly buried both reports because neither firm could prove any of his absurd claims.[54]

More than any other public figure, Trump has undermined democracy's most sacred act: voting. At an October 2022 rally, nearly two years after his re-election defeat, the former president continued to repeat his false and incendiary claims of election fraud: "I don't believe we'll ever have a fair election again." It's unclear whether Trump meant this statement as a prediction or a pledge.[55]

In 2022, the Bipartisan Policy Center profiled election deniers. Its polling showed that 33 percent of rural residents are deniers, a rate half again as high as the 21 percent of urban deniers.[56] Flipping the question around, in May 2022 the University of Chicago's Institute of Politics (IOP) asked Americans if they "generally trust our elections to be conducted fairly and accurately counted." Only 43 percent of rural respondents agreed, lower than the national average of 56 percent or the 57 percent of suburbanites and far lower than the 65 percent of urbanites who trust election results.[57]

Given their constituents' beliefs, is it any surprise that a disproportionate share of the 139 House Republicans who voted against certifying Joe Biden's 2020 election hail from rural districts? Using CityLab's district classifications, 48 of those 139 members represented "purely rural" districts, and another 55 came from mixed "rural-suburban" districts. In a chamber where 42 percent of districts are either purely rural or rural-suburban, the 103 combined members from these rural-influence districts produced 74 percent of the votes opposing certification. Just one member who voted not to certify Biden's election represented a "purely urban" district: Staten Island's Nicole Malliotakis from New York's Eleventh District.[58]

These members share another important characteristic in addition to their disproportionately rural districts. After doing a deep dive into the background of those 139 House election deniers, *The New York Times* found an interesting pattern. "Many represent districts where racial and demographic change is churning more swiftly than in other Republican areas," the reporters discovered. "But in comparison with other Republicans, the objectors represent districts where the White portion of the population is decreasing faster relative to other racial or ethnic groups."[59] Election denialism is one of the most profound dangers American democracy faces, and it runs deepest with rural voters and the House Republicans from majority-White but rapidly changing and disproportionately rural districts who represent them.

In the 2022 midterms, Republicans nominated nearly three hundred election deniers for offices including U.S. senator, governor, and secretary of state.[60] More than half these candidates lost, including every GOP secretary of state candidate from a 2020 presidential swing state. Many political observers breathed a sigh of relief. Yet more than one hundred election deniers won. Election denialism and the 2020 "Big Lie" have gained wide currency with rural citizens. Curiously, these rural voters never seem to question the electoral legitimacy of Republican officials whom they elected from the same states during the same election cycles.

Harvard political scientist Theda Skocpol argues that election denialism is designed to question not so much the legitimacy of voting outcomes as the legitimacy of certain voters. What deniers really believe, says Skocpol, is that votes of those who look, think, or pray differently from them are *inherently* illegitimate. "I don't think Stop the Steal is about ballots at all. I don't believe a lot of people really think that the votes weren't counted correctly in 2020," Skocpol said in an interview with *The Atlantic.* "They believe that urban people, metropolitan people—disproportionately young and minorities, to be sure, but frankly liberal Whites—are an illegitimate brew that's changing America in un-recognizable ways and taking it away from them. Stop the Steal is a way of saying that. Stop the Steal is a metaphor."[61]

Obama birtherism. Finally, there is the mother of all recent right-wing conspiracy theories: Obama birtherism, a fitting name for the conspiracy theory that birthed Donald Trump's presidency. In the spring of 2011, when Trump briefly considered a 2012 presidential run, the reality TV star began to question the authenticity of President Barack Obama's 1961 Hawai'i birth certificate, and thus Obama's legitimacy to serve as president. Political scientist Philip Klinkner lined up Trump's state-ments alongside poll data and media mentions of birtherism. His find-ings are stunning: During just six weeks in March and April 2011, Trump's comments coincided with a fourteen-point drop in the per-centage of Americans who believed Obama was born in the United States.[62]

To be fair, birtherism did not start with Trump: During the 2008 Democratic presidential primary, key Hillary Clinton allies circulated an anonymous email questioning Obama's birthplace,[63] and throughout that campaign and into his presidency, challenging Obama's citizenship was a constant theme of right-wing rhetoric. But Trump turbocharged the conspiracy theory: In just six weeks, he almost single-handedly con-vinced one in every seven U.S. adults that Obama was an illegitimate president.

According to Klinkner, racial resentment was the single best predic-tor of support for the birther conspiracy in 2011. Not surprisingly, five years later, birtherism was one of the strongest predictors of which Re-publicans supported Trump in the 2016 presidential primary. GOPers who believed the companion claim that Obama is a Muslim were a whopping 40 percentage points more likely to support the reality TV star.[64] For millions of Americans, racialized attitudes dovetail neatly with conspiracist beliefs.

And where was birtherism strongest? You guessed it: in rural communities. In 2009, two years *before* Trump first seized upon the issue in 2011, Public Policy Polling surveyed voters in North Carolina and Virginia about this issue. PPP concluded that birtherism is "very much a rural phenomenon"[65] after finding that rural Republicans in both states were twenty percentage points more likely than other state Republicans to believe the birther conspiracy.[66]

The evidence is overwhelming: Heartland America is home to unusually high levels of dangerous, often self-destructive conspiracism and beliefs in other fictions. Edgar Maddison Welch's story is a tragedy—for him, for his parents and daughters, and especially for the dozens of people he terrorized at the Comet Ping Pong pizza parlor in 2016. Fortunately, nobody was injured or killed that day.

But Welch's story is also a cautionary tale: Research shows that conspiracist beliefs are linked to undemocratic, even violent tendencies.[67] Nor is Welch alone: Millions of other rural White Americans also endorse wild and potentially dangerous conspiracist ideas.

THE THIRD THREAT:
ANTI-DEMOCRATIC TENDENCIES

Opposing democratic norms like checks and balances between the branches of government, the role of a free press, and citizen access to the ballot; embracing authoritarian, White nationalist, or Christian nationalist alternatives over secular, constitutional rule; believing local sheriffs can defy superseding state and national laws—each of these political beliefs shares two commonalities. One, they are undemocratic impulses that threaten the U.S. constitutional system. And two, rural Americans are more likely to express them.

Democracy requires a vigilant defense of its norms and institutions. Unfortunately, in their analyses of the 2020 American National Election Survey, political scientists Suzanne Mettler and Trevor Brown found

rural residents to be less supportive than city dwellers of core democratic principles: "[Rural Americans] were much more likely to favor
restrictions on the press, for example, and to suggest it would be helpful
if the president could unilaterally work on the country's problems without paying attention to the Congress or the courts. These indicators
point to a serious divide in the U.S. polity, one that threatens the health
of democracy."[68]

The fact that rural Americans are more likely to dismiss the need for
checks and balances on presidents or an independent media suggests
that their beliefs in constitutional principles are limited and conditional.
Rural America's favorite president agrees: Donald Trump proclaimed
that Article II of the Constitution gave him the "right to do whatever I
want as president."[69] And everyone knows how Trump feels about the
media, whom he routinely castigates as scum and enemies of the state
worthy of scorn or even violence.

Ballot access. Anti-democratic impulses are evident in the urban-
rural split on support for the core democratic principle of ballot access.
A 2021 Marist College poll asked Americans which concerned them
more, "making sure that everyone who wants to vote can do so" or "making sure that no one votes who is ineligible." Nationally, 56 percent of
respondents were more concerned about ballot access, but a shocking 41
percent were more concerned about ineligible people voting.[70]

We say "shocking" because the latter group is fretting about a phantom problem. After analyzing literally billions of votes cast by millions of
voters in hundreds of elections over multiple election cycles, the Brennan Center for Justice concluded that vote fraud amounts to at most
three out of every million votes cast. The center's findings echo results
from similar studies conducted by Columbia University, Dartmouth
University, Arizona State University, *The Washington Post,* and the U.S.
Government Accountability Office. Even Kris Kobach—a voter fraud
fabulist appointed by Donald Trump in 2017 to head a commission
tasked with finding examples of fraud—documented just 14 cases out of
84 million votes cast in twenty-two states, a rate even lower than the
Brennan Center found.[71] Voter fraud is the Freddy Krueger of American
politics, a fictional demon who appears in the fevered dreams of cranks

like MyPillow CEO Mike Lindell. Yet two out of every five Americans are more worried about this imaginary "crisis" than they are that their fellow citizens have ballot access.

As for who believes in voter fraud, the Marist Poll results are predictable: Majorities of Americans who live in big cities (68 percent), small cities (65 percent), and the suburbs (59 percent) express greater concern about eligible citizens being able to vote. Conversely, majorities of residents of small towns (51 percent) and rural areas (58 percent) are more worried about nonexistent voter fraud. The direct relationship between population density and beliefs in ballot integrity could not be more obvious.[72]

Authoritarianism and nationalism. Authoritarianism, White nationalism, and White Christian nationalism present another series of connected threats to American democracy. In the United States and other Western nations, authoritarians backed by White nationalists and Christian nationalists like Trump are increasingly emboldened. Their followers degrade democratic institutions and norms, including transparency, accountability, the rule of law, and civil liberties and rights. The impulse to follow and elevate authoritarian figures is a human reflex so innate that it may be hard-wired into humans' evolutionary biology.[73]

In her book *Strongmen: Mussolini to the Present*, Ruth Ben-Ghiat studies the characteristics common to modern authoritarians. What stands out, she says, are the ways strongmen employ powerful appeals to in-group solidarity. "For authoritarians," Ben-Ghiat explains, "only some people are 'the people,' regardless of their birthplace or citizenship status." Moreover, she explains that a strongman's "rogue nature" draws followers to him because he "proclaims law-and-order rule" for outgroups "yet enables lawlessness" for his supporters.[74] Certain people are instinctually attracted to strongmen, especially those who affirm their base supporters' political predispositions.

Among the citizenry, authoritarian personalities tend to fit a similar demographic profile. In their book *Cultural Backlash: Trump, Brexit, and Authoritarian Populism*, Pippa Norris and Ronald Inglehart provide the basic profile of authoritarian voters in the United States and other Western democracies. "Voting for authoritarian parties is strongest among the older generation, men, the less educated, white European populations, in rural areas, and among the most religious."[75] For these aging, less educated, rural White men, the authoritarian's appeal is rooted in an expectation that his (or her) hardfisted rule will benefit those whom Ben-Ghiat calls "chosen" groups.

In the U.S. case, no group enjoys a more chosen status than heartland White Americans. Which is why Trump's most devoted voters, rural Whites, so often excuse his rogue behavior, whether it is sleeping with porn stars or mocking Sen. John McCain for being captured in Vietnam. "Cults of personality are anathema to democracies," warns Sarah Longwell, founder of the Republican Accountability Project. They tend to be "based on the same things—lies, pledges of loyalty, and intolerance of dissent," she says.[76] So long as authoritarians hate the same out-groups as their followers, politicians like Trump can have all the extramarital affairs and mock all the wounded veterans they want.

Emboldened by his authoritarian followers, Trump ordered tanks to appear on the National Mall for a July 4 rally, deployed the Secret Service to clear away White House protestors so he could walk to St. John's Episcopal Church in Lafayette Square to hold a Bible aloft, and incited the January 6 domestic terrorists to attack the U.S. Capitol. The president whose electoral following was strongest in America's rural corners was the only 2016 presidential candidate, Democrat or Republican, for whom the authoritarianism personality trait predicted electoral support.[77]

Self-styled patriot groups seek to restore power as exercised primarily if not exclusively by Whites, Christians, or both. Groups like the Oath Keepers and the Three Percenters openly advocate upheaval, revolution, and violence as a necessary means to achieving this restoration. These radical, undemocratic groups find supporters in every corner of the nation, but their rural connections are indisputable. In their study of "rural rage," investigative journalists Chip Berlet and Spencer Sunshine describe the geography of violent White nationalist groups. "Patriot movement groups were active on the streets in 2017, 2018, and 2019, joining the frequently violent pro-Trump street rallies which are also attended by organized White supremacists," Berlet and Sunshine explain.

"And although the Patriot movement's tactics are still fringe, they are also inching toward the mainstream under Trump's presidency. While not exclusively a rural phenomenon, the current right-wing populist backlash against diversity and human rights has established a strong foothold in the United States in rural areas with economies based on farming, ranching, the timber industry, and mining."[78] (Northwestern University's Kathleen Belew, an expert on authoritarian and White nationalist movements, and other scholars of White nationalism disagree about the degree to which patriot movements can be classified as distinctly rural.)

As a subset of the White nationalist movement, Christian nationalism presents a related threat to U.S. democracy. In their book, *Taking Back America for God,* Samuel Perry and Andrew Whitehead explain how Christian nationalists seek to undermine secular governance by infusing Christian identity and norms into public life. Millions of Christian nationalists believe the United States should be a Christian-only or at least a Christian-dominant nation. They reject the separation of church and state and want biblical precepts to replace secular practices and constitutional law.[79]

According to a Pew poll released two weeks before the 2022 midterms, 45 percent of Americans say the United States should be a Christian nation. Among these citizens, 54 percent say that if the Bible and the will of the people conflict, the Bible "should have more influence," and 31 percent say the federal government should "stop enforcing the separation of church and state." A sizable segment of the U.S. citizenry, ranging between 15 and 25 percent, favors theocratic over secular governance.[80] Their views were neatly summarized by Colorado representative Lauren Boebert, who said she's "tired" of church-state separation and believes the "church is supposed to direct the government." Presumably, Boebert doesn't mean the Buddhist, Jewish, or Muslim church.

Oddly enough, many Christian nationalists believe simultaneously in both their dominance and their victimhood. "Americans who subscribe to white Christian nationalism see themselves as representing 'the nation,' and 'the real Americans' over and against a corrupt 'regime' of elites who would take away their rights and plunge the nation further into decadence," Perry and Whitehead conclude. "This should sound familiar."[81] It does: This persecution complex echoes many right-wing and Trump-peddled talking points about how either Whites or Christians are under siege and are therefore justified in resorting to undemocratic means to impose their will.

Combating perceived persecution motivated millions of Christian nationalists to support Trump—a man who never goes to church and who couldn't quote a single line of scripture when asked—as some sort of divine savior. "There is a very common claim that Trump is a new iteration of King Cyrus, in that he himself is not a believer, but God is using him to restore America," Sarah Posner, author of *Unholy: Why White Evangelicals Worship at the Altar of Donald Trump*, writes. "Many of his supporters continue to claim a divine mandate for his administration and its policies."[82] Among those whom Perry and Whitehead identify as movement "ambassadors"—citizens who most closely identify with Christian nationalist ideals—87 percent who both are White and hail from rural communities voted for Donald Trump in 2016.[83]

Journalist Katherine Stewart explains why Christian nationalism, cast as a religious movement, is actually a political movement. Right-wing political donors including the DeVos/Prince, Bradley, Ahmanson, Scaife, Olin, Friess, Wilks, and Green families have funneled millions of dollars into Christian nationalist organizations. "Christian nationalism is not a religious creed but, in my view, a political ideology," Stewart writes in her book *The Power Worshippers*. "It asserts that legitimate government rests *not on the consent of the governed* but on adherence to the doctrines of a specific religious, ethnic or cultural heritage. It demands that our laws be based not on the reasoned deliberation of our democratic institutions but on particular, idiosyncratic interpretations of the Bible."[84]

Who are these Christian nationalists? Not all Christian nationalists are White evangelicals and not all White evangelicals are Christian nationalists, but the groups overlap substantially. According to Samuel Perry, 58 percent of White evangelicals say the name "Christian nationalist" describes them either "well" or "very well."[85] A 2023 poll conducted jointly by PRRI and the Brookings Institution pegged that percentage at 64.[86] The fact that roughly three-fifths of White evangelicals openly admit they are Christian nationalists is alarming.

Not surprisingly, White evangelicals also express exclusionary, antidemocratic attitudes. Fifty-seven percent believe one must be Christian to be "truly American," a rate twice that of the next closest religious subgroup, White mainline Protestants, at 29 percent.[87] A remarkable 84 percent say the Bible should have "a great deal" of or at least "some" influence on U.S. laws.[88] White evangelicals are also strongly anti-immigrant: Only one in five supports a pathway to citizenship for so-called Dreamer immigrants brought to the United States as children, the lowest of any religious group. More than half of White evangelicals—higher than any other religious identity—believe the 2020 election was stolen from Donald Trump.[89] And at 27 percent, they are the religious group least likely to agree that "American culture and way of life has mostly changed for the better."[90] An almost identical 26 percent of White evangelicals—again, highest among religious groups—say that "true American patriots might have to resort to violence in order to save the country."[91]

More to our point is *where* White evangelicals reside: Forty-three percent of rural residents identify as evangelical, a rate twice the national average.[92] Consequently, Christian nationalism is "unevenly distributed around the country," explains Paul D. Miller, author of *The Religion of American Greatness: What's Wrong with Christian Nationalism*. It is "more common in the South with a strong representation in the Midwest. It is stronger in rural areas and smaller towns, less common in bigger cities."[93] White evangelism and its ugly cousin, Christian nationalism, are not exclusively rural phenomena. But Christian nationalists find unique comfort in rural pews.

Constitutional sheriffs. Rural sheriffs present yet another threat to U.S. democracy. From Western movies to *The Andy Griffith Show*, the local sheriff has long been depicted as the archetypal American hero—a strong, silent, impartial defender of the weak against various predators. But a dark trend has emerged among America's self-styled "constitutional sheriffs," who assert self-serving, invented claims that their office grants them powers superior to those of any other public official at any level of government, powers they can use in pursuit of whatever radical agenda they please. The roots of the constitutional sheriff movement trace back to the Posse Comitatus, a White supremacist and anti-Semitic movement in the 1970s that emerged from remnants of the Ku Klux Klan and introduced the notion that sheriffs are above the law.

There are roughly five thousand members of the Constitutional Sheriffs and Peace Officers Association, which, along with Protect America Now, is one of two organizations leading this nascent movement.[94] With notable exceptions like Joe Arpaio and David Clarke—both of whom gained fame as close allies of Donald Trump—few of these sheriffs are known beyond their home counties. But they are convinced they have the right to exercise extraordinary power.

Indeed, constitutional sheriffs believe that within their counties, *they are the law.* In a modern nod to the reactionary, pre–Civil War theory of "nullification" advanced by slavery defender John Calhoun, CSPOA and PAN sheriffs reject the concepts of national supremacy and state-level authority. According to the Marshall Project, roughly 10 percent of the nation's three thousand head sheriffs believe they have "interposition" powers to insert themselves between their constituents and state and national officials.[95] They reject the Supremacy Clause of the Constitution, which makes clear that federal authority exceeds that of other levels of government. To the constitutional sheriffs, it is the county that is supreme, and they are the highest authority in their counties. Being a constitutional sheriff means believing you are empowered to rule like a one-man judge and all-White jury, picking and choosing which laws and court rulings to enforce and which not.

The "one-man judge and all-White jury" line is not hyperbole: U.S. sheriffs are almost all White men. Only 5 percent are minorities, and only 3 percent are women.[96] Fully 71 percent of sheriffs describe themselves as either "conservative" or "very conservative," and most of the rest self-describe as "middle of the road."[97] Never mind that they do not look or think anything like the nation overall: Sheriffs in rural counties *are not even demographically representative of the rural counties* over which they have authority. Those connected to the CSPOA harbor unusually radical and revanchist attitudes, like the sheriff from rural Oklahoma's McCurtain County who was caught on tape joking with three other county officials about assassinating a local journalist while pining for a return to the glory days when it was still legal to lynch Black prisoners.[98]

Although they may not yet have led the kind of violent revolution against other levels of government they believe they can wage, in recent years sheriffs have begun to make their ideas clear. Egged on by the CSPOA, sheriffs in three states took it upon themselves to investigate supposed fraud in the 2020 presidential election. All three were among dozens who met in Las Vegas in 2022 with representatives from True the Vote, MyPillow's Mike Lindell, and other election conspiracists.[99] Calvin Hayden, the sheriff of rural Johnson County, Kansas, was one of the three. Eighteen months after the 2020 election, in a state Donald Trump won easily, Hayden continued to pursue what he called a "criminal prosecution" of vote fraud in his county, which Biden had carried narrowly. Hayden claimed that his office had received two hundred calls alleging election fraud. A public records search revealed just one such call.[100]

Sheriff Dar Leaf of Michigan's rural Barry County decided to investigate Dominion Voting Systems machines in his home county. Trump supporters in two other rural Michigan counties, Antrim and Cheboygan, engaged in similar efforts. Leaf coordinated his activities with Trump lawyers Sidney Powell and Stefanie Lambert, who filed a voter fraud lawsuit in Michigan that was so outrageous, the judge sanctioned both attorneys for misconduct. "The upheaval in Barry County shows how the right's misinformation-fueled efforts to control elections have spread to even the smallest towns," Reuters reported. "Here and in some other conservative communities, Trump-aligned activists have sown doubt and discord that is putting long-serving election clerks on the defensive."[101]

On three other issues—Covid-19, immigration, and violence against women—experts Emily Farris and Mirya Holman found that constitutional sheriffs not only flout state or national laws, but also harbor attitudes that often prevent them from properly administering those laws. Constitutional sheriffs were less likely to enforce Covid-19 mask mandates during the pandemic. They are more prone to allowing their animosities toward immigrants to justify enforcement activities that go "far beyond" what immigration law specifies. And their views about women make them less likely to believe reports of rape and domestic violence committed against women.[102]

Then there is the matter of gun rights, an issue on which constitutional sheriffs have defiantly planted a flag. The sheriffs are especially resistant to what's legally known as extreme risk protection orders—informally called "red flag" laws—that empower judges to order law enforcement officials to take guns from citizens who pose a demonstrated and imminent danger to other persons.[103]

The constitutional sheriff movement is gaining strength. Dangerous CSPOA-affiliated teachers are training other law enforcement officers who are entrusted to protect the citizenry. These radicals impart to trainees not only their views on the law, policing, and the use of force, but their racist, conspiratorial, and authoritarian views as well. Some express beliefs similar to those of trolls on the online bulletin board 4chan, including support for QAnon, the Proud Boys, and other White nationalist groups; the belief that the 2020 election was stolen; the most vulgar forms of Islamophobia; and the allegation that President Joe Biden is a pedophile.[104]

Right-wing money supports the movement. In 2021, the conservative Claremont Institute hosted its inaugural Sheriffs Fellowship program. *Slate*'s Jessica Pishko obtained a copy of the curriculum, which was chock-full of right-wing, Christian nationalist, and authoritarian messaging. "The office [of sheriff] is already vulnerable to extremism and . . . sheriffs can enable other extremist actors like vigilantes and militias to wreak havoc on society," Pishko writes. "Claremont provides a historical and intellectual cover for selected sheriffs to continue a march into white Christian nationalism; for Claremont, the sheriffs are elected influencers who can push their message into the mainstream."[105] And that message is clear: Sheriffs should be able to wield unfettered authority in their respective counties to carry out whatever radical agendas they want.

U.S. democracy is in peril. Ballot blockers, wannabe authoritarians, White Christian nationalists, and constitutional sheriffs each pose existential and often overlapping threats to American constitutional governance. Unfortunately, rural Whites form the tip of the spear for each of these movements.

THE FOURTH THREAT:
INTIMIDATION, HARASSMENT, AND VIOLENCE

In August 2022, a federal jury in Grand Rapids, Michigan, convicted Barry Croft and Adam Fox for their roles as ringleaders in a failed plot to kidnap Michigan Democratic governor Gretchen Whitmer. With the help of an informant, undercover FBI agents recorded videos of Croft, Fox, and nearly a dozen of their "Wolverine Watchmen" confederates making bombs and surveilling the governor's summer cottage. Two other Watchmen pled guilty to lesser charges and testified against Croft and Fox, who were convicted and sentenced to sixteen and nineteen years, respectively, in federal prison.[106]

Although he was living in the basement of a vacuum shop at the time of the failed plot, Fox hails from Potterville, Michigan, a small rural town of roughly two thousand citizens. Croft's hometown of Bear, Delaware, is a slightly bigger rural enclave of twenty thousand people. The two would-be terrorists connected through the Watchmen, a violent splinter group of the "Boogaloo" movement. U.S. Attorney Nils Kessler told the jury that the defendants' kidnapping plans were part of their grander ambition to "set off a second American civil war, a second American Revolution, something that they call the boogaloo."[107] Responding to the verdicts, Whitmer warned about the existential stakes: "Plots against public officials and threats to the FBI are a disturbing extension of radicalized domestic terrorism that festers in our nation, threatening the very foundation of our republic."[108]

Insurrectionist attacks. Famous for his scholarship on the New Deal and the "paranoid style" in U.S. politics, noted political historian Richard Hofstadter in 1970 wrote a less noticed introductory chapter in a book about key episodes of political violence entitled *American Violence: A Documentary History*. In it, Hofstadter makes two trenchant observations about patterns in political violence. His first observation pertains to who is targeted—or, rather, *not* targeted—in domestic violence episodes. His second observation concerns the perpetrators. Hofstadter writes:

> An arresting fact about American violence, and one of the keys to understanding its history, is that very little has been insurrectionary. Most of our violence has taken the form of action by one group of citizens against another group, rather than by citizens against the state. . . .
>
> One is impressed that most American violence—and this also illuminates its relationship to state power—has been initiated with a "conservative" bias. It has been unleashed against abolitionists, Catholics, radicals, workers and labor organizers, Negroes, Orientals, and other ethnic or racial or ideological minorities, and has been used ostensibly to protect the American, the Southern, the white Protestant, or simply the established middle-class way of life and morals.[109]

Hofstadter's list of targets is a bit outdated, and some of the labels he uses are inappropriate today. His second observation, however, is evergreen: As the implicit "conservative" beneficiaries of state power, White, middle-class Protestants have long targeted any out-group that dare challenge their privileged position. The Garden City terrorists who wanted to bomb Somali immigrants exemplify Hofstadter's point about how conservative violence typically targets new, foreign, or different claimants to the American dream.

But Hofstadter's first observation about violence exempting government officials and agencies no longer holds. Starting with Timothy McVeigh's 1995 bombing of the Alfred P. Murrah Federal Building, in Oklahoma City, conservative violence increasingly targets government officials, agencies, or facilities. Croft and Fox led an attempt to kidnap and kill a sitting governor. Days before the 2022 midterms, the Department of Homeland Security reported that threats issued against members of Congress rose to 9,600 in 2021, a new record and a more than tenfold increase since Donald Trump's 2016 election.[110] And, of course, millions of shocked Americans watched the January 6, 2021, domestic terrorist attacks live on TV.

Anissa Herrera learned firsthand what happens when people opt for violent threats against public officials over peaceful resolution of electoral contests. As the election administrator of rural Gillespie County, Texas, Herrera had heard the claims made by election deniers about rigged results. For the most part, those complaints seemed like little more than loose talk. Unfortunately, a subset of individuals began to harass her. "I was threatened, I've been stalked," Herrera said. By 2022, she and her fellow election officials no longer felt safe. "We have some people who are pretty fanatical and radical about things," Gillespie County judge Mark Stroeher told the local newspaper. "Unfortunately, they have driven out our elections administrator, and not just her, but the staff. Everybody has resigned."[111]

At that point, supervising the 2022 election fell to Gillespie County clerk Lindsey Brown. With only weeks to prepare and with the national media descending upon Fredericksburg, the county seat, Brown scrambled to administer the election properly. When we caught up with her at the county elections office five days before the 2022 midterms, she was upbeat, if understandably beleaguered. And as if the recent resignations did not make her supervisory duties tough enough, she was also a close friend of Herrera's and used to wait tables at the local restaurant Herrera's family owns.

Brown told us that neighboring county clerks had warned her that voters—especially those whose candidate lost the presidential race two years prior—tend to be a little more agitated during midterm cycles. But aside from one angry elderly voter and one camera crew filming inside the state-mandated, one-hundred-foot-radius boundary around polling sites, Brown encountered no problems in Gillespie County in 2022. "Elections is a whole other ball game," she said, reflecting upon election supervision relative to her more mundane responsibilities as county clerk, like building permit applications and recording tax deeds. "People are passionate and want their votes to count. And the legislature is always changing laws regarding elections."[112]

Wanting one's vote to count is a legitimate democratic reflex. Gum-

ming up the works for election officials—a tactic many Trump supporters are deploying to create administrative problems—is not.[113]
Threatening election officials is even less legitimate. Sadly, as a 2021
Brennan Center for Justice report documented, there has been a rising
number of threats issued, and sometimes carried out, by violent radicals
against innocent election officials just trying to do their jobs.[114] For Anissa Herrera and the other Gillespie County election officials who quit
in fear, the damage has been done.

Nearly two thousand miles from Gillespie County, citizens of Bonners Ferry, Idaho, were shocked to experience public threats of violence
in their small, rural town. Nestled along the Kootenai River and home to
just 2,500 residents, Bonners Ferry is the largest town and the county
seat of Boundary, Idaho's northernmost and lone Canada-bordering
county. Fewer than 13,000 people live in the county, which is 93 percent
White and 74 percent rural.[115] Boundary voters supported Trump over
Biden by a nearly three-to-one margin in 2020.

In August 2022, angry armed protestors showed up in Bonners Ferry
for a public meeting to demand that four hundred books be banned
from the local library. Many of the books on their list involved sexuality
or gender. But the list was likely generated by some person or organization outside Boundary County, because none of the four hundred books
the protestors sought to ban was even part of the library's collection.

Indeed, the protestors' agenda seemed rooted in White Christian nationalism, in particular White Christian nationalists' obsession with
forms of sexuality they regard as deviant. A parent at one town meeting
warned local officials that they were "sexual deviants" who would suffer
the consequences of heavenly wrath. Another told town officials they
"bring curses upon" themselves "from the most high."[116] A Boundary
County librarian explained that the agitators are mostly newcomers who
had come to Idaho or one of four neighboring northwestern states as
part of the American Redoubt movement. A Christian survivalist group
formed in 2011 by James Wesley Rawles, Redoubters encourage like-
minded Christians to move to sparsely populated areas in Idaho, Montana, Wyoming, or the eastern part of Oregon or Washington to create

off-the-grid and well-armed Christian communities. "In effect, we're becoming pistol-packing Amish," Rawles quipped.[117]

A small but significant number of White Christian nationalists promote violence. University of Pennsylvania religion scholar Anthea Butler, author of *White Evangelical Racism,* foresaw the January 6 domestic terrorist attack on the U.S. Capitol and the role Christian nationalists played in it. The warnings, she said, were evident a few weeks earlier, during the December 12 Jericho March near the White House. "While everybody said, 'We couldn't believe 1/6 was going to happen,' I could have told you that 1/6 was going to happen because I saw it in December, you know, when they were marching around at the Jericho March in DC," Butler told a radio interviewer. "Nobody wants to think religious people are going to take up arms, but religious people talk about violence all the time. And we've been trained because of 9/11 to think that's just Muslims. But Christians are very violent, and they like guns."[118] The Proud Boys participated in the Jericho rally at which four people were stabbed and twenty-three were arrested, including six people for assaulting police officers.[119]

These threats and acts of violence are taking place at a time when some politicians have come to look kindly on violence when it is committed by conservatives. In June 2021, Congress voted 406–21 to award the Congressional Gold Medal to police officers who had defended the U.S. Capitol Building five months earlier, on January 6, more than 150 of whom were injured. Several of those 21 "nay" votes, all Republicans, objected to the use of the word *insurrection* in the Gold Medal resolution. All but three of the 21 "nays" had also voted against certifying Joe Biden's election, and most were among the 20 votes opposing Kevin McCarthy's House Speaker bid two years later, including Arizona's Paul Gosar, Colorado's Lauren Boebert, Georgia's Andrew Clyde, Maryland's Andy Harris, Montana's Matt Rosendale, South Carolina's Ralph Norman, Texas's Louie Gohmert, and Virginia's Bob Good. Eighteen of the twenty-one House holdouts represent either "purely rural" or "rural-suburban" districts. Apparently, "backing the blue" is a conditional sentiment for some of the United States' most rural House members.[120]

Sadly, election officials, local librarians, and sitting members of Congress are not the only targets of harassment and violence. In the Trump era, radical MAGA followers have called for violence against Dr. Anthony Fauci and the Centers for Disease Control and Prevention, the Internal Revenue Service, the Federal Bureau of Investigation, and several federal judges. A right-wing loner broke into Speaker Nancy Pelosi's home and attacked her husband with a hammer. Conservatives and Republicans are not exempted from attack. Witnesses who either testified in one of Trump's two impeachment trials or with the House Select Committee to Investigate the January 6th Attacks were repeatedly harassed with profanity-laced, violent threats via phone, text, and email. From White House aide Cassidy Hutchinson to Arizona state house Speaker Rusty Bowers, a Republican, many of these victims had either supported Trump's presidential campaigns or worked in the Trump administration.[121]

Justification for violence. Where does the appetite for state-directed violence emerge? In the University of Chicago Institute of Politics poll cited earlier, Americans were asked whether they agreed that "it may be necessary at some point soon for citizens to take up arms against the government." The differences were slight, but rural Americans were most likely to agree, at 35 percent, compared with 29 percent of city dwellers and 25 percent of suburbanites.[122]

In fact, those who justify political violence number in the millions. According to University of Chicago political scientist Robert Pape and his colleagues at the Chicago Project on Security and Threats (CPOST), the tens of thousands who descended upon Washington on January 6 demanding that Donald Trump be reinstated for a second presidential term were not alone. CPOST found that 25 percent of American adults—roughly 67 million total—believe the "2020 election was stolen from Donald Trump and Joe Biden is an illegitimate president." Nine percent agree that the "use of force is justified" to restore Trump to the presidency. Overall, 8 percent agree with both statements. CPOST estimated that this 8 percent translates to roughly 21 million Americans who believe Trump should be restored to office, even if by force.[123]

Among these 21 million potential insurrectionists, CPOST estimates that approximately 8 million own a gun, 6 million said they support right-wing military groups, and 1 million said they personally knew at least one member of such groups. Fully 63 percent of them also believe racial minorities in America will "eventually have more rights than whites." And 54 percent are QAnon conspiracists who believe a "secret group of Satan-worshipping pedophiles is ruling the U.S. government."

Where do these insurrectionist-minded citizens reside? Thirty percent of the 21 million Americans who say Biden's win was illegitimate and the 27 percent who say Trump should be returned to power by force live in rural areas.[124] Those percentages are significantly higher than the estimated rural population share of 20 percent.[125] Not every citizen with violent, anti-government tendencies is rural, but rural Americans are overrepresented among those with insurrectionist tendencies.

Scholars who study partisanship are increasingly noticing not just the urban-rural fault line, but also the potential for radicalism coming from rural areas. As political scientist Lilliana Mason said when asked if she foresaw a repeat of America's first civil war, "the geographic divide is very different now. It's largely urban vs. rural, rather than North vs. South." Consequently, she says, many of today's conflicts are intra-state battles that take place at state capitals. "And then people go back home to the rural areas and get ready to go fight again." Mason worries that Republican-controlled legislatures may engage in voter suppression or install "a government that is not duly elected because the state legislatures disobeyed the actual counted votes," prompting resistance from the left. "I think the way that this gets dangerous is if we have really massive protests from Democrats met with violent counterprotesters from rural areas or Republican protesters."[126]

In recent years, terrorism in America has become primarily a right-wing phenomenon. Far-right domestic terrorist attacks in the United States have outnumbered those committed by all other groups *combined.* The two groups most prone to violence, says domestic violence expert Rachel Kleinfeld of the Carnegie Endowment for International Peace, are "white Christian evangelical Republicans [who are] outsized supporters of both political violence and the QAnon conspiracy" and "those who feel threatened by either women or minorities." Here we see how violence is linked back to the first three threats, especially in rural America, a place where White evangelism, support for QAnon, and animosity toward minorities are all higher than anywhere else in the United States.[127]

As Richard Hofstadter predicted, historically privileged citizens continue to direct their violent rhetoric and actions at whichever outgroups threaten traditional power structures: racial and religious minorities, LGBTQ+ people, immigrants, woke liberals. But Hofstadter did not foresee that once members of those in-groups conclude that the state is no longer their ally in dispensing violence, those with violent tendencies may redirect their anger toward the state itself. We take his insight one step further: Once the essential rural White "chosen" minority comes to believe it no longer commands its long-enjoyed veto power over the rest of the nation, the incentives for rural Whites to abandon support for U.S. democracy rise. And at that point, rural Whites' willingness to traffic in precisely the sort of anti-democratic, insurrectionist behaviors that Hofstadter argues have rarely occurred in American history becomes even more of a threat.

THE RURAL WHITE THREAT TO
AMERICAN DEMOCRACY

Not every rural White American espouses xenophobic, conspiratorial, undemocratic, or violent attitudes. But rural Whites are overrepresented across all four of these threats. Journalists and pundits may explain away these patterns by citing the "economic anxieties" rural Whites experience. But explanations do not justify attitudes or behaviors that imperil the world's oldest constitutional democracy.

Nor can economic anxiety explain why rural African Americans, Latinos, and Native Americans—all of whom face even greater economic and health challenges than their White neighbors—exhibit stronger democratic commitments than do rural Whites. We offer a simple explanation for this racialized aspect of the patriotic paradox: Non-White rural citizens are not now, nor have they ever been, part of what we call America's essential minority.

Unfortunately, a shockingly high percentage of that essential rural White minority so fears losing their long-enjoyed privileged status that they are willing to embrace undemocratic ideas and reactionary or even violent leaders—so long as doing so perpetuates their outsize power. These conditional patriots may pledge allegiance to the flag and to the republic for which it stands, but they do so with stipulations.

Finally, readers surely noticed that we connected Donald Trump to all four threats. This was no accident, but neither was it a stretch. Throughout his two presidential campaigns and his four years in the Oval Office in between, Trump repeatedly supported racist, conspiratorial, undemocratic, and violent beliefs and behaviors. Millions of rural White voters seem undeterred or even thrilled by the former president's statements and actions. In fact, they are the only major geo-demographic cohort among whom Trump performed *better* in the 2020 presidential contest than he did four years earlier.

With clear eyes and full hearts, rural Whites recognized Trump's exclusionary, reality-defying, undemocratic, and violent tendencies—and then rallied behind him because of, not despite, his repeated disregard for America's most sacred democratic traditions. Although we have cited here more than three dozen polls and academic studies linking rural citizens and rural Whites specifically to the four threats, perhaps the most powerful evidence that rural Whites pose a unique danger to the nation is their throaty, unmitigated defense of Donald Trump's repeated assaults on American democracy.

RACE AND RURALITY

——

LIKE THE LEADING MAN IN A FRANK CAPRA MOVIE, WILLIAM MONDALE Robinson has a name tailor-made for politics. His parents, rural southern Democrats, bestowed that middle name on him as a nod to Democratic vice president Walter Mondale. Robinson prefers it to his first name. You might say that Mondale Robinson was born to run for elected office. In 2022, he did.

After years working as an activist in national politics, the forty-four-year-old Robinson wanted a change of scenery and a change of life. He moved from Washington back to Enfield, North Carolina, the small rural city of roughly 2,200 residents where he grew up, to run for mayor. Doing so was a gamble on himself: He was trusting that the same political ideals and calls for activism he had preached for years in his nonprofit work as an electoral mobilizer would help him win.

But Robinson does not fit the traditional image of the small-town, rural southern mayoral candidate that likely comes to mind. He is African American. And Enfield, the state's poorest city and the nation's eighth poorest,[1] is majority Black and located in Halifax County, a majority-Black rural county in North Carolina's Albemarle region.

Founder of the Black Male Voter Project, Robinson spent years identifying, registering, and mobilizing apathetic and politically ignored Black men across the United States. He taught community leaders, progressive organizations, and Democratic Party officials how to do the same. In Enfield, he put his theories to the test. He and his campaign volunteers went door-to-door, repeatedly explaining his platform and making sure his supporters registered and voted. He coordinated his campaign's efforts with the team from the Rural Democracy Initiative.[2]

On May 17, 2022, Mondale Robinson was elected Enfield's new mayor, capturing 76 percent of the vote. And he did so by promoting a progressive agenda of self-empowerment on issues including livable wages, universal healthcare, and racial equity. "We reminded people that they weren't subjects of elected officials, but instead bosses of them, and they responded demanding more, showing up to city meetings in record numbers and speaking about their needs—not what the well-connected and well-monied interests in town wanted," Mondale told us. "This warmed my soul and it also saw us outperform every election on the ballot, from senate candidates to the bottom of the ticket."[3]

The challenges facing leaders like Robinson who represent rural minorities are ample and profound. Unfortunately, despite all the attention paid in recent years to the "economic anxieties" of rural White voters, the national media have mostly ignored the concerns and worries of rural African Americans, Latinos, and Native Americans. This appalling neglect is ironic because rural minorities often endure far greater economic hardships than do their rural White neighbors. We are not particularly surprised by this neglect: After all, rural folks living in the nation's small towns and counties are not part of what we call America's "essential minority."

It's easy to blame racism for the lack of attention paid to the long list of concerns and grievances felt by rural minorities. Surely, race contributes to their status as rural America's mostly ignored and invisible subpopulation. But the deeper reasons have to do with ideology and partisanship: Rural non-Whites are easily dismissed not only by Republican politicians and conservative media but even in the mainstream media, because their votes rarely determine local or statewide elections.

IGNORED AND INVISIBLE

Race and rurality in the United States intertwine in strange ways. At 76 percent, White residents constitute a clear majority of rural citizens. One-third of rural counties is more than 90 percent White, and another third is between 75 percent and 90 percent White.[4] Rural America remains the Whitest part of the country.

But the 24 percent minority share of the rural U.S. population is growing. In fact, the non-White rural population grew by 3.5 percent nationally between the 2010 and 2020 censuses, a significant increase given otherwise stagnant or shrinking rural populations. Most majority-minority counties in the United States are rural, including the vast majority of the more than one hundred majority-Black counties, another sixty-seven majority-Latino counties, plus twenty-nine majority–Native American counties. But in the vast majority of rural counties, racial minorities are numerical minorities.

African Americans, Latinos, and Native Americans nevertheless play a vital, growing role in these communities. Two-thirds of rural counties contain at least 10 percent racial minorities, and half those counties contain at least 25 percent. Rural Latino population growth is especially notable: In the four states with the largest Latino populations—Arizona, California, Florida, and Texas—the Latino growth rate in rural counties since 2000 has exceeded statewide averages.[5]

Meanwhile, in a few corners of the United States—Appalachia, New England, and pockets of the Mountain West and Pacific Coast states— rural minorities are so few that they are effectively invisible. In these places, non-White residents often feel outnumbered and misplaced, a phenomenon Dartmouth University sociologist Emily Walton calls "misrecognition." Wrongly presumed to be outsiders and routinely asked where they're from, they feel subtly and not so subtly marginalized. "While some might read these interactions as a case of people being rude or thoughtless, there's something deeply problematic about the systematic pattern of being asked to prove oneself," Walton writes. "As a consequence of misrecognition, most of the people of color I interviewed think about their small, rural New England town as a temporary destination—a place to survive, not a place to thrive."[6]

In places where minorities are more numerous and integrated, their lifestyles tend to reflect the broader rural experience. Rookie U.S. representative Don Davis's North Carolina district includes large swaths of rural communities in the northeast corner of his state. Like any politician, Davis is eager to talk about all the efforts he's making to bring economic development to his Albemarle region constituents. But the struggles of his constituents are evident, too—especially keeping young, rural African Americans from abandoning the towns where they were raised. He told us that he has talked to students, on "graduation day of all times," and had some of them "look you in the eye and say, 'I can't wait to leave.' And not stop there—and this is the most painful part—and then say, 'I'm not coming back.'" It reflects "a loss of hope that 'I cannot get a good paying job, raise my family, and live happy, peaceful, in this area.'"[7]

The rising diversification of rural America in recent decades has delivered economic benefits and new blood to many small towns and counties. Most notably, the labor contributions and consumer impacts of new, non-White residents—and immigrant populations especially—have invigorated many rural communities that had been in decline. Poultry farms in rural northern Alabama were saved by Latino laborers. In Central New York, the city of Utica blossomed after welcoming Vietnamese, Burmese, and other political refugees. After rural Iowans in Greene County lost a garbage truck manufacturing plant to Mississippi for lack of a sufficient labor pool, local leaders created a "New Vida" diversity program to lure Latino immigrants to the county, which had lost half its population since its post–World War II peak.[8] "Racial and ethnic minorities can provide a demographic and economic lifeline to struggling communities," explain Kenneth Johnson and Daniel Lichter of the University of New Hampshire's Carsey School of Public Policy. "Decades of young adult outmigration have left many rural communities with a dwindling labor force. Migrants from other areas, many from minority populations, expand the local labor force, which enhances opportunities for economic development and an expanded tax base."[9]

Although many Americans view immigrants as job-stealing interlopers, some rural Whites have begun to recognize the value of increased diversity. As a red-state liberal, Oklahoma journalist Mary Logan Wolf watched as Luther, her rural hometown of 6,500 people, declined. It "could barely sustain" its few chain restaurants—until newly arrived immigrants helped save those franchises and opened three new Mexican restaurants. Wolf believes that White Oklahomans recognize the benefits these new arrivals offer. "The immigrant labor supports the region's massive corporate hog farms, and for that reason the influx is tolerated," she admits. "No one hollers about job theft because precious few white folks are motivated to spend the day slaughtering pigs."[10]

The rise of rural minorities also affords heartland citizens opportunities to embrace diversity. "Growing racial and ethnic diversity also provides new opportunities for a more inclusive society," write Johnson and Lichter. "This is the case in rural areas, especially those experiencing chronic declines, population aging, and more deaths than births. For children, growing racial and ethnic diversity also provides new opportunities for positive interracial contact and improved race relations, for building diverse friendship networks, and for preparing them for life in an increasingly diverse nation."[11] Slowly but surely, the growth and assimilation of rural minorities are making the American heartland look a bit more like the rest of the nation.

Fast-growing Latino populations have mitigated what otherwise would have been far starker population losses, particularly but not exclusively in Sun Belt counties. "Hispanic population growth has checked long-term population decline in many rural counties, especially in Midwestern and Great Plains States where natural decrease and outmigration by young native-born adults have been reducing population in some areas since the 1950s or earlier," a 2005 report by the USDA's Economic Research Service correctly foretold. "All else being equal, over 100 nonmetro counties would have lost population between 1990 and 2000 if not for growth in the Hispanic population."[12]

Of course, the experiences of rural Whites and non-Whites differ in important ways. *The Washington Post*'s Jose A. DelReal and Scott Clement explain the divisions between rural Whites and minorities in this way: "The sense of shared identity that connects many rural Americans—which factors into rural America's sense of fairness and estrangement—is less intense among rural minorities than among rural whites." Although 78 percent of rural Whites believe other rural citizens share their values, only 64 percent of Latinos and 55 percent of African American residents in rural communities agree.[13] Polling gaps like these suggest that rural Whites and non-Whites are not fully connecting with each other.

The sad truth is that the media too often treat racial minorities as negligible if not invisible members of the U.S. rural experience. Few polls of rural Americans bother to disaggregate the differences between White and non-White rural respondents. "Narratives that erase the 24% of rural Americans who are people of color—as well as the many rural counties that are majority people of color—devalue the needs of rural people of color who face systemic barriers to opportunity . . . while giving rhetorical priority to the concerns of an imagined white monolith," warn D. W. Rowlands and Hanna Love of the Brookings Institution.[14]

Since Donald Trump's rise, the national media have devoted tremendous attention to the political grievances of rural White voters. Reporters and pundits routinely descend upon rural communities, sit down with locals at diners and sports bleachers, and listen earnestly to what downscale rural White voters have to say, but the same national media hardly notice that rural minorities exist or are aware that they have legitimate complaints of their own. The next time you see a reporter from a national newspaper or television network plop down at a local diner to interview a dozen rural African Americans, Native Americans, or Latinos about their fears and aspirations, it may actually be the first time.

Two months after Trump's inauguration, Bates University rural education expert Mara Casey Tieken issued a rare clarion call for the politicians, policymakers, and media suddenly so focused on rural Americans not to present an incomplete portrait of the heartland:

[Non-White] rural America receives even lower pay and fewer protections for its labor than does rural white America. And, as my own research shows, this rural America attends very different schools than rural white America, schools that receive far less funding and other resources.

In fact, the relationship between rural white communities and rural communities of color is much like the relationship between urban white communities and urban communities of color: separate and unequal.[15]

Small towns and counties in the American heartland are not as heterogeneous as U.S. cities and suburbs, but they are diversifying. Under slavery, segregation, or enduring forms of systemic racism, the lives and livelihoods of rural minorities have always differed from those of rural Whites. To address rural problems in a meaningful and inclusive way, politicians, policymakers, and the media must recognize rural diversity and the unique experiences of rural minorities.

UNIQUE HARDSHIPS

Like their White counterparts, minorities who live in the American heartland are struggling. But their economic hardships are severer and more persistent than those of rural Whites. With the exception of gun suicides and drug overdoses, on most every metric, rural minorities face more vexing economic and healthcare problems than their White neighbors.

Let's start with unemployment. The years following the 2007 economic crisis and subsequent Great Recession devastated rural communities. But unemployment patterns in urban and rural communities following the economic crisis moved in opposite directions depending on race. In urban areas, White unemployment rates remained lower, but by 2019, the gap between Whites and non-Whites had narrowed. In rural areas, the reverse was true: Post-recession unemployment gaps between rural Whites and non-Whites *widened*.[16] More recently, unemployment between 2019 and 2021 surged among all rural groups during the peak Covid-19 year of 2020 and then settled back down to pre-Covid levels. But in all three years, rural White unemployment was roughly one point lower than for rural Latinos and five points lower than for rural African Americans.[17]

Poverty is deeper and wider for rural minorities, too. Rural poverty disparities between Whites and non-Whites persist: The White poverty rate in 2019 (12.7 percent) was substantially lower than for African Americans (30.7 percent), Native Americans (29.6 percent), or Latinos (21.7 percent).[18] The share of rural White babies born into poverty is twenty points lower than for Latinos and a whopping 33 points lower than for African Americans.[19]

Enduring poverty is also more common in rural communities where high concentrations of non-White citizens live.[20] So-called persistently poor counties are "geographically concentrated and disproportionately located in regions with above-average populations of racial minorities, including the Mississippi Delta," explains Robin Davey Wolff, an advocate at Enterprise Community Partners, a nonprofit group that promotes affordable housing alternatives for disadvantaged communities. "Historically, rural communities of color that struggle with poverty receive less help and recognition, and as a result, many in rural areas suffer silently and alone."[21]

Rates vary among non-White rural residents, but poverty is particularly crippling and difficult to escape when people both are individually poor *and* live in a persistently poor county. This phenomenon is known as "double exposure," explains Tracey Farrigan of the USDA's Economic Research Service. "Rural residents who identify as Black or African American and American Indian or Alaska Native were particularly vulnerable to the double exposure phenomenon," Farrigan writes. "Nearly half the rural poor within these groups resided in high and persistent poverty counties in 2019."[22]

Race also limits small business development opportunities for rural minorities. The good news is that there has been an uptick in the number of minority-owned small businesses over the past few years.[23] The bad news is that the share of rural African American, Latino, and Native American–owned businesses is far lower than their national population shares.[24] Led by Virginia Democrat Tim Kaine and Mississippi Republican Roger Wicker, a bipartisan group of U.S. senators has twice introduced the Reaching America's Rural Minority Businesses bill, which would authorize the Department of Commerce to establish small-business training centers at Historically Black Colleges and Universities (HBCUs) designed specifically to stimulate small-business development among rural minorities.[25] Unfortunately, the bill hasn't come anywhere near a floor vote.

As we learned from Al Gameros, minority leaders in rural communities will try almost anything to boost their local economies. Gameros is the sixty-six-year-old Latino mayor of Globe, a small city of roughly 7,500 people in Arizona's Copper Corridor that adopted a sophisticated tourism marketing strategy. "We bought a program that tracks who comes here by cell phone," Gameros told us. That software program recognizes phones as they ping upon entering and leaving a specified perimeter surrounding Globe and then reports the phone traffic data to the city's marketing team. Thanks to this software, Gameros knows that in recent years, Globe has experienced an uptick among both young and retired out-of-town visitors.

Armed with this information, the city placed ads in the greater Phoenix metro area to target those who live within driving distance of Globe and who fit the likely tourist profile. "We rebranded our city with new marketing. We really want to be a tourist attraction and destination [that] people want to visit," Gameros boasted. "We've got bikes, we've got trail hiking, we've got UTV [utility terrain vehicle] rides. We have Besh Ba Gowah Indian ruins, and we have a winery now. So, that attracts a lot of people."[26] Globe isn't exactly booming, but its economy is far healthier than that of many of the surrounding towns in the Copper Corridor. And across the country, rural minorities face acute housing, education, and healthcare crises.

Home ownership rates in rural America far exceed national averages, and nearly half of rural homeowners own their homes "free and clear" of any mortgage. But that's largely because homes in rural areas are much cheaper than in suburbs or cities. Given higher rates of mobile home ownership, rural home values are lower than national averages. In fact, 38 percent of rural homes are worth one hundred thousand dollars or less, which means these homeowners typically have little equity at their disposal. Although rural minorities are more likely to own a home than urban minorities, there remains a twenty-point gap in home ownership rates between rural Whites, at 75 percent, and rural minorities, at 55 percent.[27]

Millions of rural minorities lack either the capital to afford a down payment or the creditworthiness to qualify for mortgages—or both. For those unable to buy a home, quality and affordable apartment rental units are sparse. "Rural minorities are more likely to live in substandard and cost-burdened housing, and are more likely to be poor," concludes a 2012 study conducted by the Washington, D.C.-based Housing Assistance Council. "The geographic isolation and relative segregation of rural minorities living in majority-minority census tracts continues to be an important component of poverty and substandard housing in many rural and small town communities."[28]

Education patterns are equally dispiriting for rural minorities. Although rural Whites graduate high school at rates higher than the national average, the 77 percent graduation rate for rural minorities falls below the national rate and is ten points lower than for their rural White classmates. The abysmal graduation rate for Native Alaskans is *less than half* the national average.[29] Whatever their racial background, rural high school graduates are less likely to go to college than their urban and suburban counterparts.[30]

According to a study by Penn State's Center for Education and Civil Rights, rural school districts with high shares of minorities are also more likely to still be segregated. Such districts often endure the departure of White families and a declining property tax base, both of which create fiscal challenges for the impoverished families of minority students in these school districts. "Exposure to poverty in rural America's public schools is more pronounced among minoritized students than white students," the report concludes. "These patterns illustrate how segregation by race often also means segregation by income as well."[31] White flight is still very real, even if it happens now within rural areas.

Rural Whites and non-Whites also experience divergent health outcomes, healthcare access, and coverage affordability. According to the Rural Health Information Hub (RHIB), rural non-Whites report higher rates of "fair or poor health" than their White neighbors. Though rates for specific maladies vary among African American, Latino, and Native American subgroups, rural non-Whites battle a variety of chronic health and mental health challenges—which isn't particularly surprising, given the limited resources available to them. Indeed, RHIB identifies the two factors that most contribute to racial differences in health problems as "inadequate access to care and the provision of substandard quality healthcare services." Although federal programs track these disparities and provide resources to mitigate them, racial health gaps across the rural United States endure.[32]

Premature deaths among rural seniors also differ by race. Rural residents are more likely to suffer from premature deaths, and the rate of mortality among rural seniors in the past half century did not fall as fast as it did in urban counties. But premature death rates are highest, and mortality declines slowest, among non-White rural seniors.[33]

A zip code–based analysis conducted by the Rural and Minority Health Research Center (RMHRC) found that rural areas with higher concentrations of minority residents tend to be farther removed from a Federally Qualified Health Center or a Rural Health Clinic and from "emergency rooms, pharmacies, trauma care, cardiac care, intensive care, substance abuse disorder treatment, and obstetrics" facilities. The study also found that distance from healthcare facilities can be particularly punitive for Native American populations. "If you are further away from that access, or further away from those services, then you are less likely to take advantage of them," says Janice Probst, lead author of the RMHRC's study.[34]

Public health experts Stacy Grundy and Beth Prusaczyk describe how the intersection of their scholarly and personal experiences illuminates rural healthcare disparities. Although they grew up in the same rural area, Grundy is Black and Prusaczyk is White. The two women noticed the glaring differences in hospital quality and access between Whites and minorities, African Americans especially. The media have reported at length on rural hospital closures, but Grundy and Prusaczyk discovered that "of the 12 existing federal policies aimed at supporting rural hospitals and preventing additional closures . . . *none* are intentional in (or even nominally identify) their efforts to prevent closures specifically among rural non-White communities."[35]

National studies confirm Grundy and Prusaczyk's observations. Between 2005 and 2015, the 105 rural hospitals that closed were more likely to have served predominantly African American and Latino populations.[36] The effects of limited or long-distance access to healthcare is not merely a matter of inconvenience to rural minorities, mind you: It can be a matter of life and death. Limited healthcare access makes rural African Americans and Native Americans more likely to develop cancer and experience negative outcomes in cancer treatment and less likely to survive a cancer diagnosis.[37]

Then there is the matter of affordability. A 2023 national study of nearly five thousand rural adults confirmed this unsurprising fact: The rural folks who most need medical care tend to be least likely to afford it. Consequently, budget-strained sick people in rural communities are more likely than their urban counterparts to forgo needed care. Researchers discovered that affordability also has racial implications: Because they are poorer on average than Whites, rural minorities "were more likely to delay or go without medical care due to cost" than rural Whites.[38]

There is a final, asymmetrical challenge rural minorities face: racism itself. There's no reason to suspect that rural White citizens who score high on what pollsters call "hostile racism" indicators somehow reserve these sentiments for outsiders. When rural schools in minority areas are most likely to be segregated, when rural hospitals that serve mostly minority patients are more likely to close, and when rural poverty is more persistent in minority areas, it is hard not to see implicit or even explicit racism at work in the heartland.

Rural Americans are battling a variety of interconnected economic and health problems. Their struggles are exacerbated by insufficient, dwindling, and hard-to-reach economic and medical resources. Sadly, on almost every measure of economic or healthcare vitality, the challenges for rural minorities are more pervasive and more punitive.

Whether anyone has noticed or cares, rural minorities are "anxious," too—and they must deal with that anxiety while living in the Whitest parts of the United States.

THE RURAL BLACK EXPERIENCE

According to the 2020 Census, there are more than one hundred majority-Black counties in the United States. Most are medium-to-small rural counties in the Deep South, almost half of which are in Georgia and Mississippi. Dozens more are crowded along both banks of the Lower Mississippi River Valley in Arkansas and Louisiana.[39]

Clustered near the Virginia border where Interstate 95 slices through North Carolina are seven majority-Black rural counties: Bertie, Edgecombe, Halifax, Hertford, Northampton, Vance, and Warren.[40] With about 55,000 residents, Halifax is the most populous, but four of the six other counties each contains roughly 20,000 residents. Like many majority-Black counties nationally, all seven lost population between 2010 and 2020.

These counties depart from the common perception that African Americans live almost exclusively in dense urban communities. The counties are small and sparsely populated. Although residents are to some degree racially self-sorted, rural Whites and African Americans in all seven counties often live in commingled neighborhoods. It wasn't always this way, of course: Trailing only the Cape Fear area, the Albemarle region was once home to the state's second-highest share of enslaved residents by population.[41]

Among the four majority-Black Albemarle counties we visited, Northampton is particularly fascinating. Named by English colonists for the Fifth Earl of Northampton, the county, with 22,000 current residents, ranks eighty-third in total population and eighty-ninth in population density among North Carolina's one hundred counties. Each of Northampton's two largest towns, Garysburg and Gaston, is home to only about a thousand people. Jackson, the county seat, is half that size. There is plenty of room and ample parking in Northampton County.

The county's racial history is clouded by dark moments. During the first half of the nineteenth century, somewhere between 40 and 60 percent of Northampton County's White families owned slaves.[42] The county seat, Jackson, is named for one of the most notoriously racist presidents in U.S. history. The county courthouse is flanked on its western edge by Thomas Bragg Drive, named for a local politician who served as the attorney general of the Confederacy. In this majority-Black county, the stain of racism lingers.

In 1959, Northampton's election board was at the center of an ugly episode in U.S. voting rights history. An African American woman named Louise Lassiter refused to abide results from the county's voter registration literacy test. Lassiter was literate, but because an election board examiner ruled that she had mispronounced a few words from a section of the state constitution, she was barred from registering.[43] Lassiter immediately appealed the decision in state and federal court.

The U.S. Supreme Court took Lassiter's case. Just six years prior to passage of the 1965 Voting Rights Act, the Court ruled unanimously in *Lassiter v. Northampton County Board of Elections* that literacy tests were constitutional so long as they were administered uniformly to all voters, regardless of race, so as not to serve as "merely a device to make racial discrimination easy."[44] But White examiners were empowered to decide who was and was not "literate." And even if the tests had been administered in a race-blind manner, they inherently discriminated against African Americans educated for generations in dilapidated, underfunded classrooms. Obviously, to make "racial discrimination easy" is precisely why the tests were created in the first place.

The Supreme Court's failure to recognize literacy tests' true purpose is stunning. More stunning is that Chief Justice Earl Warren and noted liberals Hugo Black, William O. Douglas, and Felix Frankfurter all concurred in *Lassiter*'s 9-0 decision. Just five years earlier, all four justices had ruled in *Brown v. Board of Education* that segregated schools were unequal and thus unconstitutional. The effect of the Court's puzzling decision was clear: African American voters in Northampton and other counties throughout North Carolina and the rest of the South would have to wait at least six more years to begin experiencing anything close to equal voting rights.

Electoral politics in Albemarle's majority-Black counties remain racialized today. In 2020, Democrat Joe Biden carried all seven jurisdic-
tions with between 59 and 67 percent of the vote. Voters split along
predictably racial lines, and Northampton was no exception. "If it wasn't
before, Northampton is now an inelastic county—whites by and large
vote Republican, blacks vote Democrat," wrote John Wynne of the news
site Politics North Carolina. "In 2012, it trended to the Democrats more
than any county in the state . . . probably thanks to the county's large
black population." In fact, Northampton owns a unique partisan distinction: It is the only county in the state to vote for every Democratic presidential nominee—even landslide losers George McGovern in 1972 and
Walter Mondale in 1984—over the past 120 years.[45]

Farming has long served as the economic foundation for Albemarle's
Black residents. Cotton, peanuts, lumber, soy, and tobacco are among its
key agricultural commodities. But the story of Black farming in the Albemarle region and across the United States mirrors the broader story of
rural agricultural decline—only worse.

Peaking in 1920, when there were nearly one million Black-owned
farms in the United States, Black farmland ownership has fallen in
each subsequent decade, plummeting from 7 percent of farmland a century ago to less than 1 percent now. The declining fortunes of Black
farmers resulted partly from the out-migration of African Americans
who abandoned agriculture-based rural southern economies in favor of
urban manufacturing jobs in northern cities. But there is also a well-
documented history of the U.S. Department of Agriculture's discrimi-
nating against Black farms and farmers. "For black farmers, the effect of
discrimination by the USDA has been particularly devastating," Abril
Castro and Caius Z. Willingham wrote in a 2019 Center for American
Progress report on the history of Black farming. "All told, black farmers
lost 80 percent of their land from 1910 to 2007. As the U.S. Commission
on Civil Rights concluded in a 1982 report, this pattern of discrimination virtually eliminated black farms, dealing a serious blow to rural
black communities."[46]

Today, Black farmers seem to be heading for extinction. They account for only 2 percent of all farmers, own a mere 0.5 percent of all

farmland, and produce just 0.2 percent of U.S. agricultural sales. "Overall, African-American farmers have been devastated economically, politically, and socially, and as such, [they] are more likely to commit
suicide, become depressed, and live in poverty compared to white farmers," rural scholars Andrew Laurence Carter and Adam Alexander write.
"These dire circumstances have all but eliminated African-Americans
from the contemporary agricultural landscape."[47]

U.S. senator Raphael Warnock of Georgia is pushing for federal restitution to Black farmers discriminated against by the U.S. Department
of Agriculture for decades. With fellow senators Cory Booker, Bernie
Sanders, and Elizabeth Warren, Warnock advocates for compensation
based on the 1982 U.S. Commission on Civil Rights report that chroni-
cled the USDA's discriminatory actions. In 2021, Warnock and his colleagues sponsored the Justice for Black Farmers Act.[48] It remains
unpassed. And when Congress included four billion dollars in debt relief for minority farmers in the 2021 American Rescue Plan, Republican
officials and White farmers immediately sued to stop the program, leaving it in a court-imposed limbo. Two years later, the Inflation Reduction
Act replaced the program with one providing aid to "economically distressed" farmers, which led to fears that most of the recipients of the aid
would be White.[49]

A fourth-generation farmer in Warren County, forty-one-year-old
Patrick Brown learned how to gather and hang-dry tobacco in the barn
by age nine. His mother was a teacher and principal who passed away in
2020. His father, the Reverend Dr. Arthur Brown, grew tobacco on the
family farm by day and led six congregations across Virginia and North
Carolina on nights and weekends; he died in 2023.

Patrick's early career took him away from the farming tradition that
began with his great-grandfather, who was born into slavery. After completing college, Patrick worked for nearly a decade at the Defense Intelligence Agency, where his agricultural skills were put to use spearheading
a federal program designed to help Afghan farmers offset with alternative crops the poppy plants they had customarily harvested for heroin
production.

After returning home, Brown realized he had to get creative to keep afloat the family farm he had inherited. Instead of tobacco, his farm now grows hemp, a niche commodity that qualifies for a carbon credit and yields a higher profit margin. Brown's "Hempfinity" brand of CBD and related products is growing. He has also converted a portion of the family's land once farmed by slaves into a tourist attraction.[50]

Brown explained to us how programmatic racism contributed to the near-total extinction of modern Black family farmers like him. "A lot of Black farmers are no longer able to farm because they are indebted to farm agencies or the USDA based on discriminatory practices," he said, citing the federal *Pigford* case that forms the basis for the efforts led by Senator Warnock to provide restitution to Black farmers. The case alleges that White farmers qualified for and received loan monies from federal programs faster and without having to provide the type of detailed records and tax returns required of Black applicants. Because the loans were collateralized with either farmland or equipment, Black litigants claim their farms were bankrupted by the discriminatory implementation of these loan programs.

But Brown recognizes that small, Black-owned family farms suffer many of the same predations that White-owned family farms do. Notably, family farmers have been victimized by the alliance of Big Ag, the federal government, and lending institutions that favor large, corporate-owned farms. "We are monopolized to only deal with [the] Farm Bureau for insurance," says Brown, because the Bureau is uniquely suited to settle insurance claims resulting from, say, low crop yields caused by adverse weather. As frustrating as that reliance is, Brown says the alternatives are worse. "Carolina Farm Credit? My dad used to deal with them, and I won't step my foot in their office because the structure of their loans is based on waiting for you not to pay it back so they can take whatever you collateralized to get the loan."[51]

At this point, even if Warnock could assemble a coalition in Congress to pass his restitution policy, any sums provided would likely be too little, too late to fully restore a rural farming town like Enfield, in majority-Black Halifax County. When we visited, the downtown area had a distinctly ghost town feel to it. Most storefronts were vacant and boarded up. One seafood and one Italian restaurant were open, plus a yoga studio and an "express tax" center. But the Western Auto, Jennie's Cafe, and even a Super 10 (a discount retailer selling items for ten dollars or less) were shuttered.

Mayor Mondale Robinson has his work cut out for him, but he is neither easily deterred nor maudlin about Enfield's bygone glories. "There isn't a building downtown left untouched by the systemic underinvestment in Enfield. More than ninety percent of the businesses are boarded with cheap and unskilled graffiti, trees growing in the middle and busting through the roofs," he lamented. "And while I'm bothered by this level of dilapidation, I'm not completely broken; nor am I nostalgic about what downtown Enfield was, because a short while ago, my mother was sprayed in those very streets—by fire hoses—for being downtown after the accepted time for Black people to be there."[52]

Healthcare disparities between rural Blacks and their neighbors are yet another area where the rural experience differs dramatically based on race. African Americans have shorter life expectancies, suffer disproportionately from a variety of chronic illnesses, and experience higher infant mortality rates. Congressman Don Davis, whose district includes the majority-Black Albemarle counties, can rattle off health patterns affecting his constituents without missing a beat. "We see the highest rates of infant mortality amongst African American women. We see high rates of chronic illnesses, stroke, diabetes."[53]

For rural residents, the fight over Medicaid expansion has been painful, both literally and figuratively. For rural African Americans in North Carolina's Albemarle region, the consequences have sometimes even been lethal. Political resistance to expanding Medicaid in the Tar Heel State had been strong. When we reported from there during the latter stages of the state's debate over expansion, the rural Democrats we spoke to could barely contain their frustration. "We need it. We need it. We need it," said Northampton County commissioner Geneva Riddick-Faulkner, who explained that her poor, rural, majority-Black county lacked not only a hospital but even an urgent care center. Many of her constituents weren't eligible for the state's existing Medicaid program, but they also couldn't afford the insurance their employers offered. Riddick-Faulkner spoke of people who needed insulin and couldn't afford it, which left them to use their relatives' supply or buy it on the black market.[54]

The legislators who dealt with the issue in the state capital of Raleigh told us their Republican counterparts knew perfectly well the benefits it would bring. Rep. Shelly Willingham, an African American legislator who represents Bertie and Edgecombe counties, said that when he talked about the issue privately with Republicans, "they'll tell you they accept the fact that it's needed." But they "didn't want to give the impression that they're helping to support this socialized medicine stuff"— not because their own constituents wouldn't benefit as much as Willingham's but because they fear a primary challenge from the right.[55]

The Republican resisters asked what would happen if the state took billions of dollars from the federal government to give people insurance and then, one day, the feds stopped sending the money. "Then they say, 'Well, we don't want to be giving Medicaid to people who don't work,'" said state senator Kandie Smith. "They will vote against their own family." But the real root of the resistance that dragged on for so long, Smith told us, was the man who signed the ACA, a law still informally known as Obamacare. "You know what it boils down to? A Black man introduced all this," she said. "That's why."[56]

A number of factors—a couple of key Republicans changing their position, pressure from the business community, and the weight of public opinion that overwhelmingly supported expansion—finally broke through that resistance, and in early 2023 the legislature voted to accept the expansion. But while they waited, hundreds of thousands of North Carolinians went without insurance, rural hospitals were endangered, and thousands of lives were lost. According to one estimate, 350 North Carolinians died every year who would have survived had the Medicaid expansion been accepted immediately.[57] Over a decade of delay, that's more victims than died in the September 11 attacks.

Educational challenges for rural African Americans are pervasive, too. School districts in rural Black areas are often substandard and starved for vital resources. In fourteen of the nineteen counties in his North Carolina congressional district, Davis said, 100 percent of the school districts are classified as Title I schools by the federal government, which means they're poor enough to qualify for various forms of assistance.[58]

Where they aren't getting enough assistance is from the state of North Carolina. In 1994, students from five poor rural counties sued the state, saying that because of inadequate funding and overstretched schools, they were being denied the North Carolina State Constitution's guarantee of a "sound basic education." As of this writing, nearly thirty years later, what is referred to as the *Leandro* case is not resolved, despite the plaintiffs' winning repeatedly in court and the state being ordered to appropriate money to improve the schools. Each time, the state legislature appealed, resisted, refused to provide the funds, and found new grounds to avoid complying with court orders. In the latest twist, after the GOP took control of the state's supreme court in the 2022 election, Republicans in the legislature sought to have the case reheard by that court, which their party now controlled, in the hope that the new majority would reverse the prior decision ordering the state to give more aid to those poor districts.[59]

From disparate resources to unvarnished racism, rural African Americans continue to fight many of the same political and social battles their urban counterparts do. But the rural Black experience differs in important ways. The devastation of rural Black family farming has been more calamitous than family farm declines nationally. Rural Black families who did not abandon rural areas for industrial cities during the Great Migration have experienced struggles even worse than those of rural Whites, including an interconnected set of employment, poverty, and healthcare problems.

THE RURAL LATINO EXPERIENCE

Latinos are now the largest racial minority in the United States. They are not yet the largest minority group in rural America, but thanks to their rapid immigration and higher birth rates, Latinos very soon will surpass African Americans to become the largest racial minority in the rural United States, too.

Although most Latinos are clustered in large urban areas, 67 of the

101 majority-Latino counties per the 2020 Census are rural. Of these 67 counties we identified, 49 are in Texas alone and 8 of the remaining 18 are in New Mexico. To be fair, Texas's 254 counties are the most of any state, and many of them feature very small populations. But Latinos accounted for a stunning 95 percent of Texas's population growth between 2010 and 2020. Although half the Lone Star State's Latino citizens reside in the state's five largest counties—Harris, Dallas, Tarrant, Bexar, and Travis—a significant chunk of that growth occurred in rural parts of the state.

Because rural Latino population baselines are so much smaller than in urban areas, Latino growth *rates* in rural counties are much higher. This is especially true outside the Sun Belt, as evident in the surge in Latino county shares across the Rust Belt states in the Northeast and Midwest. In fact, the ten counties with the fastest Latino growth rates since 2010 all have populations under 39,000. Although five of these counties are southern—Charlton County, Georgia; Pickens County, Alabama; plus three parishes in Louisiana—they're anomalies because these counties contain federal prisons where Latino felons are counted for census purposes. More reflective of broader trends are the other five fastest-growing counties, all of which are in Michigan or the Dakotas. Driven by North Dakota's oil boom demand for labor, McKenzie County's Latino population increased elevenfold in the last decade, and Williams County increased ninefold. That's right: The two fastest-growing Latino counties in the nation are in rural North Dakota.[60]

Rural Whites who fear the steady expansion of Latino populations beyond urban areas into rural communities can direct their ire at the president who signed the Immigration Reform and Control Act in 1986: Ronald Reagan. "The amnesty provisions included in the [act] gave Latinos a new freedom to move outside immigrant enclaves, positioning them to take advantage of new opportunities for low-wage jobs in other parts of the country," conclude rural Latino scholars Rogelio Saenz and Cruz Torres.[61] With the encouragement of corporate recruiters, hundreds of thousands of Latinos have since moved into smaller rural communities where locals often refuse to work in dangerous jobs like food processing, oil and timber extraction, and textile manufacturing. From

homes to hummus—if not for skilled and relatively low-paid Latino laborers, especially in the construction and agricultural sectors, the price
of almost everything Americans buy would be significantly higher.

Wisconsin's renowned dairy industry and Alabama's chicken producers are case studies in how beleaguered rural towns and counties
have revitalized thanks to Latino arrivals. "Jobs in the dairy industry are
diminishing and many of the jobs that still exist are now worked by Mexicans and Mexican Americans," writes University of Wisconsin–Green
Bay professor Jon Shelton. "Any progressive future must incorporate
Latinos in the process of reversing the decline—caused largely by conservative policies—in working people's standards of living."[62] Three decades after a poultry processing plant opened in Russellville, Alabama,
Latinos are now 40 percent of the city's nearly 11,000 residents. Their
arrival has radically transformed the town. "Russellville has like nine
tiendas Latinas [Latino-owned stores], three of which are Guatemalan,"
twenty-four-year-old Salvador Blanco told the *Los Angeles Times* in
2022. "But it's also the same town that's 30 minutes south of Florence,
which is where I live and you can't get a Jim Crow statue in front of the
courthouse taken down."[63]

Compared to national averages, rural Latinos are more likely to be of
Mexican descent. In addition to stemming what otherwise might be
even deeper population losses, the influx of Latinos into rural areas
since passage of the 1986 immigration reform law has had another important impact: Their arrival has expanded the rural labor pool and
boosted local economies. A report issued by the U.S. Congress's Joint
Economic Committee states, "Higher immigration levels and state-to-
state migration of Latino workers is critical to the economy as a way to
increase labor force participation rates, especially in newly developing
rural areas."[64]

Despite their positive impact on rural communities, Latinos in the
heartland share many of the same struggles that other rural minorities
do. According to a *Stateline* study, nearly half of rural Latino babies, 47
percent, are born into poverty. One in eight rural Latino families receives
some form of government assistance, and half of rural Latino families
receive food stamps.[65] Sadly—and ironically, given their importance to

farm production—rural Latinos are more likely than their urban counterparts to experience food insecurity. "Rural Latino communities often
work on the farms that grow the nation's food, yet their living circumstances and geographic locations create barriers to accessing healthy
foods and perpetuate a cycle of food insecurity for them," concludes a
2023 report by UnidosUS, a Washington, D.C.-based Latino advocacy
organization.[66]

In contrast to rural African Americans descended from slaves
brought here by force or rural Native Americans whose ancestors arrived long before White settlers did, rural Latinos confront a particular
kind of racism associated with being relative newcomers to rural communities. Because of their disadvantaged cultural position, language
barriers, and citizenship issues, rural Latinos have historically not demanded workplace protections and equality.

Reflecting on his experience representing rural Latinos in Phoenix,
former Arizona state senator Pete Rios told us he witnessed how different the level of political engagement was among rural Latino workers.
Those working in unskilled and nonunion jobs, especially in the farm
fields, were the least empowered. "A lot of my Latino compadres did not
want to get involved in politics," Rios recalled. "They had a fear—an
actual fear—of authority. They would say they didn't want to get fired
because Rancher Smith did not want them to get involved in politics."
And these farmhands, Rios told us, were citizens—not undocumented
workers, nor registered with temporary guestworker programs. At the
other end of the spectrum were unionized copper mine workers from
the Copper Corridor region east of Phoenix. "The one group that I
found was raring to go, and most of them were Latinos, were the mine
workers," he said. "All of the Copper Corridor was pretty well unionized
and together." Somewhere in the middle, said Rios, were prison workers, who were unionized but had less power than private-sector mine
workers because Arizona law prohibits public-sector union employees
like those working in state prisons from striking.[67]

The recency and manner by which many Latinos arrived in the
United States sometimes creates legal issues for them when they move
into long-isolated, predominantly White rural towns and counties. In

her 2017 study of police departments' racial profiling of Latinos in North Carolina, Carmen Huerta-Bapat found that profiling gaps in routine traffic stops of White and Latino drivers fell steadily statewide, but mostly because of changes in urban police departments supervised by Democratic politicians. In rural, more Republican parts of the Tar Heel State, racialized patterns in profiling persisted, especially in counties "led by popularly elected Republican sheriffs."[68]

Within a few years, Latinos will surpass African Americans to become the largest rural minority population. As their populations swell and continue to expand into more rural settings, Latinos' labor and consumer activities are reviving dormant rural communities in need of precisely the sort of infusion that immigrants have long provided to urban and suburban communities across the United States.

THE RURAL NATIVE AMERICAN EXPERIENCE

No racial group in the United States is more rural than Native Americans. Depending upon how rurality is defined, as many as half of Native Americans live in rural communities,[69] a share far higher than for any other racial or ethnic group. In stark contrast to Latinos and especially African Americans, millions of whom live in major U.S. cities or sprawling suburbs, the Native American population is uniquely rural.

The rurality of Native American populations—except in cases where specificity requires, we use the term *Native American* rather than *American Indian/Alaska Native* (AI/AN)—did not occur by accident, of course. The systematic and racist displacement of Native American peoples onto remote, rural spaces created a painful, discriminatory, and enduring "out of sight, out of mind" effect. "I would say the major challenge is that, to the American public, Indian people are invisible," laments Michael Bird, a Pueblo Indian from New Mexico and the first Native American president of the American Public Health Association. "They don't see us, they don't think about us, and they don't know the history."[70] If Bird's comment seems exaggerated, think again: According to a 2018 report published by Reclaiming Native Truth, a majority of Americans and 62 percent who live outside so-called Indian Country admit that they are completely unacquainted with the 5.2 million Native Americans who are members of the 573 tribes officially recognized by the federal government.[71]

Proximity to tribal communities may make citizens more familiar with Native American populations, but not necessarily more favorable toward them. In fact, views of tribal communities are likely to be harsher among their neighbors. The Reclaiming Native Truth report concludes, "Bias toward Native Americans changes from region to region, with the greatest bias showing among people who live near Indian Country. This may be in part because areas in and around Indian Country tend to be more rural and politically conservative." Because so many rural Native Americans live on far-removed tribal reservations, *invisible* is a term frequently used to describe them and their social and political experiences. This invisibility is meant to be metaphorical, but for many Americans—especially in eastern portions of the United States far from the Indian Country of the Plains and Western states—Native Americans are rarely if ever seen in the literal sense, either.

Worse, the default association of contemporary Native Americans with the casino industry reinforces crude, comforting myths that tribal members are getting rich from gambling receipts. In fact, only a small sliver of Native Americans profits from casinos. During his 1993 congressional testimony on the issue of Native American gambling rights, none other than Donald Trump tried to cast himself as a victim of reverse discrimination because Native Americans use their special federal status to build casinos on designated lands. Trump complained that people claiming Native American ancestry "don't look Indian" to him. And then he told California representative George Miller this: "You're saying only Indians can have the reservations, only Indians can have the gaming. So why aren't you approving it for everybody? Why are you being discriminatory? Why is it that the Indians don't pay tax, but everybody else does? I do." Not only did Trump demonstrate his ignorance about the citizenship status of Native Americans but, as the nation would later learn, he routinely brags about how "smart" he is for paying little or no taxes.[72]

Setting tribal citizens apart from the U.S. economy and culture for centuries has caused incalculable damage. On almost every economic, health, housing, education, or other measure of vitality and wellness, Native Americans rank at or near the bottom. Given how much rural prosperity is anchored to urban proximity, is it any wonder that Native American citizens—the Americans most set apart from their fellow countrymen—have enjoyed far less economic and health-related progress than other citizens?

Let's start with economic indicators. According to the Red Road, a nonprofit that promotes Native American empowerment, Native Americans have the highest poverty rate in the nation, the lowest workforce participation rate, and a median household income roughly 30 percent lower than the national average. One-quarter of Native Americans suffers from food insecurity, twice the national rate. Keep in mind, these statistics would be even worse were non-rural tribal populations removed from the calculations.[73]

The housing situation Native Americans face is bleak: Forty percent of Native American homes on reservations are considered substandard, half are unconnected to public sewer systems, and 16 percent of unconnected units have no indoor plumbing. Until thirty years ago, it was illegal to secure home mortgages on reservations. Even today, it remains difficult for aspiring Native American home buyers not otherwise disqualified because of bad credit ratings or a lack of money for a down payment to secure mortgages.[74] In 2021, *The Wall Street Journal*'s Ben Eisen explained the legal needle that Native Americans must thread to become homeowners. "Traditional mortgages in the U.S. are secured by two valuable pieces of collateral: the home itself and the land on which it sits," Eisen writes. "But in Indian Country, swaths of land are held in trust, preventing lenders from staking a claim if the homeowner stops paying."[75] The debilitating effects of the forced relocation of tribal peoples onto reservations is an enduring form of socioeconomic discrimination no other American group has faced.

The healthcare situation for rural tribes is even more dire. Since 1955, the U.S. Department of Health and Human Services has delivered direct-to-patient healthcare to Native American citizens via the Indian Health Service (IHS). Through care facilities it manages on or adjacent to reservations organized into ten geographic service areas, the IHS serves roughly 2.6 million Native Americans living in the United States.

IHS investments are insufficient to meet the needs of target populations. Consider this staggering fact: IHS spending per recipient on Native American healthcare is less than half what the Federal Bureau of Prisons spends on incarcerated felons. Although Native American patients have access to other resources, including both tribal and public health departments within their communities, Native Americans continue to suffer from the lowest life expectancy of any racial or ethnic group: On average, they die 5.5 years younger than other Americans. Most appalling is the fact that, because these disparities result largely from deaths from preventable diseases, additional state or federal investments in early or preventative care would dramatically reduce the number of premature deaths among Native citizens.[76]

The IHS is fully aware of the reasons for these dramatic and pervasive health disparities. "Lower life expectancy and the disproportionate disease burden exist perhaps because of inadequate education, disproportionate poverty, discrimination in the delivery of health services, and cultural differences. These are broad quality of life issues rooted in economic adversity and poor social conditions," the IHS website states. "American Indians and Alaska Natives continue to die at higher rates than other Americans in many categories, including [from] chronic liver disease and cirrhosis, diabetes mellitus, unintentional injuries, assault/homicide, intentional self-harm/suicide, and chronic lower respiratory diseases."[77]

Suicide rates are staggering within Native American communities and roughly 50 percent higher than for White Americans. A variety of factors contributes to Native American suicides, including both economic despair and insufficient mental health resources. Alcohol is often an accelerant: In roughly half of all Native American suicides, the victims were intoxicated. Suicide is reaching epidemic proportions among Native American youths. "Childhood adversity is also associated with AI/AN suicidal behavior and ideation. Young AI/AN men—in particular those who are unemployed, do not complete schooling, or both—and those with a history of trauma are at greater risk for suicide attempts," researchers of one 2015 public health study concluded. "Compared with other ethnocultural groups, AI/AN youths have more severe problems with anxiety, victimization, substance abuse, and depression, which may contribute to suicidality."[78] A report issued by GoodRx Research found that more than 113,000 Native Americans live in one of 492 counties designated as "mental health deserts" that feature fewer than one psychiatrist or psychologist for every 30,000 residents.[79]

We caught a quick glimpse of despair during our visit to Chinle, a remote city in Apache County, Arizona. There, Shawna Claw, a forty-one-year-old candidate for a Navajo Council seat in 2022, told us that her Chinle Chapter (the Navajo unit of local geography) shares one regional hospital with twenty-three other chapters. As she handed campaign leaflets to Navajo voters, Claw pointed across an unpaved parking lot to a building a hundred yards away that previously served as the area's lone drug and alcohol treatment facility. Now the building is shuttered because its foundation was deemed unstable, a casualty of the unstable floodplain upon which it sits. Claw said locals can obtain outpatient services, but that these resources are severely inadequate given the rates of alcohol and drug addiction on tribal lands. Almost on cue, about ten minutes later, a dented pickup truck with three middle-aged men inside it pulled up and summoned Claw in Navajo. After a brief exchange with them, she returned to our conversation. "You see," she whispered. "Those men are drunk right now. They should not be driving around." It was not yet 10 A.M.[80]

The rural Native American experience includes many successes, some of which are the by-product of new ventures, others of which stem from federal exemptions that authorize tribes to own and operate casinos. Since 1999, the Saint Regis Mohawk Tribe (SRMT) has operated a casino, hotel, and entertainment venue in Akwesasne, a small town in Upstate New York a stone's throw from the Canadian border.

The SRMT recently capitalized on yet another unique opportunity: marijuana sales. After New York State authorized tribes to sell cannabis, the SRMT in 2021 issued its first licenses to grow and sell cannabis products. Mohawk reservation retailers can also sell tobacco products at cheaper, tax-free prices. The lures of gambling, marijuana, and cheap cigarettes draw tourists and buyers from across the state and from Vermont and other nearby states and Canada. In October 2022, actor Jim Belushi, who owns and operates a major marijuana farm at his Northern California ranch, presided over a ribbon-cutting ceremony to open his farm's new Akwesasne dispensary outlet.[81]

The growth of Akwesasne's cannabis industry generates income and wealth not only for tribal entrepreneurs and citizens but also for non-tribal locals. We visited two cannabis dispensaries in Akwesasne, both staffed by young men in their mid-twenties. The first vendor was a native Mohawk, but the other was a White resident named Austin who had grown up and lived in nearby Malone. Austin works at Weedway, which is owned by Rick Hamelin, proprietor of a large Speedway gas station and commercial plaza across the street. Hamelin's firm, First Americans LLC, was one of the original three proprietors to whom the SRMT issued a "conditional cultivation license" in 2021.[82]

Emergent industries like gambling and marijuana have spurred needed economic development in certain Native American rural communities. But the economic impacts are limited and cannot possibly reverse centuries of systematic deprivation resulting from relocating Native American populations onto reservations far removed from most of the rest of U.S. society.

RURAL RAPPROCHEMENT

Douglas Burns is an Iowa blogger and columnist for the rural *Carroll Times Herald* in Carroll County, home to about twenty thousand residents in the west-central part of the Hawkeye State. In 2022, Burns penned a powerful column in which he urged rural citizens to rethink their attitudes toward diversity. "For too many rural Americans, the term diversity is synonymous with otherness because residents of remote regions don't realize that we, too, are underrepresented and misunderstood," he wrote. "Policies and structures strand and marginalize us."

We might quibble with his "underrepresented" complaint, but Burns offers an otherwise compelling and earnest plea. Although we are not certain his referent group in mind for rural Americans is White, Burns calls upon heartland folks to seek out and build coalitions with other dispossessed groups. "We rural Americans need to focus on correcting this, finding allies in other demographics who are similarly left out of the modern American economy and higher education and top levels of the judiciary—and yes, even my profession, journalism, where rural voices can be absent or hard to find in key power centers."[83]

We echo Burns's call for rural Americans to think broadly about where they can find suitable allies to join their efforts at remedying what ails rural communities. But anxious rural White voters need not venture into racially diverse, urban polyglots to garner sympathy for feeling "underrepresented and misunderstood." For rural Whites from Maine to Montana to Mississippi, there is ample diversity in rural communities and plenty of potential allies among their dispossessed non-White neighbors—most of whom face the same economic, social, political, and health-related problems as rural Whites do.

Although many of the challenges rural minorities face are similar to—if a bit more daunting than—those of their White neighbors, shared experiences have never qualified minorities for inclusion as part of America's essential minority. "In defining rural white America as rural America, pundits, academics and lawmakers are perpetuating an incomplete and simplistic story about the many people who make up rural America and what they want and need," warns Bates College professor Mara Casey Tieken. "Ironically, this story—so often told by liberals trying to explain the recent rise in undisguised nativism and xenophobia—serves to re-privilege whiteness. Whiteness is assumed; other races are shoved even further to the margins."[84]

Despite the dual burden of their numerical and racial minority statuses, the one in four rural citizens who is a minority is no more or less rural than members of the dominant White majority. Sadly, minorities garner little to no attention from a media that purports to concern itself with rural anxieties. The economic, healthcare, and cultural concerns of rural minorities matter, too, and no rural renaissance can be complete without their inclusion. For that reason alone—to say nothing of the political benefits to be reaped from building a truly pan-rural movement—

rapprochement among rural residents of every race, color, and creed presents an opportunity for rural citizens to speak with one voice. Unfortunately, if the partisan and electoral divides within rural communities are any indication, a multiracial rural revival is unlikely to emerge soon.

DESPAIR, DISTRACTION, DISILLUSIONMENT, AND DEMOCRATIC DECLINE

—

We pretty much own rural and
small town America.

—MITCH MCCONNELL, SENATE REPUBLICAN LEADER[1]

CONGRESSMAN CHIP ROY REPRESENTS TEXAS'S TWENTY-FIRST Congressional District, which begins in the suburbs of San Antonio and Austin and then stretches 150 miles west into more sparsely populated areas of Central Texas. After the 2020 Census, state Republicans redrew the district's lines, taking it from one that leaned slightly Republican to one that leaned strongly Republican. This meant that Roy's chances of losing re-election went from slim to none.

A few days before the 2022 election, we caught up with Roy at an event at a restaurant in the tiny unincorporated town of Hunt. He and a group of campaign staffers rolled in with a spring in their step and matching white collared shirts, each with Roy's name and an American flag embroidered on it, as befitting an incumbent with a hefty war chest who knew he was going to win. After he delivered an inside-baseball discussion of congressional strategy to the crowd of seventy-five supporters, he gave us a few minutes to talk. We asked him if there was a particular agenda he was pursuing that would enable his rural constituents to get what they needed from Washington and how their needs might be different from those of his suburban constituents.

At first, Roy seemed a little confused by the question. "You're talking about appropriations?" he said, something in which, as a staunchly anti-spending conservative, he's not that interested. When we said that it could include anything, he ticked off issues he said were of concern to all his constituents, including illegal immigration and inflation, and then went on to explain why he usually *opposes* the enormous Farm Bill passed periodically by Congress, which is the vehicle for many of the copious subsidies given to farmers. (Roy doesn't like the bill because it's where food stamps are funded.)

In other words, like many of his colleagues who represent districts that cover rural areas, Roy has no particular rural agenda. Four days after we spoke to him, he pulverized his earnest but underfunded Democratic opponent, a twenty-eight-year-old Latina who had managed to raise only a tiny fraction of the money Roy had.[2] He then returned to Washington, D.C., and led a revolt against Kevin McCarthy's bid to be Speaker of the House, humiliating McCarthy and extracting a series of promises that helped lead to the debt ceiling crisis of 2023.

Chip Roy is an ideologue, in ways that are both good and bad. He has a firm set of principles he holds to; special interests will be unlikely to buy his support for something he doesn't agree with. But he is also so intensely opposed to the idea of an active, effective government that he'll happily push the country toward economic catastrophe as a tool to extract concessions on domestic spending. He's an advocate of the insurrectionist view of the Second Amendment, that the amendment's core purpose is to provide a means for the violent overthrow of the system the Constitution created;[3] this view is ahistorical, ignorant of the text of the Constitution itself (which, in multiple places, forbids armed resistance to the government), and reflective of a shocking degree of entitlement for a White man who has never in his life experienced anything resembling actual government oppression. If you go to Roy's website and read his press releases, you'll find lots of culture war posturing on abortion and "wokeness" in the military, but you won't find announcements of grants obtained for the local hospital or new initiatives to bring jobs to rural

Texas. As one local Democratic activist in Gillespie County told us when we asked about politicians staging repeated photo ops in which they don khaki shirts and gaze determinedly across the Rio Grande, Roy "probably spends more time at the border than in his district."[4] (Roy's district does not border Mexico.)

For Roy and the legions of politicians like him at all levels of government who represent rural White Americans, everything is working out fine. Their positions get more secure with each passing election, even as their constituents' problems go unaddressed.

The four factors we identified in this book as the foundation of America's rural problem provide a political strategy for those who benefit from the status quo. The deep challenges affecting rural Americans—in economic opportunity, healthcare, education, infrastructure, and more—keep so many of them dissatisfied and disgruntled. Their elevated status as the essential minority provides a means to pander to them even as the distance between what they get and what they feel they deserve widens. Their outsize electoral power enables Republicans to retain control of government, often to such a degree that the party is all but exempted from electoral competition. And they are represented at all levels by politicians who use these structural, material, and cultural conditions to manipulate rural Americans in ways that translate into little or no improvement in their lives—and often make those lives worse.

For those politicians, the threats we have identified coming from rural White America—racism and xenophobia, conspiracism, anti-democratic beliefs, and the justification of violence—are not threats at all. They're either not a problem to worry about or, even worse, tools that can be used to maintain the support of those voters and aim their anger in whatever direction the politicians find most advantageous.

RURAL AMERICA'S PARTY PROBLEM

With the rural/urban political divide as stark as it is today, it's easy to forget that it wasn't always this way. In fact, for much of our history, rural and urban Americans did not vote all that differently in the aggregate; Republican presidential candidates would usually outpoll Democratic candidates by just a couple of points in rural areas. Beginning with the 2000 election, however, rural and urban votes began drifting apart, and that separation is now a chasm.[5] In 2016, 62 percent of rural Whites supported Donald Trump. Two years later, in the Democratic sweep of the 2018 midterms, 64 percent of rural Whites backed Republican House candidates. Then 71 percent voted for Trump in 2020, and 74 percent voted GOP in 2022.[6]

This divergence made rural America less politically competitive, giving both parties little incentive to devote substantial resources to winning votes there. Yet it's only Democrats who are endlessly lectured about "ignoring" rural America, and they do largely ignore it—if all you're talking about is politics and not policy. In many places, there is scant Democratic presence; the party has little or no organization, and if there is a Democrat at all on the ballot in many races, they may just be a placeholder, someone who agreed to have their name entered but doesn't do much campaigning.

Unfortunately, this leaves rural liberals—of whom there are plenty—with neither genuine representation nor a connection to other like-minded people around them. While many Democratic leaders are driven by a cold logic that considers only the next election and sees no point in trying to compete in rural America, others are trying to change their party's mind on the subject. "If you're losing a district thirty to seventy and don't want to lose it the next time twenty-five to seventy-five, part of the strategy has to begin with getting the thirty percent to believe that they're a substantial presence in those communities, that there are people out there like them," Greg Speed, president of the progressive organizing group America Votes, told us. "A forty-point margin is a bad loss in an election. Thirty percent of a community is a huge percentage of that community. Our problem begins with actual Democrats in these communities feeling under siege."[7]

What isn't as widely understood is that Republicans ignore many rural areas, too, for essentially the same reason as Democrats: They know the races there won't be competitive, so they don't need to bother. "For the most part, Republicans rack up big margins in red areas by default," says Wisconsin Democratic Party chair Ben Wikler. One of his goals when he took the helm of the party was to change its long-term prospects in rural areas of the state by competing everywhere, and in 2022, for the first time in many years, Democrats fielded a state representative candidate in every district, even those where they had little chance of winning. Those candidates found a barren political landscape. "Candidate after candidate would tell me that they were working their socks off and never seeing any evidence of a real campaign on the Republican side," Wikler told us. "And some of those candidates right before the election told me that they were really confident they'd win, because they knew their opponent had essentially done nothing, had barely filed any fundraising, had no meaningful field presence to speak of. And yet the Republicans would still win by these massive margins."[8] There are statewide races where rural outreach makes a difference; in the 2023 election for a vital state supreme court seat, Wisconsin Democrats won in part by improving their margins in rural areas of the state. But those opportunities don't come around often.

Nevertheless, when it comes to policy, Democrats at both the state and federal level never stop trying to help rural America, as politically unrequited as their efforts might be. Every Democratic presidential campaign puts out some kind of rural agenda, full of policies and programs and economic development ideas. And when they take office, they back it up with dollars; when Democrats pass a big spending bill, it is likely not just to make a point of directing money to rural areas, but also to ensure that resources are in place to help rural communities access funding and navigate federal bureaucracies.[9]

You will search in vain for similar Republican initiatives to revitalize urban centers, yet nobody accuses the GOP of "ignoring" urban America or demands that the party genuflect before the urban citizens who vote against it in such substantial numbers. In fact, the GOP's overt hostility toward cities is taken as a given, something barely worth remarking upon—but it has electoral effects. When Democrat Donna Deegan won the 2023 mayoral election in Jacksonville, Florida, the number of Republican mayors in America's twenty largest cities was reduced to *one*.

The Republican animosity toward cities not only does nothing to help rural Americans; at times, it even undermines them. For instance, recent years have seen a dramatic increase in "pre-emption," in which state legislatures pass laws forbidding local governments from setting rules in particular policy areas. The legislature might bar municipalities from increasing their local minimum wage, or protecting renters from eviction, or setting higher worker safety standards.

As the parties have polarized geographically and Republican hostility toward cities has increased, GOP-controlled legislatures have turned to pre-emption as a weapon to wield against their own liberal-leaning cities, which almost every red state has. Those cities are often the most dynamic, fastest-growing parts of the state—for instance, the five largest cities in Texas account for over half the state's GDP[10]—but if anything, this only increases the resentment conservatives feel toward them.

Which is one of the reasons states like Texas and Florida have passed one pre-emption law after another meant to tie the hands of local officials, often on hot-button issues such as LGBTQ+ rights, but also on issues like housing and payday lending that aren't as likely to grab headlines. When states do so, however, they also restrict the freedom of local governments in small towns and rural areas to craft ordinances to serve their constituents' interests. "The cities are the ones who have the most ordinances," Luis Figueroa of the progressive public policy group Every Texan told us when Republicans in the state passed a sweeping pre-emption law in 2023. "But these are going to affect rural areas as well," when their mayors and city councils find that their hands have been tied by state legislators looking to stick it to Houston, San Antonio, and Austin. Republicans' contempt for cities is so commonplace now that it has become an easy way to signal one's conservative bona fides to the GOP base. Those who want attention and votes know they can obtain them by telling people that New York, San Francisco, or Chicago are hellholes that embody everything ordinary Americans should hate and fear.

On the ground, anti-government ideology makes life worse for rural people in a hundred ways. Who, for instance, is going to provide vital infrastructure if the government doesn't do it, or does it badly? In December 2022, *The Texas Tribune* reported, "Aging infrastructure, coupled with inflation driving up costs of supplies, has left Texas' water infrastructure increasingly brittle. This year, there have been at least

2,457 boil-water notices issued across the state—an average of seven per day," most of them in rural areas.[11] Somehow, Republican rule has not only failed to turn rural Texas into a paradise, it hasn't even given it a reliable water supply.

On issue after issue, rural Americans are getting not nearly enough or nothing at all from the Republicans who represent them. More than that, they are often actively harmed by the party's policy positions and ideological commitments. Republicans press for school vouchers that take money away from public schools and direct it to private schools, but in many rural areas, there simply are no private schools; if the local public schools are starved for resources, the whole community suffers. The GOP is the party of climate denial, yet farmers are more affected by climate change than almost anyone else, from peach farmers in Georgia[12] to hay farmers in Upstate New York,[13] seeing their crops devastated by warming temperatures and weather disasters.

Or consider abortion. Republican-run states passed a wave of draconian restrictions in the wake of the Supreme Court ruling overturning *Roe v. Wade*. These restrictions are certain not only to increase unwanted pregnancies in rural areas, with all the attendant impacts on the economic lives of women and families, but also to have wider negative effects on rural people's ability to access healthcare. In Sandpoint, Idaho, for instance, ob-gyns fleeing the state after being threatened with criminal penalties for providing care led to the closing of the only maternity ward in an entire rural region.[14]

Then there's broadband internet service, one of the most vital services a community needs to create and sustain economic vitality. As of 2022, seventeen states had severe restrictions or outright bans on municipalities providing their own broadband service to residents, even in places where private companies don't find it profitable to install high-speed internet access.[15] In most cases, these bans have been spearheaded by Republican legislators at the behest of the telecommunication companies. In 2021, congressional Republicans introduced legislation that would "prohibit a State or political subdivision thereof from providing or offering for sale to the public retail or wholesale broadband internet access service," claiming with a straight face that relieving telecoms of competition from municipal providers would "promote competition."[16] And if you live in a rural area where none of the telecoms wants to give you service? Too bad.

Attacks on higher education help Republicans win elections, but they hurt rural college students, who so often struggle to afford college.[17] In late 2022, *The Washington Post* reported on a wave of rural universities cutting back majors, in large part because states had slashed funding for education; humanities and sciences were being eliminated in favor of more "practical" fields. "It's saying to us that they don't value us, that our towns are doomed to be train stops," said a student majoring in history and political science, both of which were shut down.[18]

Rural Americans can usually expect their practical concerns to fall on deaf Republican ears, while Democrats are eager to help, whether out of sincere concern for rural America's fate or a (usually) doomed effort to win back some lost votes. Every Democratic presidential nominee puts out some kind of plan to aid rural America, and progressive groups do the same. The website of the Center for American Progress, the largest left-leaning think tank, contains dozens of articles on the challenges facing rural America and possible solutions; white papers like the "Rural New Deal," a project of the Progressive Democrats of America and the Rural Urban Bridge Initiative, abound. The American Rescue Plan, passed early in 2021 without a single Republican vote in either the House or Senate, was positively brimming with benefits for rural America. It provided money for rural healthcare, schools, emergency services, workforce development, broadband, and water and sewer systems. Did Joe Biden and the Democrats get credit from people in those communities? No. Rural folks took the money, of course, but quickly forgot who had obtained it for them.

When you ask them directly about the things government does for them—including the things Republicans try the hardest to destroy—rural Americans are usually aware of what they need, even if they're less clear on who might help them get it. In a 2017 Kaiser Family Foundation poll, 68 percent of rural residents said Medicaid is "important to their community," a higher number than urban or suburban residents.[19] Yet the electorate in those same communities gives overwhelming support to the party that tried to kick millions of people off Medicaid by repealing the Affordable Care Act and that continually looks for ways to undermine the program.

Even if you were to narrow the scope of what rural Americans want from government to some basic, collective benefits—not food stamps but hospitals, not tax credits but new sewers—their anti-government feelings deprive them of those, too. Did Donald Trump and Republicans give them infrastructure legislation that would enable them to get bridges and roads repaired, or replace lead water pipes, or spread broadband? No, they didn't. It took the election of a Democratic government to get those things for them. The Trump administration did nothing to respond to the "right to repair" movement, which wants farmers to be able to make repairs to their own equipment so they don't have to wait for expensive and time-consuming visits from dealer representatives every time a tractor or combine breaks down. It was Joe Biden who signed an executive order to have the Federal Trade Commission take steps to curb this restrictive practice.[20] It was Colorado governor Jared Polis, a progressive Democrat in a state that Democrats dominate, who in 2023 signed the first state-level legislation guaranteeing a right to repair for agricultural equipment.

And as sociologist Robert Wuthnow said about his lengthy research on rural areas in every corner of the country, "We found town managers and elected officials who were frustrated over the generalized anger toward Washington because it inhibited practical solutions from being pursued. These officials knew they had to secure grants from the federal government, for instance, but found it difficult to do that when local elections were won by far-right candidates."[21]

Everywhere you look, Republican ideological goals are having their intended effects in rural America, which winds up making life worse. In 2017, a pair of researchers examined rural counties to determine where upward mobility was most common—in other words, where economic opportunity existed and the American dream was more of a reality. In the end, they identified three factors that would have the greatest effect in promoting mobility in rural America: strong schools, good broadband, and the availability of family planning so women were less likely to have unwanted pregnancies before they were economically ready to have children.[22]

None of this should come as a surprise. Yet on all three counts, the GOP, the party that dominates rural America, is directly undermining its ability to create upward mobility. Republicans denigrate and defund public schools. They actively work to prevent municipalities from setting up their own broadband systems. And they undermine family planning at every turn, from promoting counterproductive "abstinence-only" education, to filing lawsuits to prevent people from getting contraceptives covered by insurance, to outlawing abortion everywhere they can.

Meanwhile, these same politicians feed rural Americans a brand of authoritarian populism, one that generates anger at "elites" yet is remarkably disconnected from the economic power relations in society. This kind of populism seeks a class war, but one whose victory is to be found not in a redistribution of power or in policies that lift up those who struggle, but in the discrediting of cultural elites while money and power are kept in the hands of the traditional economic overclass.[23]

Authoritarian populism is distinct from other variants of populism because it not only focuses on a conflict between "the people" and the elite but also rejects democracy, as democracy might enable those who are not like "us" to win and hold power. Wherever one of these rightist movements emerges in today's world, whether it's Trumpism in America, Brexit in Britain, the National Rally in France, Viktor Orbán's Fidesz party in Hungary,[24] or the AfD in Germany, chances are it will have its most fervent support in rural areas. And not just rural areas, but the places that have been left behind by economic transitions. Recent elections have shown that in areas that have successfully adapted to the modern economy, moderate candidates do better, but in places that have struggled economically, far-right candidates dominate.[25]

So, like all right-wing parties that depend on rural voters, the Republican Party has an interest in maintaining, not alleviating, their struggles. Rural voters who are satisfied and optimistic might consider the entreaties of both parties, but the more dissatisfied and angrier they are, the more they'll stick with the GOP. Come Election Day, despair is a Republican candidate's chief asset, because that despair is easiest to convert into anger, and that anger into votes.

At the same time, Republicans know quite well that they benefit when politics in rural areas has a kind of hollowness to it. Rural areas have fewer sources of local news and fewer opportunities for political participation.[26] The relative lack of political activity is a by-product of various forces, but it derives from at least one very intentional strategy: the attempt to destroy collective bargaining in America. While that long war has certainly been waged to serve the economic interests of the wealthy and corporations, it also has had a very particular political purpose.

The economic benefits of union membership have been widely understood for decades: Union members earn more money and get more generous benefits than their nonunion counterparts. And because unions set standards even nonunionized employers have an incentive to meet, their benefits are spread even to those who aren't members.[27] Just as important, labor unions *politicize* people in the best sense, by making them understand their own struggles in a broader context. They tell you that your problem isn't that your boss is a jerk, even if he is; your problem is much bigger than that. It's about the way power is distributed both on the job and in our society as a whole, through the laws and regulations that affect you every day. Most threatening of all, labor unions tell you that you have common cause with other people who are in a similar position, even if they have a different skin color or speak a different language or worship a different god, and that if you work together, you can take some of that power back.

One of the key weapons against labor unions that conservatives have wielded is "right-to-work" laws, which hinder union organizing by outlawing contracts in which everyone in a workplace is required to pay dues to the union that negotiates on their behalf. This starves the union of funds and gives a powerful incentive for workers not to bother joining, making organizing much harder. Republicans then gain in multiple ways; because unions usually support Democrats, the lack of unions in an area will deprive the party of financial support and volunteers. A group of scholars analyzed neighboring counties where one had a right-to-work law and the other did not and found that not only did right-to-work laws dampen voter turnout and significantly lower Democratic vote share, but "the weakening of unions also has large downstream effects: fewer working-class candidates serve in state legislatures and Congress, while state policy moves in a more conservative direction."[28] Support for unions recently surged to its highest level since 1965. A truly representative set of rural politicians would respond accordingly—but good luck finding a Republican official, rural or otherwise, who has declared he has reversed his long-standing opposition to collective bargaining.

Elite Republicans understand this well; destroying unions has a broad spectrum of benefits for them and their plutocratic patrons, including convincing people that the economic status quo, no matter how bad it gets, is something that can't be changed by ordinary people. The party and its media advocates continually defend the distribution of wealth in America by insisting that it correlates perfectly with virtue: If you work hard, then you'll succeed, and if you haven't succeeded, then you've gotten just what you deserve.

But rural people know, or certainly *ought* to know, what a lie this is. Not only are our country and the world full of people who got rich because of who their parents were or any of a panoply of advantages that go under the preposterous name of "meritocracy," but rural communities everywhere are brimming with people who work incredibly hard yet can't get ahead. Where does the farm family who wakes at 4 A.M. every day to labor in their fields yet who can't make the payments on their loans fit into this picture of work leading inevitably to success? Where do the people who spent decades on an assembly line only to watch the factory pick up and move when it was bought by a private equity firm fit into that picture? What about those trying to make ends meet in poorly paid retail jobs with few other opportunities where they live? Don't those people work hard? If so, then why hasn't this perfect system rewarded them?

Republicans deal with this contradiction by telling rural people that, yes, they struggle, and, yes, the Republican Party will do little if anything practical for them, but the answer can be found in directing all their resentment and hatred to a different set of targets: immigrants, racial minorities, college professors, urbanites, and "woke" liberals of all kinds. Republicans whip up torrents of feigned outrage at "elites," convincing regular people to focus their energy into the most inane of controversies so they won't notice what really matters. There is no end to those controversies and no material goal each one serves; if the libs have been properly owned, the right has won a battle and the next one will soon be cued up.

So, when Bud Light partners with a transgender influencer to sell a few more cases of beer, Fox News and the rest of conservative media swing into action, thumping desks and threatening boycotts, without mentioning that the brand's parent company, Anheuser Busch, gives millions of dollars to the Republican Party. Your problems must be the fault of Bud Light, so go out and make a video of yourself shooting a few cans of the stuff. The stores in your hometown are all shuttered? It must be because a Wall Street bank tweeted out an image of a Pride flag.

This directs the focus of politics to issues marked by apparently irreconcilable differences between the parties, where questions of government officials' performance become almost irrelevant. If you've been persuaded that the greatest threat to your way of life is a trans girl on the other side of the state who wants to play on her middle school softball team, not only won't you ever consider voting for a Democrat, but you won't ask much of your Republican representatives, either. You won't hold them accountable for the condition of your streets or the lack of economic opportunities in your town. And you won't believe that politics is a place where you can work to make things better.

You won't turn your pain into action and demands for change; you'll just turn it into the poison of bitterness and rage. That's just how the Republican Party wants rural people: angry and resentful at famous liberals and impersonal forces that are thousands of miles away and endlessly cynical about the prospects for politics to change their communities. You could imagine elected Republicans who reflect their constituents' cultural beliefs *and* also work hard to craft and implement policies that would improve their lives, but those politicians are awfully thin on the ground.

If they want to change this miserable state of affairs, rural people need to start by realizing they are the foundation of conservative Republican power in America. Without them, the conservative project and the GOP would be lost. Then they have to ask: What are we getting for the support we give to the Republican Party? Are we getting revitalized main streets, more economic opportunity, better infrastructure, better schools, a more promising future for our children?

Right now, the answer is clearly no. They're getting a punch in the face, and next November, they'll go back to the polls and say, "Thank you, sir. May I have another?" We call this vicious political circle the *despair, distraction, disillusionment, democratic decline spiral.* Each of these four stages leads to the next and then circles back around again.

First, despair inevitably sets in once jobs disappear, wages stagnate, benefits vanish, healthcare facilities close, and young people leave after graduation in search of greener pastures. Unable, but also mostly unwilling, to cure what ails their constituents, strategic politicians concerned with their own power divert their constituents' attention away from their suffering by ginning up grievance-fueled culture war distractions. Because those wars are never won, and because the material miseries are left unaddressed, rural folks become increasingly disillusioned. At this point, they start wondering whether the foundations, principles, and norms of U.S. democracy are worth defending and begin engaging with demagogues who offer tempting alternatives. With each successive iteration, the problems of rural communities deepen, the opportunity for politicians to manipulate their resentments grows, rural grievances fester, and democratic commitments further deteriorate.

Feeling disempowered despite wielding magnified power, rural voters respond to this spiral by lashing out at the polls or in the streets— whereupon the four threats we earlier delineated (antagonisms toward out-groups, anti-science conspiracism, anti-democratic urges, and the justification of violence) morph from mere sentiments into behaviors that threaten the institutions that preserve, protect, and defend our pluralist constitutional democracy. Feeling less control with each passing year, the essential minority becomes alienated from democracy, resistant to good-faith policy compromises, and more permissive of transgressive government behaviors like stealing state secrets, unleashing tear gas on citizens, or denying the legitimacy of partisan opponents by refusing to honor the peaceful transfer of power.

In the prologue we posed two related questions: What does the essential rural minority expect in exchange for its continued commitment to pluralist democracy, and what happens if those expectations are unmet? The former is difficult to answer: Other than Republicans prevailing in every election and liberalism disappearing from American civic and cultural life, it can be difficult to discern what precisely White rural voters want. But the answer to the second question is clearer: The world's oldest constitutional democracy will be imperiled. Scholars of democratic decline make clear that democracies fail gradually and then all of a sudden. Anyone who denies the steady diminishment of democratic principles, norms, and institutions witnessed of late, and especially since Trump's rise, is suffering from a greater level of self-denial than those rural citizens who refuse to hold their own rural, White, mostly male, conservative Republican officials responsible for exacerbating the despair, distraction, and disillusionment they experience.

THE MISSING PIECE OF RURAL POLITICS

The way to end the Republican Party's exploitation of rural communities is not as simple as convincing them that they should all vote for Democrats (though some of them surely should). For many, the positions of the Democratic Party on issues such as abortion and LGBTQ+ rights will always be unacceptable. What those rural White voters need to do is not to vote Democratic but to get themselves better Republicans.

There are multiple ways rural citizens can move toward a better economic future, and some methods will work better in some places than in others. But more than anything else, breaking the dangerous cycle in which rural misery leads to anti-democratic revanchism will require *a new rural political movement*.

Although rural consciousness and rural White resentment are pervasive, there is no rural movement. There are small nonprofits and think tanks whose mission is to improve life in rural America. There are a few innovative independent news outlets covering rural issues, like *The Daily Yonder*. But what rural America lacks is a real movement, especially in one key component: *demands*. Rural America has many advocates, but they don't organize around a set of demands in the way that the anti-abortion movement or the environmental movement or the gun rights movement or the LGBTQ+ rights movement has.

In fact, rural Whites are the *only* significant part of either party's coalition that has no coherent set of demands, for all the power they hold. While those coalitions are made up both of identity groups (Blacks, evangelicals) and issue groups (environmentalists, gun advocates), all have their own policy agendas, specific things they want their party to advocate for and the nation's laws to reflect. Rural Whites have no such agenda.

The lack of a movement with a clear agenda breaks the vital link between influence at the ballot box and concrete results, the policy and economic changes that might actually improve people's lives. Movements help candidates get elected, but when the election is over, their members continue to make demands of the officeholders they helped, always with the threat that if the politicians don't deliver, the movement may turn on them. Without that movement, there's no way to hold the politicians accountable. Yet rural voters won't ask whether the politicians delivered on the promises they made in the last campaign, when they came before them and said, "I will fight to accomplish these things you have told me you want."

The lack of a rural movement is what allows rural people to be so easily exploited. Think of the contrast between how rural Americans' needs are considered and how each party takes into account the interests of the movements within their respective coalitions. When Republicans win an election and prepare to govern, the people and groups that helped them win—corporations, gun advocates, anti-abortion groups, and so on—are at the table when the spoils are divided. Appointments, appropriations, the legislative agenda—all must be done in close consultation with those groups. Every White House, Republican or Democratic, has a significant number of people assigned to the care and feeding of the party's constituencies, so that those constituencies feel listened to and so the White House knows exactly what their demands are. But where are rural people in this system?

They're an afterthought, because they aren't organized and have no movement to represent them. There is no demographic group in America as loyal to one political party as rural Whites are to the GOP that gets less out of the deal. Chip Roy's puzzlement when asked if he had a rural agenda ("You're talking about appropriations?") demonstrates this disconnect.

If they created a movement, rural Americans—and rural Whites especially—would have an extraordinary opportunity to be courted by both parties. Imagine a future in which rural Americans' needs and demands were a central component of the national political debate, and both parties labored relentlessly to convince rural voters they had something to offer them. If those voters had clearly defined demands, Republicans would *have* to satisfy them, and Democrats would *want* to satisfy them. Rural voters are already embedded within the GOP, and Democrats are desperate to win more rural votes. Yet, at the moment, rural voters are squandering their position by asking the parties for nothing.

A rural movement could do something else for rural people: give them a different and more constructive outlook on politics. The toxic rage and resentment festering in so many White rural areas is even starker when one compares it to what one finds among non-White rural Americans.

Black, Latino, and Native rural Americans find themselves in even worse conditions than their White rural counterparts, suffering from poverty, substance abuse, and lack of resources and opportunity. And unlike most rural Whites, they've experienced generations of discrimination and abuse from federal and state governments. But they haven't abandoned their belief in the democratic process. They aren't threatening election officials, or planning violence against people they don't like, or plotting to overthrow the government.

Their willingness, even eagerness, to work within our democratic system is something characteristic of Americans who don't just suffer from deep problems but who are the victims of genuine discrimination: They are often those with the *most* faith in the United States and its system of government. The civil rights movement, the women's movement, the gay rights movement—all were undertaken by people who believed they could effect change with organizing, activism, and moral persuasion. Those people didn't respond to every short-term setback by threatening violence. They didn't storm the Capitol Building or show up at their local statehouse with AR-15s strapped across their chests.

Activism within the democratic system is also an instruction, one that affects how people view the opportunities for change. The civil rights movement gave Black Americans a model of political engagement at both the individual and collective level, whether they personally participated in the movement or not. Black people know how change happens and how their situation can be improved: They boycott and march and organize, and the NAACP files lawsuits, and people who represent Black Americans get elected to office, and legislation is passed. It may not always work, and progress can be slow, but there exists a well-understood structure in which political action takes place.

Rural Whites have no similar model with which to understand how politics is done and how it might affect their lives. There is no prominent National Association for the Advancement of Rural People lobbying and filing lawsuits on their behalf. There are no national days of protest to press for their demands. There are no big political fights over the future of rural America with which they can engage. Politics now is not a place of shared struggle where meaningful victories might be achieved; it's a vehicle for nothing more than the occasional grunt of rage.

The first step to creating a potent political movement must be rural Whites' acknowledgment that they've been blaming the wrong people for their problems. What we said at the outset of this book bears repeating: Hollywood didn't kill the family farm and send manufacturing jobs overseas. College professors didn't pour mountains of opioids into rural communities. Immigrants didn't shutter rural hospitals and let rural infrastructure decay. The outsiders and liberals at whom so many rural

Whites point their anger are not the ones who have held them back—and as long as they keep believing that they are, rural people won't develop an effective form of politics.

We won't presume to tell rural Americans exactly what policies they should be asking for; that's something any movement has to decide on its own. There are plenty of ideas out there in think tank reports and economic papers, and there are people in rural areas working hard to fashion a new future. Some have focused on creating a recreation-based economy to replace the old one based on resource extraction. Others have welcomed the immigrants moving into the heartland as an engine of revitalization, rather than fearing and rejecting them. Still others are agitating to resist the predations of corporate consolidation. All these are worthy efforts.

But it's hard to find agreement on what a positive future for rural America would look like. Ask urbanists—or just people who live in cities—what they envision for the future of their communities, and you'll find a great deal of agreement: ample public transportation, walkability, green buildings, more integration of residential and commercial spaces, more affordable housing, more extensive tree canopy in neighborhoods that lack it, and so on. It's hard to find a similar consensus vision for rural America that goes beyond nostalgia for a past that can't be reclaimed.

Assembling that vision and rallying people around it is a daunting enterprise. But rural Americans have a tool at their disposal that no other group has: History, geography, political structures built for a very different world, and the efforts of today's Republican Party to create a lock on power afford rural people the ability to change their own circumstances. With all their outsize influence, rural folk can demand a better deal from their leaders. They can tell their politicians that shutting down abortion clinics and banning books about queer kids from schools is not enough. Rather than blaming outside forces for their difficulties, they can turn things around themselves.

But it's absolutely crucial that any rural movement is not a *White* rural movement, but one that includes the interests and voices of all people who live in rural America, including the quarter of them who aren't

White. Black, Latino, and Native rural Americans have their own dis-tinct struggles but share many problems with rural Whites.

Demographic change is coming to rural America whether its White population wants it or not, even if it has been slower than in the rest of the country. Although rural America is still about three-quarters White, the median rural county saw its non-White population increase by 3.5 percentage points between the 2010 and 2020 censuses.[29] According to 2020 Census data, the adult rural population is 21.6 percent non-White, while the under-eighteen rural population is 32.5 percent non-White.[30]

This steadily increasing diversity can have both positive and negative effects, however. It may produce more political competitiveness, which forces politicians to be responsive as they compete for votes. But it can also spark a backlash; anti-immigrant sentiment and racial resentment are often most intense neither where there are no non-White people nor where there are large numbers of them, but in places that used to be nearly all-White and where the non-White population is *growing.*[31]

Such demographic change is inevitable. Like the country as a whole, rural America will be more diverse tomorrow than it is today, just as today it is more diverse than it was yesterday. If rural Americans created a similarly diverse movement, it could help defuse some of that backlash by showing that rural folk have common cause not just with people nearby or with people who look like them, but with everyone who lives in a rural area anywhere in the country, no matter who they are. The stronger those bonds become, the more results they will produce. A rural movement that is all White will remain mired in the same patholo-gies and missed opportunities that plague rural Americans today.

Past need not be prologue, but so far, rural Whites as a group haven't shown the inclination to create a movement with a vision for the future, let alone one that sees increasing rural diversity as an asset and not a problem. Instead, they appear to be going farther and farther down a dark path. Their resentments feed the idea that they are surrounded by enemies who must be destroyed if they themselves are to survive. They're increasingly drawn to politicians who view democracy not as a treasured value, but as an impediment to getting what they want, one that can and should be discarded. They're told that their ugliest selves are their truest selves, and too many of them believe it. Unless they can see their way clear to a different path, not only will their own lives not improve, but they'll keep dragging the country down with them. The result could be the most frightening political crisis in the United States since the Civil War.

In 2024 and beyond, whenever Republicans lose an election, they will say to their supporters broadly and to rural Whites in particular, *Look what they took from you. The election was rigged and power stolen from you, its rightful possessors. Democracy has failed you, your enemies have seized control and are coming to annihilate you, and the only answer is to hack away at the foundations of the system that allowed such a thing to occur.* This will be the refrain repeated not only by Donald Trump but by a hundred politicians and media figures who stand beside him. The question is whether rural people will accept these untruths and act upon them.

THE OPPORTUNITY

"The United States was born in the country and has moved to the city," historian Richard Hofstadter wrote in 1960.[32] That migration, with the center of gravity shifting away from rural areas and toward cities and suburbs, is a defining theme of American economic, political, and cultural history. But even as many kinds of power and influence centered themselves in and around cities, rural Americans' political power was not only maintained but enhanced. But because so much of what they see around them testifies to a lack of power, rural residents often fail to appreciate this fact. They live amid economic precarity, many of them (especially the older ones) feel alienated from popular culture, and they have so much trouble envisioning a prosperous future that they cling to nostalgia for a past that was seldom as rosy as they remember.

But as imperfect as it was, that past made space for optimism. Every boarded-up shop or empty building tells two stories, one about the present and one about the past. In the now, such sights speak of disappointment, resignation, and loss, but they also show what once was. Every abandoned factory was once churning out products, a place where a proprietor built a business and people came to buy what they wanted. Every main street in decline had to decline from somewhere higher.

The question is not whether the past can be recaptured but whether there can be a better future in rural America. But it has to start with rural Americans using the power they possess to create it.

As we said at the outset, we wrote this book not to denigrate or mock our fellow Americans who live in rural areas. We have family and friends who live there and ancestors who are buried there. We have traveled plenty to rural towns and counties—not just in researching this book but during personal travels, for the enjoyment of the scenery, food, music, festivals, and our fellow Americans. But we haven't shied away from hard truths, either. No one has more at stake in the issues we've explored than rural people do. Unfortunately, there are powerful individuals and organizations who see the problems of rural America as their own path to profit, in both dollars and votes. They want rural people to stew in a toxic combination of bitterness and impotence. They want them to remain ignorant of their own capacity to make positive change, to ignore the real sources of their problems, and to cultivate their worst impulses.

It does not have to be that way. We have said that rural White Americans have been treated as the essential minority, but they are essential in another way: Without them, we cannot forge a future as a stable pluralist democracy. Creating a better future for rural America, both economically and politically, ought to be a national priority. If it isn't, many of the problems that plague us now will only worsen.

In 1803, Thomas Jefferson wrote to a friend of his desire for promising young men to "return to the farms of their fathers" to reinvigorate American agriculture, "a calling now languishing under contempt & oppression." Jefferson went on to pour some of his own contempt on American cities, which he said threatened to become "here, as in Europe, the sinks of voluntary misery."[33]

Today, the sinks of voluntary—or involuntary—misery are too often found in rural areas across the country, where opportunities are slight and anger festers. But that can change. Rural people, and rural Whites especially, have the means to pull themselves and the United States of America back from the brink. They must—but it is not their problem alone. No matter where you live or who you are, every American has a stake in what happens to our rural brethren and their communities. The survival of our democracy depends on it.

AUTHORS' NOTE

———

WHAT WE MEAN WHEN WE TALK
ABOUT "RURAL"

Wहात constitutes "rural" and who qualifies as a rural American? The short but unsatisfying answer is that it depends on whom you ask.

Rurality is a place-based distinction, but not entirely nor exclusively so. Some scholars, for example, study and measure what they call "rural consciousness," an exhibited identity or belief system that most people who grew up in rural communities carry with them years and even decades after they left their rural hometowns to move to suburban or urban areas. Conversely, many people who move or retire to rural communities may exhibit little if any degree of rural consciousness because they are recent arrivals who brought an enduring suburban or urban identity with them.

Meanwhile, what qualifies any geographic community—a town or small city, even a county or entire state—as "rural" is also a matter of some dispute. Even federal agencies do not agree on how to define and categorize rural citizens. The U.S. Department of Agriculture uses a classification scheme based on rural-urban commuting area codes. But the Centers for Disease Control and Prevention, the Health Resources and Services Administration's Federal Office of Rural Health Policy, and the Office of Management and Budget each uses its own classification scheme.[1] It overstates the matter to describe this dissensus as an apples-and-oranges comparison; rather, it's more like oranges, tangerines, and clementines—citrus fruits of varying sizes and flavors. Scholars Kenneth M. Johnson and Daniel T. Lichter warn that a recent Census Bureau re-definition of what constitutes a "metropolitan statistical area" will alter how citizens are classified based upon their place of residence.[2]

There is also the equally complicated matter of how various researchers and institutions classify rural people and other geographic subgroups. To the best of our knowledge, among scholars, data scientists, and pollsters, the most common way to group citizens by place of residence is into three broad subgroups: rural, suburban, and urban. However, some pollsters dichotomize citizens or voters as either metro or nonmetro. In the other direction, some scholars and think tanks use five or more categories; Kenneth M. Johnson and Dante Scala developed a geographical spectrum with nine subgroups arrayed along a spectrum from the most rural to the most urban.[3] How Americans self-describe their residency also varies: According to a 2017 U.S. Housing and Urban Development survey, 27 percent of Americans said they live in urban communities, 52 percent said suburban, and 21 percent said rural; results from a poll conducted by the Pew Research Center one year later were 25, 43, and 30 percent, respectively.[4]

Given these differences and disagreements as to what makes citizens rural—their identity, their address, or both—we remained agnostic throughout our research and writing by merely reporting the categories and definitions that each pollster, scholar, or researcher used. That is, when we cited a poll result distinguishing among the attitudes of "urban, suburban, and rural" citizens, it is because the pollster grouped citizens trichotomously; when we used the labels "metro" and "nonmetro," that study's results or poll's cross tabs were reported dichotomously. Simply put, we found ourselves at the mercy of the choices made by the researchers who collected, sorted, classified, and tabulated their results.

However, as a back-of-the-napkin baseline—and in cases where a specific classification scheme was absent or irrelevant—our default preference was to classify and discuss citizens as either urban, suburban, or rural. Although we have seen estimates for the "rural" population in this simplest, trichotomous classification scheme range from as low as 14 percent to as high as 33 percent of the national total, we prefer 20 percent as the baseline share of the U.S. population classified as rural. That's one-fifth of all American citizens. And given that about one in four rural Americans is non-White, we've reached the assumption that approximately 15 percent of the national population is both rural and White, with the remaining 5 percent rural non-White.

A final point about how place intersects with race: Readers will notice that sometimes we report a poll data point or other statistic as simply "rural" and at other times "rural White." Again, with a few exceptions, this is because we are at the mercy of whether pollsters and researchers had big enough samples to report rural attitudes by racial subgroup. Too often, national poll samples are too small for pollsters to break down rural voters by race. Assuming the 20 percent estimate for the rural population nationwide, a national poll with a sample of roughly one thousand respondents will include about two hundred rural respondents, only fifty of whom (one in four) will be rural non-Whites. These subsamples are too small from which to draw statistical inferences about the difference between rural Whites and rural non-Whites.

All this leads to a very crucial point about data sufficiency and our book's arguments and conclusions: The too-small rural respondent subsample issue more likely than not *understates* many of our conclusions about the contemporary threats posed to U.S. democracy by rural Whites. Let us explain why.

For much of this book, we focus on rural Whites because, as we demonstrate, they exert magnified voting power and mythic status and—most worrisome—their commitments to U.S. democracy have deteriorated recently. Where appropriate and where data are available, of course, we distinguish between poll findings that apply to rural respondents overall and findings that apply to rural Whites only. Because so few polls include large enough subsamples of non-White rural adults to elicit their opinions, however, we are often forced to discuss or describe the attitudes and beliefs of all rural citizens, White and non-White combined. But lumping all rural voters together tends to obscure the percentages or results that apply solely to rural White voters.

For example, according to a 2018 Pew Research Center survey, 46 percent of White rural citizens say they value diversity in their communities—the lowest share of any geographic-racial subgroup.[5] By comparison, 71 percent of rural minorities value diversity, a twenty-five-point difference. The pro-diversity attitudes of rural non-Whites thus lift the overall rural share supporting diversity to 54 percent.

But polls like Pew's that include the racial splits are rare. A poll too small to allow for a racial breakdown would simply report that a 54 percent majority of rural Americans support diversity, when in fact that majority exists *only* because of the far higher support for diversity by the one-in-four rural citizens who is non-White. Likewise, consider that rural Americans are more likely to claim the election "was stolen from Trump." Specifically, a 2021 Public Religion Research Institute survey found that a combined 47 percent of rural Americans either "completely" (26 percent) or "mostly" (21 percent) agreed that the election was stolen, compared with a combined 30 percent of suburbanites and 22 percent of urban dwellers.[6] These regional differences are statistically significant. But we know from racial differences in attitudes about the 2020 election that Whites believe it was stolen at far higher rates than non-Whites. Consequently, the overall rural share who believe the election was stolen is *lowered* by the inclusion of non-White rural voters, whereas the suburban and urban shares who believe it was stolen are *raised* by the presence of White suburban and urban respondents. In this way, stated differences between rural and either suburban or urban adults are technically accurate, but they mask the wider opinion disparities on key issues that exist between, say, rural Whites and urban non-Whites.

We do not blame pollsters for failing to spend the enormous sums it would take to gather large enough racial subsamples for rural respondents. We merely note that the absence of these racial breakdowns, when coupled with pundits' reflex to falsely equate "rural" and "White," tends to mask the weaker democratic sentiments exhibited by White rural Americans behind the stronger democratic sentiments expressed by their non-White rural neighbors. This is another way of saying that insufficiently large subsamples in most national polls and studies almost always *understate* the actual degree to which rural Whites pose the threats to American democracy we identify in this book. Given these data limitations, the actual threat emanating from rural White corners of the nation is surely more dire than we depict in our book's findings and warnings.

ACKNOWLEDGMENTS

—

ANY BOOK IS A COLLECTIVE EFFORT, AND OURS IS NO EXCEPTION. WE owe eternal thanks to those who helped us along the way.

In our reporting for this book, a number of people not only provided their own insights but connected us with others who could share their stories. We are particularly indebted to Cathy Collier, Pete Rios, Mondale Robinson, Heather Wolford, Hannah Smith, and Keith McKeever, each of whom helped connect us to people in the five states where we conducted interviews.

We are also indebted to several pollsters who either provided us previously unreported place-based cross tabs or, in a few cases, calculated cross tab results specifically for us: Natalie Jackson at the Public Religion Research Institute; Neil Newhouse, Luke Jackson, Koran Addo, and Alicia Sams of the University of Chicago's Institute of Politics; Patrick Murray at the Monmouth University Poll; Tom Jensen from Public Policy Polling; and David Lazer at The COVID States Project Poll.

A number of researchers and journalists also directed our attention to findings of relevance to our inquiry, including Aditya Dasgupta, University of California, Merced; Marc Edelman, CUNY; Ashley Jardina, Duke University; Kristen Lunz Trujillo, Harvard Kennedy School of Government; Matthew MacWilliams, Johns Hopkins University; Keith Orejel, Wilmington College; Sarah Posner, Recovering Truth; Meri

Power-Ayer, Suffolk University Political Research Center; Dante Scala, University of New Hampshire; and Mara Casey Tieken, Bates College.

We are grateful to countless friends and family members who took time to read parts of the original book proposal or drafts of the manuscript to provide useful insights and feedback.

Our agent, Will Lippincott, is a man of heroic wisdom, patience, and skill; without him the book would never have come to fruition. Finally, we are extremely grateful for the guidance of our editors at Random House, Mark Warner and Molly Turpin, and the rest of the Random House team, all of whom made the book better.

NOTES

CHAPTER 1. ESSENTIAL MINORITY, EXISTENTIAL THREAT

1. In 1993, Democrats held an extraordinary 32–2 majority in the state senate; three decades later, Republicans held a 31–3 majority.
2. Truman and Letitia Chafin, interview with the authors, Williamson, W.V., April 3, 2023.
3. One episode in this period is known as the Matewan Massacre (or the Battle of Matewan), in which miners and their allies had a shootout with members of the Baldwin–Felts Detective Agency, who had been sent to put them back in their place. The event was dramatized in the 1987 John Sayles film *Matewan*. The Mine Wars culminated in the Battle of Blair Mountain in 1921, the largest insurrection on American soil since the Civil War. Thousands of miners faced off against an army led by Logan County sheriff Don Chafin, who in his official capacity was essentially the coal companies' enforcer, a task he carried out with enthusiastic brutality. The conflict ended only when President Warren Harding ordered the West Virginia National Guard to move in and restore order.
4. The most important pieces of legislation were the National Industrial Recovery Act in 1933 and the National Labor Relations Act in 1935.
5. One key development was the spread of the Joy Loading Machine, which would gather coal, move it on a conveyor belt, and deposit it in a coal car, actions that previously had to be done by large numbers of men with shovels.
6. Raymond Chafin, interview with the authors, Williamson, W.V., April 7, 2023.
7. West Virginia Office of Miners' Health Safety and Training, "2021 Production and Employment—Broken Down by County," table, n.d.
8. This happened just twelve years after John Kerry won a comfortable victory there; only two of the fifty-five counties in the state voted more strongly for Kerry. In 2016, only three of the fifty-five voted more strongly for Trump than Mingo did.
9. Public Religion Research Institute, "Competing Visions of America: An Evolving Identity or a Culture Under Attack?", PRRI, November 1, 2021, Question 7a. We thank PRRI's Natalie Jackson and Sean Sands, who produced for us, upon request, the urban/suburban/rural splits from this poll that were not made available in the versions of results and cross tabs produced for the public.
10. *Washington Post*/Kaiser Family Foundation Poll of Rural and Small-town America, conducted April 13–May 1, 2017, Question 49.
11. Kim Parker et al., "What Unites and Divides Urban, Suburban and Rural Communities," Pew Research Center, May 22, 2018.

12. Eli Yokley, "The Culture War Has Democrats Facing Electoral Demise in Rural America. Can They Stop the Bleeding?" *Morning Consult,* February 22, 2022.

13. B. Kal Munis, "Us Over Here Versus Them Over There . . . Literally: Measuring Place Resentment in American Politics," *Political Behavior* 44 (2022): 1057–78.

14. Kim Parker et al., "What Unites and Divides Urban, Suburban and Rural Communities," Pew Research Center, May 22, 2018; see Section 3 results.

15. Public Religion Research Institute, "Competing Visions of America: An Evolving Identity or a Culture Under Attack? Findings from the 2021 American Values Survey," November 1, 2021, Question 34a.

16. Public Religion Research Institute, "Understanding QAnon's Connection to American Politics, Religion, and Media Consumption," May 27, 2021.

17. Public Policy Polling, "Birthers Very Much a Rural Phenomenon," August 11, 2009.

18. Suzanne Mettler and Trevor Brown, "The Growing Rural-Urban Political Divide and Democratic Vulnerability," *Annals of the American Academy of Political and Social Science* 699, No. 1 (January 2022): 130–42.

19. Parker et al., "What Unites and Divides Urban, Suburban and Rural Communities," see Section 2.

20. Public Religion Research Institute, "Survey: Two-Thirds of White Evangelicals, Most Republicans Sympathetic to Christian Nationalism," February 8, 2023.

21. Maurice Chammah, "Does Your Sheriff Think He's More Powerful Than the President?" The Marshall Project, October 18, 2022.

22. Matthew D. Nelsen and Christopher D. Petsko, "Race and White Rural Consciousness," *American Political Science Review* 19, No. 4 (December 2021): 1205–18.

23. Robert A. Pape, "21 Million Americans Say Biden Is 'Illegitimate' and Trump Should Be Restored by Violence, Survey Finds," *The Conversation,* September 23, 2021.

24. Public Religion Research, "Competing Visions of America," Question 34d; cross tabs for place identity computed and provided to authors directly by PRRI's Natalie Jackson.

25. Ben Kamisar, "Attitudes on Jan. 6 Capitol Attack Settle in Along Familiar Partisan Lines," NBC News, August 24, 2021.

CHAPTER 2. RURAL RUIN

1. Calculated by authors, courtesy of data provided by Ballotpedia, "Election Results, 2020: Pivot Counties in the 2020 Presidential Election," see ballotpedia.org/Election _results,_2020:_Pivot_Counties_in_the_2020_presidential_election. The three counties with longer streaks are Clay, Minnesota; Blaine, Montana; and Clallam, Washington.

2. Details and quotes derived in this section are from separate interviews with Roy Holzer, Wilmington Town Hall, Wilmington, N.Y., March 22, 2023; and Shaun Gillilland, Willsboro Town Hall, Willsboro, N.Y., March 22, 2023.

3. Tim Henderson, "Shrinking Rural America Faces State Power Struggle," *Stateline,* August 10, 2021.

4. Elizabeth A. Dobis et al., "Rural America at a Glance, 2021 Edition," Economic Information Bulletin No. 230, Economic Research Service, U.S. Department of Agriculture, November 2021.

5. Paul Mackun, Joshua Comenetz, and Lindsay Spell, "Around Four-Fifths of All U.S. Metro Areas Grew Between 2010 and 2020," U.S. Census Bureau, August 12, 2021; and Economic Research Service, "Ag and Food Statistics: Charting the Essentials," U.S. Department of Agriculture, February 2020.

6. *Washington Post*/Kaiser Family Foundation Poll of Rural and Small-town America, Question 40.

7. Patrick J. Carr and Maria Kefalas, *Hollowing Out the Middle: The Rural Brain Drain and What It Means for America* (New York: Beacon Press, 2010).

8. Jessica D. Ulrich-Schad and Cynthia M. Duncan, "People and Places Left Behind: Work,

Culture, and Politics in the Rural United States," Conference Paper No. 64, ERPI 2018 International Conference on Authoritarian Populism and the Rural World, International Institute of Social Studies in The Hague, Netherlands, March 17–18, 2018, Table 2.

9. Gracy Olmstead, "How to Keep Young People from Fleeing Small Towns for Big Cities," *The Week,* August 6, 2018.

10. Mila Besich, interview with the authors, Superior, Arizona, November 7, 2022.

11. Shawna Claw, interview with the authors, Chinle, Arizona, November 8, 2022.

12. Navajo Nation Council, "Navajo Nation Unofficial Election Results, 2022: General Election," Tuesday, November 8, 2022.

13. Andrea Stewart, interview with the authors, Malone, N.Y., March 20, 2023.

14. Farmington population estimate based on decade population figure nearest to Manchin's birth year. "West Virginia Governor Cool to School Consolidation," *Education Week,* April 12, 2005.

15. Kristi Eaton, "Relocation Programs Continue to Grow in Numbers in Rural America," *Daily Yonder,* January 18, 2023.

16. Chris Morris, "West Virginia Is Close to Giving $25,000 to Ex-Residents to Move Back," *Fortune,* February 28, 2023.

17. Sarah Melotte, "Is Rural America Growing Again? Recent Data Suggests 'Yes,'" *Daily Yonder,* February 2, 2023.

18. Sarah Melotte, "Rural Counties with the Most Population Loss Voted the Most Democratic in 2020," *Daily Yonder,* September 20, 2022.

19. "The Megaphone of Main Street: The Small Business Rural/Urban Divide," SCORE, February 16, 2023.

20. Olugbenga Ajilore and Caius Z. Willingham, "The Path to Rural Resilience in America," Center for American Progress, September 21, 2020.

21. Eduardo Porter, "The Hard Truths of Trying to 'Save' the Rural Economy," *New York Times,* December 14, 2018.

22. Justin McCarthy, "U.S. Approval of Labor Unions at Highest Point Since 1965," Gallup, August 30, 2022.

23. Jazmin Orozco Rodriguez, "After a Brief Pandemic Reprieve, Rural Workers Return to Life Without Paid Leave," Kaiser Health News, January 18, 2023.

24. David B. Danbom, *Born in the Country: A History of Rural America* (Baltimore, Md.: Johns Hopkins University Press, 1995), 233.

25. Economic Research Service, "Inflation-Adjusted Price Indices for Corn, Wheat, and Soybeans Show Long-Term Declines," U.S. Department of Agriculture, April 23, 2019.

26. Ryan McCrimmon, "'Here's Your Check': Trump's Massive Payouts to Farmers Will Be Hard to Pull Back," Politico, July 14, 2020.

27. Claire Kelloway and Sarah Miller, "Food and Power: Addressing Monopolization in America's Food Systems," Open Markets Institute, March 2019.

28. Union of Concerned Scientists, "Bigger Farms, Bigger Problems," April 14, 2021.

29. Union of Concerned Scientists, "Bigger Farms, Bigger Problems"; Danbom, *Born in the Country,* 229. Danbom cites the current figure at 7 percent in his book, which was first published in 1995.

30. Kirk Kardashian, "Many of Vermont's Dairy Farms Have Shuttered, and the Forecast Is for Still Fewer—and Much Larger—Operations," *Seven Days,* May 31, 2023.

31. Isabel Soisson, "Rural Advocates Want to Take on Monopoly Power and Help Family Farmers," *Dogwood,* May 8, 2023.

32. As recently as 1997, Northampton ranked first in the state and thirteenth nationally in county-wide peanut production, but has since slipped to fifth overall in North Carolina. See files.nc.gov/ncdcr/nr/NP0516.pdf, p. 46, note 21, and www.nass.usda.gov/Statistics _by_State/North_Carolina/Publications/County_Estimates/Peanut.pdf.

33. Bob Allsbrook, interview with the authors, Aunt Ruby's Peanuts gift shop, Enfield, N.C., February 16, 2023.

34. Aditya Dasgupta and Elena Ruiz Ramirez, "Explaining Rural Conservatism: Political Consequences of Technological Change in the Great Plains," Working Paper, SocArXiv, December 30, 2020.

35. Curt Meine quoted in Dan Kaufman, "Is It Time to Break Up Big Ag?" *New Yorker*, August 17, 2021.

36. Lina Khan, "Obama's Game of Chicken," *Washington Monthly*, November 9, 2012.

37. Katherine Cramer, *The Politics of Resentment: Rural Consciousness in Wisconsin and the Rise of Scott Walker* (Chicago: University of Chicago Press, 2016).

38. U.S. Bureau of Labor Statistics, "All Employees, Coal Mining, CES1021210001," table, retrieved from FRED, Federal Reserve Bank of St. Louis, August 31, 2023.

39. Hillary Clinton quoted in Lauren Carroll, "In Context: Hillary Clinton's Comments About Coal Jobs," Politifact, May 10, 2016.

40. "Trump Receives Warm Welcome in Coal Country," video clip, *Washington Post*, May 6, 2016.

41. U.S. Bureau of Labor Statistics, "All Employees, Coal Mining, CES1021210001."

42. *Washington Post*/Kaiser Family Foundation Poll of Rural and Small-town America, Question 37.

43. Steven Beda, "The Divide Between Rural and Urban America, in 6 Charts," The Conversation, March 20, 2017.

44. Al Cross quoted in Frank Morris, "How Dollar General Is Transforming Rural America," NPR, December 11, 2017.

45. Chris McGreal, "Where Even Walmart Won't Go: How Dollar General Took Over Rural America," *Guardian*, August 13, 2018.

46. Aallyah Wright, "The Movement to Stop Dollar Stores from Suffocating Black Communities," Capital B News, May 17, 2023.

47. CDC Newsroom, "CDC: More Obesity in U.S. Rural Counties than in Urban Counties," press release, Centers for Disease Control and Prevention, June 14, 2018.

48. Michael Corkery, "Dollar General Is Deemed a 'Severe Violator' by the Labor Dept.," *New York Times*, March 28, 2023.

49. For an account of how the corporation overwhelms workers looking for nothing more than a little extra pay and humane treatment, see Greg Jaffe, "The Worker Revolt Comes to a Dollar General in Connecticut," *Washington Post*, December 11, 2021.

50. Michael Corkery, "As Dollar Stores Proliferate, Some Communities Say No," *New York Times*, March 1, 2023.

51. Michael Corkery, "Will a Dollar General Ruin a Rural Crossroads?" *New York Times*, June 2, 2023.

52. R. Rasker et al., "The Economic Importance of Air Travel in High-Amenity Rural Areas," *Journal of Rural Studies* 25 (2009): 343–53.

53. Aubrey Byron, "Getting from Here to There in Rural America," Strong Towns, November 1, 2018.

54. Tessa Conroy and Stephan Weiler, "Rural Americans Aren't Included in Inflation Figures. For Them, the Cost of Living May Be Rising," *Daily Yonder*, February 8, 2023.

55. Tom Peterson, "This Region Has the Fewest Electric Vehicles. Here's Why," *Stateline*, March 6, 2023.

56. Alan Morgan quoted in "The Power of Connection: Reversing Social Isolation in Rural America: Highlights and Key Findings of the 2018 Connectivity Summit on Rural Aging," Portland, Me., August 7 and 8, 2018.

57. "SBJ Unpacks: Lake Placid's $500 Million Makeover," *Sports Business Journal*, January 11, 2023; Aaron Cerbone, "SLK Gets $8.5M from State for Terminal Upgrade," *Adirondack Daily Enterprise*, September 19, 2022; "Governor Hochul Announces Completion of Saranac Lake Civic Center's Nearly $7 Million Upgrade," press release, Office of New York State Governor Kathy Hochul, January 5, 2023.

58. Gillilland interview, March 22, 2023.

59. Center for Business and Economic Research at Marshall University, *The Economic and Fiscal Impact of the Hatfield-McCoy Trail System in West Virginia—2021,* Final Report, prepared for Hatfield-McCoy Regional Recreation Authority, April 11, 2022.

60. Duncan Slade, "Less Money, Fewer Jobs: After Two Decades, WV's ATV Trails Have Fallen Far Short of Initial Projections," *Mountain State Spotlight,* August 24, 2021.

61. Larry DeBoer quoted in Brian Wallheimer, "Study: Rural-Urban Fiscal Divide Grows in Response to Decades of State Tax Overhauls," "Agriculture News" press release, Purdue University, July 15, 2020; Larry DeBoer, *Capacity-Cost Indexes for Indiana Local Governments 2002 and 2018,* report, Indiana Fiscal Policy Institute, June 2020.

62. Ajilore and Willingham, "The Path to Rural Resilience in America."

63. Headwaters Economics, "Fiscal Policy Is Failing Rural America: Understanding Barriers to Economic Development, Conservation, and Renewable Energy," Headwaters Economics, October 2020.

64. Besich interview with the authors.

65. U.S. Department of Agriculture, "Rural Development" homepage, "Programs & Services" tab, subtab listing for "All Programs," www.rd.usda.gov/programs-services/all-programs.

66. Anthony F. Pipa and Natalie Geismar, "Reimagining Rural Policy: Organizing Federal Assistance to Maximize Rural Prosperity," Brookings Institution, November 19, 2020.

67. Nick Hanauer, "Democrats Need to Fix Rural Economies—and Get the Credit for It," *American Prospect,* March 24, 2022.

68. Economic Research Service, "Federal Tax Policies and Low-Income Rural Households," ERS Report Summary, U.S. Department of Agriculture, May 2011.

69. Shreya Paul, Marisa Rafal, and Andrew J. Houtenville, "2021 Annual Disability Statistics Compendium: 2021," Section 10: Rural, University of New Hampshire's Institute on Disability, see Table 10.1; Terrence McCoy, "Did You Know in Rural America, Disability Benefit Rates Are Twice as High as in Urban Areas?," *Washington Post,* July 22, 2017.

70. Data on federal spending from the USDA's Economic Research Service can be found at www.ers.usda.gov/data-products/federal-funds.

71. Holly Taylor, "Courthouse Construction Set to Begin in Spring of 2022," *Roanoke-Chowan News Herald,* December 21, 2021.

72. American Hospital Association, "AHA Report: Rural Hospital Closures Threaten Patient Access to Care," AHA, September 8, 2022.

73. Dunc Williams, Jr., et al., "Rural Hospital Mergers Increased Between 2005 and 2016— What Did Those Hospitals Look Like?" *Journal of Health Care Organization, Provision, and Financing,* July 18, 2020, doi:10.1177/0046958020935666.

74. Liz Carey, "Experts: National Physician Shortage Will Hit Rural Areas Harder," *Daily Yonder,* March 13, 2023.

75. Liz Carey, "Under Half of Rural Hospitals Offer Labor and Delivery Services, Putting Rural Moms at Risk, Report Says," *Daily Yonder,* May 9, 2023.

76. H. Joanna Jiang et al., "Risk of Closure Among Independent and Multihospital-Affiliated Rural Hospitals," *JAMA Health Forum* 3, No. 7 (July 1, 2022).

77. Cecilia Nowell, "How to Kill a Rural Hospital," *Nation,* September 5–12, 2022.

78. Jeffrey H. Dorfman and Anne M. Mandich, "Senior Migration: Spatial Considerations of Amenity and Health Access Drivers," *Journal of Regional Science* 56, No. 1 (2016): 99–136.

79. The exact figures for median distance increases for general inpatient (from 3.4 to 23.9 miles) and emergency facilities (from 3.3 to 24.2) are not identical, but both round to about seven to one. Government Accountability Office, "Affected Residents Had Reduced Access to Health Care Services," Report GAO 21-93, GAO, December 2020.

80. Pooja Salhotra, "Texans Are Dying on State Highways Every Day—Especially in Rural 'Dead Zones,'" *Texas Tribune,* December 21, 2022.

81. Salako Abiodun, Fred Ullrich, and Keith J. Mueller, "Update: Independently Owned Phar-

macy Closures in Rural America, 2003–2018," Rural Policy Brief No. 2018-2, Iowa City: RUPRI Center for Rural Health Policy Analysis at the University of Iowa.

82. Salako Abiodun, Fred Ullrich, and Keith J. Mueller, "Issues Confronting Rural Pharmacies after a Decade of Medicare Part D," Rural Policy Brief No. 2017-3, Iowa City: RUPRI Center for Rural Health Policy Analysis at the University of Iowa.

83. Markian Hawryluk, "The Last Drugstore: Rural America Is Losing Its Pharmacies," *Washington Post,* November 10, 2021.

84. Hawryluk, "The Last Drugstore."

85. Kimberly Donahue, "Williamson Memorial Hospital to Reopen with $2 Million in Federal Funding," WCAZ News Channel 3, September 29, 2022.

86. Based on the authors' conversations with the pharmacy manager of the Jackson, North Carolina, branch of the Futrell Pharmacy chain, August 5, 2022.

87. Based on in-person conversation with Robin Humphreys, community health liaison for Baylor Scott and White, Llano, Texas, November 4, 2022.

88. Citizens Advocates website, "About Us" tab, citizenadvocates.net/about-us/.

89. Carolyn Y. Johnson, "Poll Shows Obamacare Started Looking a Lot Better After the Election," *Washington Post,* December 1, 2016.

90. Ezra Klein, "Racists Are Likelier to Oppose Health Reform When They Think About Obama," Vox, May 23, 2014.

91. For instance, one study found that "nativism was an independent and significant predictor of opposition to health care reform and that this effect held for both Republicans as well as Democrats, although the relationship is stronger for Republicans" (Benjamin R. Knoll and Jordan Shewmaker, " 'Simply Un-American': Nativism and Support for Health Care Reform," *Political Behavior* 37 [2015]: 87–108); another found that "racial attitudes had a significantly larger impact on health care opinions in the fall of 2009 than they had in cross-sectional surveys from the past two decades and in panel data collected before Obama became the face of the policy. Moreover, the experiments embedded in one of those re-interview surveys found healthcare policies were significantly more racialized when attributed to President Obama than they were when these same proposals were framed as President Clinton's 1993 reform efforts" (Michael Tesler, "The Spillover of Racialization into Healthcare: How President Obama Polarized Public Opinion by Racial Attitudes and Race," *American Journal of Political Science* 56 [2012]: 690–704).

92. David Mushinski, Alexandra Bernasek, and Stephan Weiler, "Job Lock in Rural Versus Urban Labor Markets," *Growth and Change: A Journal of Urban and Regional Policy* 46, No. 2 (2015): 253–73.

93. Jennifer Cheeseman Day, "Rates of Uninsured Fall in Rural Counties, Remain Higher than Urban Counties," U.S. Census Bureau, April 9, 2019; Gina Turrini et al., "Access to Affordable Care in Rural America: Current Trends and Key Challenges," Office of Health Policy, Department of Health and Human Services, July 9, 2021.

94. Turrini, "Access to Affordable Care in Rural America," see Table 1, p. 3.

95. "Transcript: Gov. Tate Reeves Delivers 2023 State of the State Address," *Mississippi Today,* January 30, 2023.

96. Kayode Crown, "As Mississippi Hospitals Fail, Leaders Kill Medicaid Expansion Efforts Again," *Mississippi Free Press,* February 2, 2023.

97. Liz Carey, "Nearly Half of All Rural Hospitals Are Operating in the Red," *Daily Yonder,* March 8, 2023.

98. Shannon M. Monnat, "The Contributions of Socioeconomic and Opioid Supply Factors to U.S. Drug Mortality Rates: Urban-Rural and Within-Rural Differences," *Journal of Rural Studies* 68 (2019): 319–35.

99. Sarah Jones, "Yes, Virginia, There Is a Crisis," *Democracy: A Journal of Ideas* 50 (Fall 2018): 78–84.

100. Lindsey Bever, "A Town of 3,200 Was Flooded with Nearly 21 Million Pain Pills as Addiction Crisis Worsened, Lawmakers Say," *Washington Post,* January 31, 2018.

101. Center for American Progress, "Gun Violence in Rural America," September 26, 2022.

102. Dan Frosch, Kris Maher, and Zusha Elinson, "Murder Rates Soar in Rural America," *Wall Street Journal*, June 19, 2022.

103. Colin Woodard, "The Surprising Geography of Gun Violence," *Politico Magazine*, April 23, 2023.

104. John Gramlich, "What the Data Says About Gun Deaths in the U.S.," Pew Research Center, February 3, 2022; T. H. Chan School of Public Health, "Lethality of Suicide Methods: Case Fatality Rates by Suicide Method, 8 U.S. States, 1989–1997," Harvard University, Cambridge, Mass.

105. For instance, according to data in the CDC's WONDER database, 89 percent of gun suicide victims in 2020 were White; the figure in 2019 was 91 percent.

106. Kim Parker et al., "The Demographics of Gun Ownership," Pew Research Center, June 22, 2017.

107. Data taken from the Census Bureau's state rankings based on rural population share, www .census.gov/newsroom/blogs/random-samplings/2016/12/life_off_the_highway.html; and Heather Saunders, "Do States with Easier Access to Guns Have More Suicide Deaths by Firearm?" Kaiser Family Foundation, July 18, 2022.

108. Turrini, "Access to Affordable Care in Rural America," 7–8.

109. Shelby Harris and Sarah Melotte, "'We Are Not Thought Of'—Lack of Maternal Care Threatens Health of Western N.C. Mothers," *Daily Yonder*, January 17, 2023.

110. Centers for Disease Control and Prevention, "Pregnancy Mortality Surveillance System," CDC, n.d.; and Peter T. Merkt et al., "Urban-Rural Differences in Pregnancy-Related Deaths, United States, 2011–2016," *American Journal of Obstetrics and Gynecology*, Vol. 225, Issue 2, August 2021.

111. Claire Suddath, "A Very Dangerous Place to Be Pregnant Is Getting Even Scarier," *Bloomberg Businessweek*, August 4, 2022.

112. Steven H. Woolf and Heidi Schoomaker, "Life Expectancy and Mortality Rates in the United States, 1959–2017," *Journal of the American Medical Association* 322, No. 20 (2019): 1996–2016.

113. Gina Kolata and Sabrina Tavernise, "It's Not Just Poor White People Driving a Decline in Life Expectancy," *New York Times*, November 26, 2019; Joel Achenbach, "'There's Something Terribly Wrong': Americans Are Dying Young at Alarming Rates," *Washington Post*, November 26, 2019.

114. Philip Bump, "Trump Praised West Virginia for Keeping Coronavirus Out. That's Not How This Works," *Washington Post*, March 17, 2020.

115. Ryan Saelee, Ph.D., et al, "Disparities in COVID-19 Vaccination Coverage Between Urban and Rural Counties—United States, December 14, 2020 to January 31, 2022," Centers for Disease Control and Prevention, *Morbidity and Mortality Weekly Report* 71, No. 9 (March 4, 2022): 335–40.

116. Daniel Wood and Geoff Brumfiel, "Pro-Trump Counties Now Have Far Higher COVID Death Rates: Misinformation Is to Blame," *Morning Edition*, NPR, December 5, 2021.

117. Michael Miller, "Third COVID-19 Wave Hit Rural America Especially Hard," UC News, University of Cincinnati, February 10, 2022.

118. Bradley Jones, "The Changing Political Geography of COVID-19 over the Last Two Years," Pew Research Center, March 3, 2022.

119. Monica Potts, "Why Being Anti-Science Is Now Part of Many Rural Americans' Identity," FiveThirtyEight, April 25, 2022.

120. Sarah Melotte, "Rural Covid-19 Deaths Drop for the Fourth Consecutive Week," *Daily Yonder*, October 20, 2022.

121. Rankings courtesy of the *New York Times* coronavirus tracker site, effective on May 30, 2023, www.nytimes.com/interactive/2021/us/covid-cases.html.

122. Michelle Samuels, "US Covid Deaths May Be Undercounted by 36 Percent," Boston University School of Public Health.

123. Abigail Abrams and Alana Abramson, "How the Biden Administration Plans to Convince Skeptical Republicans to Get Vaccinated," *Time,* April 21, 2021.
124. Kathleen J. Frydl, "The Oxy Electorate," *Medium,* November 16, 2016.
125. Will Wilkinson, "The Density Divide: Urbanization, Polarization and Populist Backlash," Niskanen Center, June 2019, p. 9, Figure 2.
126. Porter, "The Hard Truths of Trying to 'Save' the Rural Economy."

CHAPTER 3. THE GREATEST POLITICAL HAND EVER DEALT

1. Jimmy Carter, "The First Campaign: An Excerpt from Jimmy Carter's New Memoir, 'A Full Life,'" *Atlanta Magazine,* August 13, 2015.
2. Jimmy Carter, *Turning Point: A Candidate, a State, and a Nation Coming of Age* (New York: Crown, 1992), xxiv.
3. Emily Badger, "As American as Apple Pie? The Rural Vote's Disproportionate Slice of Power," *New York Times,* November 20, 2016.
4. United States Census Bureau, "2020 Population and Housing State Data," August 12, 2021.
5. Matthew Yglesias, "American Democracy's Senate Problem, Explained," Vox, December 17, 2019.
6. Nate Silver, "The Senate's Rural Skew Makes It Very Hard for Democrats to Win the Supreme Court," FiveThirtyEight, September 20, 2020. Note that the FiveThirtyEight piece uses a different measure of rurality than ours.
7. Yglesias, "American Democracy's Senate Problem, Explained."
8. Calculated by authors using the 2010 U.S. Census Bureau data and rankings for states based on urban/rural population shares: United States Census Bureau, "2010 Census Urban and Rural Classification and Urban Area Criteria," and United States Census Bureau, "Life Off the Highway: A Snapshot of Rural America."
9. Lee Drutman, "The Crisis of Senate Legitimacy," chap. 14 in Sean Theriault, ed., *Disruption: The Senate During the Trump Era* (New York: Oxford University Press, forthcoming).
10. These figures are based on 2022 Census population estimates. Because citizens of the District of Columbia are deprived of representation in Congress, we did not include its population in these totals.
11. Adam Liptak, "Smaller States Find Outsize Clout Growing in Senate," *New York Times,* March 11, 2013.
12. Hillary Rodham Clinton, "Give New York Its Fair Share of Homeland Money," *New York Times,* August 22, 2004.
13. Richard Johnson and Lisa L. Miller, "The Conservative Policy Bias of U.S. Senate Malapportionment," *PS: Political Science and Politics* 56, No. 1 (September 2022): 10–17.
14. The need for two amendments has been debated by constitutional legal scholars, but that debate is purely academic, given that neither the first nor the second amendment needed would ever receive the consent of the small states.
15. Amy Walter, "The Republican Electoral College Advantage," *The Cook Political Report,* July 22, 2022.
16. Technically, Trump received 304 electors in the final official count, but only because some electors refused to vote for him. But the total in the states he won on Election Night was the same 306 as Biden's was four years later in the states Biden carried.
17. Calculated by the authors using the 2010 U.S. Census Bureau data and rankings for states based on urban/rural population shares and members of Congress elected in 2020: United States Census, "2010 Census Urban and Rural Classification and Urban Area Criteria."
18. Trent England, "Rural Americans Would Be Serfs If We Abolished the Electoral College," op-ed, *USA Today,* May 23, 2019.
19. Murtaza Hussain, "Secret Donors to Nonprofit Pushing Trump's 'Big Lie' Election Conspiracy Revealed," The Intercept, August 7, 2021.

20. The Heritage Foundation's ebook can be found at thf_media.s3.amazonaws.com/2020/ Events/2020_08_0201_EssentialElectoralCollege_Ebook.pdf.

21. John Molinaro and Solveig Spjeldnes, "The Electoral College and the Rural-Urban Divide," Aspen Institute blog post, February 1, 2021.

22. Jim Inhofe, "Only 'Sore Losers' Want to Abolish Electoral College," *The Daily Signal,* April 26, 2021.

23. In his introduction to *Securing Democracy: Why We Have an Electoral College* (by Gary Gregg II of the Intercollegiate Studies Institute), a 2001 collection of essays meant to justify George W. Bush's win in 2000, McConnell writes, "One analysis even showed that Bush won areas with a landmass of more than 2.4 million square miles, while Gore garnered winning margins with a landmass of just over 580,000. The men who created the Electoral College would have well understood this situation."

24. Rebecca Salzer and Jocelyn Kiley, "Majority of Americans Continue to Favor Moving Away from Electoral College," Pew Research Center, August 5, 2022.

25. Salzer and Kiley, "Majority of Americans Continue to Favor Moving Away from Electoral College."

26. Jocelyn Kiley, "Majority of Americans Continue to Favor Moving Away from Electoral College," Pew Research Center report, September 25, 2023.

27. Philip Bump, "A Remarkable GOP Admission: Undermining the Electoral College Threatens Our Best Path to the White House," *Washington Post,* January 4, 2021; "Joint Statement Concerning January 6 Attempt to Overturn the Results of the Election," press release issued by Rep. Thomas Massie, January 3, 2021.

28. Elena Mejia and Amelia Thomson-DeVeaux, "How Biden Could Appoint More Judges than Trump," FiveThirtyEight, January 3, 2023.

29. *Reynolds v. Sims,* 377 U.S. 533 (1964).

30. "Obama to NYC Supporters: 'Move to North Dakota,'" Reuters, May 14, 2014.

31. Nathaniel Rakich and Dhrumil Mehta, "Trump Is Only Popular in Rural Areas," FiveThirtyEight, December 7, 2018.

32. "American Democracy's Built-in Bias Towards Rural Republicans," *The Economist,* July 12, 2018.

33. "American Democracy's Built-in Bias Towards Rural Republicans."

34. Geoffrey Skelley, "The Suburbs—All Kinds of Suburbs—Delivered the House to Democrats," FiveThirtyEight, November 8, 2018.

35. Demetrios Pogkas et al., "How Democrats Broke the House Map Republicans Drew," Bloomberg, November 10, 2018.

36. District summaries reported in "How the Suburbs Will Swing the Midterm Election," by Richard Florida and David Montgomery, Bloomberg, October 5, 2018; original CityLab spreadsheet available online here: github.com/theatlantic/citylab-data/blob/master/citylab -congress/citylab_cdi.csv.

37. Mettler and Brown, "The Growing Rural-Urban Political Divide and Democratic Vulnerability," 130–42.

38. Philip Bump and Lenny Bronner, "What the Urban-Rural Split in the 118th Congress Will Look Like," *Washington Post,* September 29, 2022.

39. Sean Trende, "In Pennsylvania, the Gerrymander of the Decade?" Real Clear Politics, December 14, 2011.

40. Joseph Ax, "Alabama to Ask US Supreme Court to Keep Republican-drawn Electoral Map," Reuters, September 5, 2023.

41. 595 U.S. ___ (2022), 21A375 John H. Merrill, *Alabama Secretary of State et al. v. Evan Milligan et al.,* initial decision issued by Justice Brett Kavanaugh to stay ruling on the case, February 7, 2022.

42. "Federal Court Strikes Down South Carolina Congressional District," Democracy Docket, January 6, 2023.

43. Richard L. Hasen quoted in Michael Wines, "Maps in Four States Were Ruled Illegal Ger-

rymanders. They're Being Used Anyway," *New York Times,* August 8, 2022; Nicholas Fandos, "Democrats Lose Control of N.Y. Election Maps, as Top Court Rejects Appeal," *New York Times,* April 27, 2022.

44. Domingo Garcia quoted in Michael Hardy, "The Reign of the 3%," *Texas Monthly,* November 22, p. 117.

45. Michael Li, interview with the authors, October 27, 2022.

46. Kandie Smith, interview with the authors, Greenville, N.C., February 17, 2023.

47. Shelly Willingham, interview with the authors, Tarboro, N.C., February 17, 2023.

48. Some estimates peg a different inflection decade for the switch from a rural majority to a minority, but here we rely upon the Census Bureau's use of 1920 as the inflection decade. See "Urban and Rural Areas," History, United States Census.

49. Frances Lee quoted in Badger, "As American as Apple Pie?"

50. Jonathan A. Rodden, *Why Cities Lose: The Deep Roots of the Urban-Rural Political Divide* (New York: Basic Books, 2019), 1–5.

51. Griff Palmer and Michael Cooper, "How Maps Helped Republicans Keep an Edge in the House," *New York Times,* December 14, 2012.

52. Robin Vos and Scott Fitzgerald quoted in Bruce Thompson, "Vos and Fitzgerald Trash Urban Voters," *Urban Milwaukee,* December 26, 2018.

53. Emily Badger, "Are Rural Voters the 'Real' Voters? Wisconsin Republicans Seem to Think So," *New York Times,* December 6, 2018.

54. Ben Wikler, interview with the authors, January 18, 2023.

55. Jane Mayer, "State Legislatures Are Torching Democracy," *New Yorker,* August 15, 2022.

56. David Pepper, *Laboratories of Autocracy: A Wake-Up Call from Behind the Lines* (Cincinnati: St. Helena Press, 2021), 173–82.

57. Gerald Gamm and Thad Kousser, "No Strength in Numbers: The Failure of Big-City Bills in American State Legislatures, 1880–2000," *American Political Science Review* 107, No. 4 (2013): 663–78; Gerald Gamm and Thad Kousser, "The Last Shall Be Last: Ethnic, Racial, and Nativist Bias in Distributive Politics," *Legislative Studies Quarterly,* January 30, 2023.

58. Patrick Flavin and Gregory Shufeldt, "Explaining State Preemption of Local Laws: Political, Institutional, and Demographic Factors," *Publius: The Journal of Federalism* 50, No. 2 (Spring 2020): 280–309.

59. Chloe Maxmin and Canyon Woodward, *Dirt Road Revival: How to Rebuild Rural Politics and Why Our Future Depends on It* (Boston: Beacon Press, 2022), 22–23.

60. Michael Li and Chris Leaverton, "Gerrymandering Competitive Districts to Near Extinction," Brennan Center for Justice, August 11, 2022.

61. Nolan McCarty, Keith T. Poole, and Howard Rosenthal, "Does Gerrymandering Cause Polarization?" *American Journal of Political Science* 53, No. 3 (2009): 666–80.

62. David Leonhardt, "'A Crisis Coming': The Twin Threats to American Democracy," *New York Times,* September 17, 2022.

63. Thomas F. Schaller, "Md. Secessionists: Have You Considered West Virginia?" *Baltimore Sun,* September 18, 2013; Mike Baker and Hilary Swift, "Oregon's Rural-Urban Divide Sparks Talk of Secession," *New York Times,* March 18, 2023; Colby Galliher and Edison Forman, "County Secession: Local Efforts to Redraw Political Borders," Brookings Institution, January 10, 2023.

64. Philip Bump, "The Ongoing Political Effort to Separate America's Cities from America," *Washington Post,* August 2, 2022.

65. Elaine Godfrey, "'Stop the Steal' Is a Metaphor," interview of Theda Skocpol, *Atlantic,* August 12, 2022.

66. Morning Consult poll, January 15–16, 2022, Table MCWA 14_4, p. 96. The rural percentage was computed by combining results for the exhaustive "rural under 45" and "rural 45+" subsets (350 / 1076 = 32.5 percent).

67. Melanie Lawson, "Texas Senate Votes to Allow Gov. Abbott to Overturn Harris County Elections," KTRK (ABC News 13, Houston), May 4, 2023.

68. Will Wilkinson, "The Density Divide: Urbanization, Polarization and Populist Backlash," report, Niskanen Center, June 2019, p. 77.

CHAPTER 4. CULTURES AT WAR

1. Letter from Thomas Jefferson to John Jay, August 13, 1785. It may be found at founders .archives.gov/documents/Jefferson/01-08-02-0333.
2. Mark Leibovich, "Palin Visits a 'Pro-America' Kind of Town," *New York Times*, October 17, 2008.
3. Or, as one pair of researchers put it, "Rural America is sometimes viewed as a kind of safety deposit box that stores America's fundamental values." Daniel T. Lichter and David L. Brown, "Rural America in an Urban Society: Changing Spatial and Social Boundaries," *Annual Review of Sociology* 37 (2011): 565–92.
4. See Mark Shucksmith, "Re-imagining the Rural: from Rural Idyll to Good Countryside," *Journal of Rural Studies* 59 (April 2018).
5. David B. Danbom, *Born in the Country: A History of Rural America* (Baltimore, Md.: Johns Hopkins University Press, 2017).
6. James C. Davis et al., "Rural America at a Glance," USDA Economic Research Service, November 2022.
7. This ad can be seen at youtu.be/2Kft22BHIak.
8. Andrew Wendler and Austin Irwin, "Ford's F-Series Pickup Truck History, from the Model TT to Today," *Car and Driver*, September 24, 2022.
9. The 1920 Census reported that the farm population was nearly 32 million, or 30 percent of the population of 105 million.
10. Brett Berk, "You Don't Need a Full-Size Pickup Truck, You Need a Cowboy Costume," The Drive, March 15, 2019.
11. Mark Metzler Sawin, interview with the authors, October 19, 2022.
12. Though it sounds like a joke, the supposed power of testicle tanning to restore one's manhood is indeed a topic of discussion in a documentary Carlson created in 2022 called *The End of Men*, on Fox Nation.
13. Greg Sargent, "As Vile as It Gets: J.D. Vance Goes Full 'Great Replacement Theory,'" *Washington Post*, April 6, 2022.
14. J. D. Vance, *Hillbilly Elegy: A Memoir of a Family and a Culture in Crisis* (New York: HarperCollins, 2016), 57.
15. Vance quoted in Jim Hoft, "Ohio Senate Candidate J. D. Vance Talks Biden's Ministry of Truth, J6 Prisoners, Ukraine War Cries, Mitch McConnell, and Trump's Endorsement with Gateway Pundit," GatewayPundit, April 29, 2022.
16. Vance writes, "She'd begun taking prescription narcotics not long after we moved to Preble County. I believe the problem started with a legitimate prescription, but soon enough, Mom was stealing from her patients and getting so high that turning an emergency room into a skating rink seemed like a good idea. Papaw's death turned a semi-functioning addict into a woman unable to follow the basic norms of adult behavior" (*Hillbilly Elegy*, 113).
17. Ryan Lizza and Rachael Bade, "POLITICO Playbook: The Book J. D. Vance Doesn't Want You to Read," Politico, May 5, 2022.
18. For proof of who really deserves blame for the opioid crisis, look no further than who was forced by the courts to pay settlement monies to West Virginia, the state that suffered more than any other from the opioid crisis. In May 2023, the sum of those settlements surpassed a whopping $1 billion. In addition to money from Purdue's bankruptcy settlement, those who have to pony up include pharmaceutical companies Allergan, Janssen, Johnson and Johnson, and Teva; opioid distributors Cardinal Health, AmeriSourceBergen, and McKesson; plus major pharmacy retailers Walmart, Kroger, CVS, Walgreens, and Rite Aid. In other words, the drugs that unleashed incalculable misery and death upon rural America were made, distributed, and sold by U.S. companies operating within our nation's borders.

Somebody should alert Vance—who won his Senate seat in 2022 on the strength of big margins in Ohio's rural White counties—that not a single Mexican entity or immigrant made the list.

19. McKay Coppins, "What Mitt Romney Saw in the Senate," *The Atlantic,* September 13, 2023.

20. Thomas Frank, *What's the Matter with Kansas? How Conservatives Won the Heart of America* (New York: Picador, 2005).

21. Parker et al., "What Unites and Divides Urban, Rural, and Suburban Communities."

22. Lydia Saad, "Country Living Enjoys Renewed Appeal in U.S.," Gallup, January 5, 2021.

23. Kim Parker, Juliana Menasce Horowitz, and Rachel Minkin, "Americans Are Less Likely than Before COVID-19 to Want to Live in Cities, More Likely to Prefer Suburbs," Pew Research Center, December 16, 2021.

24. Nancy Isenberg, *White Trash: The 400-Year Untold History of Class in America* (New York: Viking, 2016), 135.

25. There are moments when Hollywood has turned a more empathetic gaze on the country. For instance, at the 1985 Academy Awards, Sally Field won the Best Actress trophy for her role in *Places in the Heart,* the story of a woman bravely struggling to hold on to her farm and her family in the face of hard times. Among those whom Field beat out were Jessica Lange, nominated for her role in *Country,* the story of a woman bravely struggling to hold on to her farm and her family in the face of hard times; and Sissy Spacek, nominated for her role in *The River,* in which she plays a woman bravely struggling to hold on to her farm and her family in the face of hard times.

26. You can see these tropes in movies like *Doc Hollywood* and TV shows such as *Northern Exposure.*

27. There is, however, an irony in how small towns are portrayed in these movies. As Dylan Reid noted in the Canadian urbanist magazine *Spacing,* they're almost urban. "The towns portrayed in these Christmas movies possess the walkability, active public spaces, and low motor vehicle presence that urbanists strive for. They have thriving, walkable main streets full of independent retail shops tightly packed together. Every building faces on to the street, and everyone strolls along the sidewalks and interacts with each other in person." In the small towns of these movies, there isn't a dollar store or a fast-food joint—staples of the real rural America—in sight. (Dylan Reid, "The Secret Small-Town Urbanism of TV Christmas Movies," *Spacing,* December 17, 2019.)

28. Anthony Nadler, "Political Identity and the Therapeutic Work of U.S. Conservative Media," *International Journal of Communication* 16 (2022): 2622.

29. Annie Gowan, "Censorship Battles' New Frontier: Your Public Library," *Washington Post,* April 17, 2022.

30. Interview with the authors, November 3, 2022.

31. Paul Waldman and Greg Sargent, "A Rural Texas County Just Blinked on Library Closures. Pressure Worked," *Washington Post,* April 14, 2023. The commission decided that day not to shutter the libraries; when we finished this book, the lawsuit was ongoing.

32. PEN America, "Banned in the USA: The Growing Movement to Censor Books in Schools," September 19, 2022.

33. American Library Association, "American Library Association Reports Record Number of Demands to Censor Library Books and Materials in 2022," news release, March 22, 2023.

34. Teresa Moss, "Fund Cut Passes for Craighead County Libraries," *Northwest Arkansas Democrat-Gazette,* November 9, 2022.

35. Brooke Leigh Howard, "Tennessee Library Director Quits After Furor over LGBT+ Books," *Daily Beast,* October 28, 2022.

36. Molly Bolan, "A Library Struck by Controversy that Began Over a Book It Didn't Own," *Route Fifty,* September 1, 2022.

37. Danielle Paquette, "A Mich. Library Refused to Remove an LGBTQ Book. The Town Defunded It," *Washington Post,* August 24, 2022.

38. Kathy Zappitello, interview with the authors, November 30, 2022.

39. "Newspapers Fact Sheet," Pew Research Center, June 29, 2021.
40. Penny Abernathy, "The State of Local News: The 2022 Report," *Northwestern/Medill Local News Initiative,* June 29, 2022.
41. Nancy Gibbs, "Newspapers Are Disappearing Where Democracy Needs Them Most," *Washington Post,* December 27, 2022.
42. Danny Hayes and Jennifer L. Lawless, "The Decline of Local News and Its Effects: New Evidence from Longitudinal Data," *Journal of Politics* 80, No. 1 (January 2018).
43. Paul Fanlund, "Diving Deep into Wisconsin's 'Media Ecology,'" *Capital Times,* June 15, 2018.
44. Scott Ellison, "God and Man at a Southern Appalachian Community College: Cognitive Dissonance and the Cultural Logics of Conservative News Talk Radio Programming," *Review of Education, Pedagogy, and Cultural Studies* 36, No. 2 (2014): 90–108.
45. Tim Sullivan, "No Longer the Fringe: Small-Town Voters Fear for America," Associated Press, November 30, 2022.
46. Tina Sfondeles, "High-rise in a 'Hellhole'? Republican Bailey Living on North Michigan Avenue to 'Immerse' Himself in the City He Keeps Dissing," *Chicago Sun-Times,* September 13, 2022.
47. Presidential debate, September 26, 2016.
48. Tyler Monroe and Rob Savillo, "Fox's Coverage of Violent Crime Dropped After the Midterms," Media Matters for America, November 17, 2022.
49. *All Things Considered,* October 20, 2022.
50. Dan Frosch, Kris Maher, and Zusha Elinson, "Rural America Reels from Violent Crime. 'People Lost Their Ever-Lovin' Minds,'" *Wall Street Journal,* June 10, 2022. This was one of the few stories about the rural crime wave that appeared in mainstream news outlets.
51. "We Fact-checked the Oklahoma Governor's Debate Between Kevin Stitt and Joy Hofmeister," *The Frontier,* October 21, 2022.
52. Blake Masters quoted in Matt Stieb, "Blake Masters Has a Lot of Thoughts About Black People," *New York Magazine,* August 30, 2022.
53. *The Ingraham Angle,* Fox News, April 1, 2022.
54. Mayhill Fowler, "Obama Exclusive (Audio): On V.P. and Foreign Policy, Courting the Working Class, and Hard-Pressed Pennsylvanians," *Huffington Post,* April 19, 2008.
55. Ronald Inglehart, *The Silent Revolution: Changing Values and Political Styles Among Western Publics* (Princeton, N.J.: Princeton University Press, 1977).
56. For more on this, see Will Wilkinson, "The Density Divide and the Southernification of Rural America," Model Citizen, Substack.com, August 30, 2021; for a discussion of the flag's presence in Vermont, one of the bluest and northernmost states, see Emily Corwin, "Why Do Some Vermonters Display the Confederate Flag?" Vermont Public Radio, July 17, 2020.
57. W.E.B. Du Bois, *Black Reconstruction: An Essay Toward a History of the Part Which Black Folk Played in the Attempt to Reconstruct Democracy in America, 1860–1880* (New York: Harcourt, Brace and Company, 1935), 700–701.

CHAPTER 5. THE UNLIKELY KING OF RURAL AMERICA

1. Amanda Emery, "Man Mows 58,000-Square-Foot 'TRUMP' Sign into Lawn to Show Support," MLive.com, September 28, 2016.
2. Doug Koehn quoted in Marc Ramirez, "Rancher Plows Mile-Long Tribute to Donald Trump on His Colorado Land," *Dallas Morning News,* February 5, 2017.
3. A series of reforms both parties instituted after the 1968 election transformed the nominating process, taking it out of the smoke-filled back rooms and into the hands of voters. This elevated the importance of the Iowa caucuses and the New Hampshire primary, providing the winners essential momentum that translated into news coverage, contributions, and future victories.

4. Sam Frizell, "Hillary Clinton Calls for Greater Investment in Rural America," *Time*, August 26, 2015.
5. Dee Davis quoted in Helena Bottemiller Evich, "Revenge of the Rural Voter," Politico, November 13, 2016.
6. *With All Due Respect*, aired August 26, 2015, on Bloomberg TV.
7. Rove advised Crossroads GPS, the Koch-funded organization, to invest eight hundred thousand dollars in Stefanik's campaign. Kenneth P. Vogel, "Karl Rove and the Modern Money Machine," *Politico Magazine*, July/August 2014.
8. Griff Witte, "A Moderate Congresswoman Went All-in for Trump. Her Constituents Think They Know Why," *Washington Post*, December 13, 2019.
9. Ryan Bort, "High-Ranking Republican Pushes 'Great Replacement' Rhetoric Two Days After White Supremacist Mass Shooting," *Rolling Stone*, May 16, 2022.
10. Karen Edwards, interview with the authors, Harrietstown Town Hall, Saranac Lake, March 21, 2023.
11. Bernadette Hogan and Jesse O'Neill, "Trump Says Rep. Elise Stefanik Could Be President in 2028 at Palm Beach Fundraiser," *New York Post*, January 12, 2022.
12. Ta-Nehisi Coates, "The First White President," *The Atlantic*, October 2017.
13. We tallied these results based on the census's "Urban-Rural Continuum Codes," which are revised every ten years. Because the 2023 revision was released too late to be included in our analysis, we used the 2013 codes.
14. The ad, which was created by the Democratic PAC Priorities USA, can be seen at youtu.be/oLooJwjo3JU.
15. Charles Mahtesian, "Rural Turnout Plummets in 2012," *Politico*, November 30, 2012.
16. Charles Mahtesian, "How the Felon Won," *Politico*, May 9, 2012.
17. The only exceptions were Beaver County, Oklahoma, where Trump got 1,993 votes in 2016 and 1,968 votes in 2020; and Martin County, Kentucky, where he got 3,503 votes in 2016 and 3,496 votes in 2020.
18. Don Albrecht, "Rural/Urban Differences: Persistence or Decline," *Rural Sociology* 87, No. 4 (May 2022): 1137–54.
19. On one of the many occasions in which he extolled his own intelligence, Trump said in response to a question about which foreign policy advisers he relied on, "I'm speaking with myself, number one, because I have a very good brain and I've said a lot of things" (*Morning Joe*, aired March 16, 2016, on MSNBC).
20. One characteristic passage: In his 2015 speech honoring the fiftieth anniversary of Bloody Sunday in Selma, Alabama, Obama said, "What greater form of patriotism is there than the belief that America is not yet finished, that we are strong enough to be self-critical, that each successive generation can look upon our imperfections and decide that it is in our power to remake this nation to more closely align with our highest ideals?"
21. Corey Robin, *The Reactionary Mind: Conservatism from Edmund Burke to Sarah Palin* (New York: Oxford University Press, 2011), 4.
22. "'This Deal Will Make Me Look Terrible': Full Transcripts of Trump's Calls with Mexico and Australia," *Washington Post*, August 3, 2017.
23. Diana Mutz, "Status Threat, Not Economic Hardship, Explains the 2016 Presidential Vote," *PNAS* 115, No. 19 (2018): 4330–39.
24. Kristin Lunz Trujillo and Zack Crowley, "Symbolic Versus Material Concerns of Rural Consciousness in the United States," *Political Geography* 96 (June 2022).
25. Shannon M. Monnat and David L. Brown, "More than a Rural Revolt: Landscapes of Despair and the 2016 Presidential Election," *Journal of Rural Studies* 55 (October 2017): 227–36.
26. Ann Oberhauser, Dan Krier, and Abdi Kusow, "Political Moderation and Polarization in the Heartland: Economics, Rurality, and Social Identity in the 2016 U.S. Presidential Election," *Sociological Quarterly* 60, No. 4 (2019): 1–21.
27. Lilliana Mason, Julie Wronski, and John V. Kane, "Activating Animus: The Uniquely Social Roots of Trump Support," *American Political Science Review* 115, No. 4 (2021): 1–9.

28. John Sides, Michael Tesler, and Lynn Vavreck, *Identity Crisis: The 2016 Presidential Campaign and the Battle for the Meaning of America* (Princeton, N.J.: Princeton University Press, 2018), 71.

29. According to polls conducted by Sides, Tesler, and Vavreck, 39 percent of White Obama voters in 2012 disagreed with the statement "Generations of slavery and discrimination have created conditions that make it difficult for blacks to work their way out of the lower class," and 28 percent agreed with the statement "It's really a matter of some people not trying hard enough. If blacks would only try harder they could be just as well off as whites." Sides, Tesler, and Vavreck, *Identity Crisis,* 166.

30. See Lucy Madison, "Romney on Immigration: I'm for 'Self-deportation,'" CBS News, January 24, 2012.

31. Trump quoted in Salvador Hernandez, "Trump Escalates Attack on American-Born Judge: 'He's a Mexican,'" BuzzFeed, June 3, 2016.

32. Jeremy Diamond, "Trump on Protester: 'Maybe He Should Have Been Roughed Up,'" CNN, November 23, 2015.

33. Sam Reisman, "Trump Tells Crowd to 'Knock the Crap Out' of Protesters, Offers to Pay Legal Fees," Mediaite, February 1, 2016.

34. Nicholas Valentino and Fabian Guy Neuner, "The Changing Norms of Racial Political Rhetoric and the End of Racial Priming," *Journal of Politics* 80, No. 3 (November 2016): 757–71.

35. Helena Bottemiller Evich, "Revenge of the Rural Voter," Politico, November 13, 2016.

36. Kristin Lunz Trujillo, "Rural Identity as a Contributing Factor to Anti-Intellectualism in the U.S.," *Political Behavior* 44 (2022).

37. Trump rally in Charleston, West Virginia, August 21, 2018.

38. Matt Grossman and Daniel Thaler, "Mass-Elite Divides in Aversion to Social Change and Support for Donald Trump," *American Politics Research* 46, No. 5 (September 2018): 753–84.

39. Anonymous Hillary Clinton supporter quoted in Emily Van Duyn, "Hidden Democracy: Political Dissent in Rural America," *Journal of Communication* 68 (2018): 965–87.

40. Kandie Smith, interview with the authors, Greenville, N.C., February 17, 2023.

41. Geneva Riddick-Faulkner, interview with the authors, Jackson, N.C., February 17, 2023.

42. *Time* Staff, "President Trump at U.S. Coast Guard Commencement: 'Adversity Makes You Stronger,'" *Time,* May 17, 2017.

43. Trump's November 15, 2022, quote in Maggie Haberman @maggieNYT, "I'm a victim, I will tell you, I'm a victim," Trump says, Twitter, November 16, 2022.

44. Miles T. Armaly and Adam M. Enders, "'Why Me?' The Role of Perceived Victimhood in American Politics," *Political Behavior* 44 (2022): 1583–609.

45. Niraj Chokshi, "The 100-Plus Times Donald Trump Assured Us that America Is a Laughingstock," *Washington Post,* January 27, 2016.

46. See Richard E. Nisbett and Dov Cohen, *Culture of Honor: The Psychology of Violence in the South* (Boulder, Colo.: Westview Press, 1996).

47. Matthew R. Lee and Graham Ousey, "Reconsidering the Culture and Violence Connection: Strategies of Action in the Rural South," *Journal of Interpersonal Violence* 26, No. 5 (May 2010): 899–929.

48. Donald Trump and Bill Zanker, *Think Big and Kick Ass in Business and Life* (New York: Harper Business, 2011), 197–98.

49. "Whereas Trump's sensitivity to slights in college-educated Democratic communities is regarded as a sign of a thin skin and possibly a disordered mind, that same sensitivity is regarded as normal—even admirable—in the Democratic communities we studied," they wrote. Stephanie Muravchik and Jon A. Shields, *Trump's Democrats* (Washington, D.C.: Brookings Institution Press, 2020), 8.

50. Though teen parenthood has steadily fallen in the United States for years, the gap between rural and urban teens has remained steady. See Brady E. Hamilton, Ph.D.; Lauren M. Ros-

sen, Ph.D.; and Amy M. Branum, Ph.D., "Teen Birth Rates for Urban and Rural Areas in the United States, 2007–2015," NCHS *Data Brief,* No. 264, National Center for Biotechnology Information, November 2016, 1–8.

51. Maggie Astor, "Colorado County Clerk Indicted in Voting Security Breach Investigation," *New York Times,* March 9, 2022.
52. Emma Brown and Amy Gardner, "Georgia County Under Scrutiny After Claim of Post-Election Breach," *Washington Post,* May 13, 2022.
53. Sam Metz, "Election Conspiracies Grip Nevada Community, Sowing Distrust," Associated Press, July 29, 2022.
54. Richard Hasen, interview with the authors via email, October 31, 2022.
55. Speech in Delaware, Ohio, April 23, 2022.
56. Speech at the Conservative Political Action Conference, Gaylord National Resort and Convention Center, National Harbor, Md., March 4, 2023.

CHAPTER 6. CONDITIONAL PATRIOTS

1. Quotes spliced together from FBI recordings, as reported in Mike Levine, "Becoming a Domestic Terrorist: How 3 Self-Styled 'Patriots' Were Led to Lethal Plot," ABC News, November 1, 2021; Frank Morris, "Mosque Bombing Plot Rattles Immigrants in Kansas' 'Meat Triangle,'" NPR, March 20, 2018; and Jessica Pressler and Benjamin Rasmussen, "The Plot to Bomb Garden City, Kansas," *New York Magazine,* December 2017.
2. "Patrick Eugene Stein," bio, Extremist Leaders, Counter Extremism Project, n.d.
3. "Sovereign citizen movement entry," Southern Poverty Law Center, n.d.
4. *The Informant: Fear and Faith in the Heartland,* ABC News documentary series, hosted by George Stephanopoulos (Hulu, 2021).
5. Robert O'Harrow, Jr., Andrew Ba Tran, and Derek Hawkins, "The Rise of Domestic Extremism in America," *Washington Post,* April 12, 2021.
6. Betsy Woodruff Swan, "DHS Draft Document: White Supremacists Are Greatest Terror Threat," Politico, September 4, 2020; Matt Zapotosky, "Wray Says FBI Has Recorded About 100 Domestic Terrorism Arrests in Fiscal 2019 and Many Investigations Involve White Supremacy," *Washington Post,* July 23, 2019.
7. 18 USC Chapter 113B: TERRORISM, uscode.house.gov/view.xhtml?path=/prelim @title18/part1/chapter113B&edition=prelim.
8. Jose A. DelReal and Scott Clement, "Rural Divide," *Washington Post,* June 17, 2017; "*Washington Post*/Kaiser Family Foundation Rural and Small-Town America Poll," conducted April 13–May 1, 2017.
9. B. Kal Munis, "Us Over Here Versus Them Over There . . . Literally: Measuring Place Resentment in American Politics," *Political Behavior* 44, No. 3 (2022): 1057–78.
10. B. Kal Munis and Nicholas Jacobs, "Place-Based Resentment in Contemporary U.S. Elections: The Individual Sources of America's Urban-Rural Divide," *Political Research Quarterly* 76, No. 3 (2022): 1102–18.
11. Kal Munis and Nicholas Jacobs, "Why Resentful Rural Americans Vote Republican," *Washington Post,* October 20, 2022.
12. Mark Murray, "Trump, Clinton Voters Divided Over a Changing America," NBC News, www.nbcnews.com/politics/first-read/trump-clinton-voters-divided-over-changing -america-n798926.
13. Parker et al., "What Unites and Divides Urban, Suburban and Rural Communities," Section 5, p. 62 ("only 46 percent") and Section 2, p. 30 ("white Americans benefit").
14. "Fear of Muslims in American Society Chapman University Survey of American Fears," poll, Chapman University, released October 16, 2018.
15. Parker et al., "What Unites and Divides Urban, Suburban and Rural Communities."
16. Trevor Brown, Suzanne Mettler, and Samantha Puzzi, "When Rural and Urban Become

'Us' versus 'Them': How a Growing Divide Is Reshaping American Politics," *The Forum* 19, No. 3 (2021): 365–93.

17. "LGBTQ Youth in Small Towns and Rural Areas," *Research Brief,* The Trevor Project, November 2021.

18. Brown, Mettler, and Puzzi, "When Rural and Urban Become 'Us' versus 'Them,'" Figure 2.

19. Lisa R. Pruitt, "What Republicans Know (and Democrats Don't) About the White Working Class," Politico, June 26, 2022.

20. Robert Wuthnow quoted in Sean Illing, "A Princeton Sociologist Spent 8 Years Asking Rural Americans Why They're So Pissed Off," Vox, June 30, 2018.

21. Katherine Cramer, *The Politics of Resentment: Rural Consciousness in Wisconsin and the Rise of Scott Walker* (Chicago: University of Chicago Press, 2016), 85.

22. Katherine Cramer, interview with the authors, January 10, 2023.

23. Matthew D. Nelsen and Christopher D. Petsko, "Race and White Rural Consciousness," *American Political Science Review* 19, No. 4 (December 2021): 1205–18.

24. Rural Objective PAC Battleground Poll conducted by YouGov Blue, April 29–May 13, 2021.

25. *Washington Post*/Kaiser Family Foundation Rural and Small-Town America poll.

26. Parker et al., "What Unites and Divides Urban, Suburban and Rural Communities."

27. Llano County Tea Party meeting, VFW Post 370, Llano, Texas, November 3, 2022.

28. Public Religion Research Institute, "Competing Visions of America."

29. Katherine Fennelly and Christopher Federico, "Rural Residence as a Determinant of Attitudes Toward U.S. Immigration Policy," *International Migration* 46 (2008): 151–90, see Table 1.

30. Boris Podobnik, Marko Jusup, and H. Eugene Stanley, "Predicting the Rise of Right-wing Populism in Response to Unbalanced Immigration," *Physics and Society,* December 4, 2016.

31. Taylor Orth, "From Millionaires to Muslims, Small Subgroups of the Population Seem Much Larger to Many Americans," YouGov.com, March 15, 2022; and "Perils of Perception: A 40-Country Study," poll and slide deck, Game Changers/Ipsos, 2016.

32. Ashley Jardina, *White Identity Politics* (New York: Cambridge University Press, 2019), 273.

33. Although the share of non-White members of Congress is rising, only 26 percent of U.S. House members and 11 percent of senators of the 117th Congress elected in 2020 were non-White: Katherine Schaeffer, "The Changing Face of Congress in 8 Charts," Pew Research Center, February 7, 2023; in state legislatures, not a single state in 2021 had a share of minority state legislators higher than the statewide minority population percentage: Renuka Rayasam et al., "Why State Legislatures Are Still Very White—and Very Male," Politico, February 23, 2021.

34. Dana Wilkie, "How DE&I Evolved in the C-Suite," Society for Human Resource Management, n.d.

35. Jardina, *White Identity Politics,* 273–74.

36. *Washington Post*/Kaiser Family Foundation Rural and Small-town America poll, Question 2.

37. *Washington Post*/Kaiser Family Foundation Rural and Small-town America poll, Question 70.

38. Dante Chinni, "What Your Travel May Say About Your Politics," NBC News, September 7, 2015; Richard Florida, "America's Great Passport Divide," *Atlantic,* March 15, 2011.

39. Ian Mackey quoted in "Gay Missouri Lawmaker Confronts Colleague: 'Gentlemen, I Am Not Afraid of You Anymore,'" CNN, April 15, 2022; Hickory County statistics drawn from U.S. Census Bureau's 2020 "Quick Facts" website.

40. Will Wilkinson, "The Density Divide: Urbanization, Polarization and Populist Backlash," report, Niskanen Center, June 2019.

41. Ezra Klein, *Why We're Polarized* (New York: Avid Reader Press/Simon & Schuster, 2020).

42. Lilliana Mason, Julie Wronski, and John V. Kane, "Activating Animus: The Uniquely Social

Roots of Trump Support," *American Political Science Review* 115, No. 4 (November 2021): 1508–16.

43. Masha Gessen, *Surviving Autocracy* (New York: Riverhead Books, 2020), 218.

44. Adam Goldman, "The Comet Ping Pong Gunman Answers Our Reporter's Questions," *New York Times,* December 7, 2016; Keith L. Alexander and Susan Svrluga, "'I Am Sure He Is Sorry for Any Heartaches He Has Caused,' Mother of Alleged 'Pizzagate' Gunman Says," *Washington Post,* December 13, 2016; Michael E. Miller, "Pizzagate's Violent Legacy," *Washington Post,* February 16, 2021.

45. Department of Justice, "North Carolina Man Sentenced to Four-Year Prison Term for Armed Assault at Northwest Washington Pizza Restaurant," press release, United States Attorney's Office, District of Columbia, June 22, 2017.

46. Adam Enders et al., "Are Republicans and Conservatives More Likely to Believe Conspiracy Theories?" *Political Behavior* (2022), 1–24.

47. Karen M. Douglas et al., "Understanding Conspiracy Theories," *Advances in Political Psychology* 40 (2019): 3–35; Joseph E. Uscinski and Joseph M. Parent, *American Conspiracy Theories* (New York: Oxford University Press, 2014); Greg Miller, "The Enduring Allure of Conspiracies," *Knowable Magazine,* January 14, 2021; Joseph E. Uscinski et al., "The Psychological and Political Correlates of Conspiracy Theory Beliefs," *Scientific Reports* 12, No. 21672 (2022).

48. Public Religion Research Institute, "Understanding QAnon's Connection to American Politics, Religion, and Media Consumption."

49. Public Religion Research Institute, "Understanding Qanon's Connection to American Politics, Religion, and Media Consumption."

50. Ipsos, "More than 1 in 3 Americans Believe a 'Deep State' Is Working to Undermine Trump," poll, Ipsos, December 30, 2020. Summary quote excerpted from Christopher T. Conner and Nicholas MacMurray, "The Perfect Storm: A Subcultural Analysis of the QAnon Movement," *Critical Sociology* 48, No. 6 (2022): 1049–71.

51. Robert Jones quoted in Giovanni Russonello, "QAnon Now as Popular in U.S. as Some Major Religions, Poll Suggests," *New York Times,* May 27, 2021.

52. Trujillo, "Rural Identity as a Contributing Factor to Anti-Intellectualism in the U.S."

53. Public Religion Research Institute, "Competing Visions of America," Question 34a. The breakout was 26 percent "completely" and 21 percent "mostly."

54. Josh Dawsey, "A Second Firm Hired by Trump Campaign Found No Evidence of Election Fraud," *Washington Post,* April 27, 2023.

55. Alexandra Hutzler, "Experts Say Trump, Election Deniers Eroding Trust in Democracy. Can It Be Restored?" *ABC News,* October 7, 2022.

56. Katie Harbath et al., "New Survey Data on Who Americans Look to for Election Information," Bipartisan Policy Center, November 2, 2022.

57. Institute of Politics (IOP), National Online Study No. 220265, University of Chicago, May 19–23, 2022, Table 15-2, Banner 2, p. 86 of cross tabs provided by IOP directly to authors, PDF available upon request. See also IOP's public release, "Our Precarious Democracy: Extreme Polarization and Alienation in Our Politics," n.d. (hereafter cited as: IOP National Online Study No. 220265).

58. District geography statistics calculated by authors using the roll call list of the 139 House Republicans and CityLab's district ratings. The other 36 House GOP districts broke down as follows: 20 "sparsely suburban"; 13 "densely suburban"; 2 "urban-suburban"; and 1 "purely urban." github.com/theatlantic/citylab-data/blob/master/citylab-congress/citylab_cdi.csv.

59. Steve Eder, David D. Kirkpatrick, and Mike McIntire, "They Legitimized the Myth of a Stolen Election—and Reaped the Rewards," *New York Times,* October 3, 2022.

60. Amy Gardner, "A Majority of GOP Nominees—299 in All—Deny the 2020 Election Results," *Washington Post,* October 6, 2022.

61. Theda Skocpol quoted in Godfrey, "'Stop the Steal' Is a Metaphor."

62. Philip Klinkner, "The Causes and Consequences of 'Birtherism,'" paper presented at the 2014 Annual Meeting of the Western Political Science Association, Sheraton Hotel, Seattle, Wash., April 17–19, 2014.

63. Ben Smith and Byron Tau, "Birtherism: Where It All Began," Politico, April 22, 2011.

64. Results from *USA Today*/Gallup poll, 2011 cited in Michael Tesler, "Birtherism Was Why So Many Republicans Liked Trump in the First Place," *Washington Post,* September 19, 2016.

65. Public Policy Polling, "Birthers Very Much a Rural Phenomenon," blog, PPP, August 11, 2009.

66. Cross tabs were provided to us upon request by Tom Jensen at PPP. For readability purposes and because the two-state results were so similar, we collapsed and averaged the results in North Carolina and Virginia for the "urban" and "suburban" subgroups and again for the "rural" and "small town" subgroups. The exact results for North Carolina were urban, 65 percent; suburban, 67 percent; rural, 44 percent; and small town, 46 percent. For Virginia, they were urban, 65 percent; suburban, 67 percent; rural, 44 percent; and small town, 46 percent.

67. Bettina Rottweiler and Paul Gill, "Conspiracy Beliefs and Violent Extremist Intentions: The Contingent Effects of Self-Efficacy, Self-Control and Law-Related Morality," *Terrorism and Political Violence* 34, No. 7 (2020): 1485–504.

68. Mettler and Brown, "The Growing Rural-Urban Political Divide and Democratic Vulnerability," 130–42.

69. Michael Brice-Saddler, "While Bemoaning Mueller Probe, Trump Falsely Says the Constitution Gives Him 'The Right to Do Whatever I Want,'" *Washington Post,* July 23, 2019.

70. Marist Poll, conducted on behalf of NPR/*PBS Newshour,* June 22–29, 2021.

71. "Debunking the Voter Fraud Myth," Brennan Center for Justice, January 31, 2017.

72. 2021 Marist Poll.

73. Albert Somit and Steven Peterson, *Darwinism, Dominance, and Democracy: The Biological Bases of Authoritarianism* (Westport, Conn.: Praeger, 1997).

74. Ruth Ben-Ghiat, *Strongmen: Mussolini to the Present* (New York: W.W. Norton and Company, 2020), quotes from pp. 251 and 256, respectively.

75. Pippa Norris and Ronald Inglehart, *Cultural Backlash: Trump, Brexit, and Authoritarian Populism* (Cambridge, U.K.: Cambridge University Press, 2019), 280.

76. Sarah Longwell, "Elevating Pro-Democracy Republicans," *Democracy: A Journal of Ideas* 66 (Fall 2022): 51–57.

77. University of Massachusetts, Amherst, Poll, December 2015, conducted by and cited in Matthew MacWilliams, "The One Weird Trait that Predicts Whether You're a Trump Supporter," Politico, January 17, 2016.

78. Chip Berlet and Spencer Sunshine, "Rural Rage: The Roots of Right-Wing Populism in the United States," *The Journal of Peasant Studies* 46, No. 3 (2019): 480–513.

79. Andrew L. Whitehead and Samuel L. Perry, *Taking Back America for God: Christian Nationalism in the United States* (New York: Oxford University Press, 2020).

80. Gregory A. Smith, Michael Rotolo, and Patricia Tevington, "45% of Americans Say U.S. Should Be a 'Christian Nation,'" Pew Research Center, October 27, 2022.

81. Samuel L. Perry and Andrew Whitehead, "Why White Christian Nationalism Isn't Going Away," *Time,* November 13, 2022.

82. Quoted in Eric C. Miller, "Trump's Unholy Alliances: An Interview with Sarah Posner," *Religion & Politics,* July 29, 2020.

83. Whitehead and Perry, *Taking America Back for God,* see chap. 1 and esp. Table 1.1.

84. Katherine Stewart, *The Power Worshippers: Inside the Dangerous Rise of Religious Nationalism* (New York: Bloomsbury, 2019), 4–8, emphasis added.

85. Samuel Perry @profsamperry, tweet, Twitter, 3:57 P.M., November 30, 2022.

86. "Survey: Two-Thirds of White Evangelicals, Most Republicans Sympathetic to Christian Nationalism," PRRI press release, February 8, 2023.

87. Bruce Stokes, "What It Takes to Truly Be 'One of Us,'" Pew Research Center, February 1, 2017.

88. Smith, Rotolo, and Tevington, "45% of Americans Say U.S. Should Be a 'Christian Nation.'"

89. Public Religion Research Institute, October 2022 poll results, reported in "Challenges in Moving Toward a More Inclusive Democracy: Findings from the 2022 American Values Survey," PRRI, October 27, 2022. The exact percentages for Dreamer opposition and stolen 2020 election are, respectively, 21 percent and 54 percent.

90. PRRI's 2015 American Values Survey, as reported in Robert P. Jones, *The End of White Christian America* (New York: Simon & Schuster, 2016), Figure 3.2, p. 86.

91. Public Religion Research Institute, "Competing Visions of America."

92. Brown, Mettler, and Puzzi, "When Rural and Urban Become 'Us' versus 'Them,'" see Table 1.

93. Paul D. Miller quoted in Morgan Lee, "Christian Nationalism Is Worse Than You Think," *Christianity Today,* January 13, 2021.

94. Chammah, "Does Your Sheriff Think He's More Powerful than the President?"

95. Chammah, "Does Your Sheriff Think He's More Powerful than the President?"

96. "Confronting the Demographics of Power: America's Sheriffs," Reflective Democracy Campaign, Women Donors Network, June 2020.

97. Maurice Chammah, "We Surveyed U.S. Sheriffs. See Their Views on Power, Race and Immigration," The Marshall Project, October 18, 2022.

98. Jonathan Edwards, "Okla. Governor Calls on Officials to Resign After 'Horrid' Audio Emerges," *Washington Post,* April 18, 2023.

99. Alexandra Berzon and Nick Corasaniti, "2020 Election Deniers Seek Out Powerful Allies: County Sheriffs," *New York Times,* July 25, 2022.

100. Steve Vockrodt, "Johnson County Sheriff Claimed He Got 200 Tips of Election Fraud. A Records Request Yielded Only One," KCUR Radio, July 28, 2022.

101. Peter Eisler and Nathan Layne, "Inside One Far-Right Sheriff's Crusade to Prove Trump's Bogus Voter-Fraud Claims," Reuters, July 29, 2022.

102. On mask mandates, see Emily M. Farris and Mirya R. Holman, "Sheriffs, Right-Wing Extremism, and the Limits of U.S. Federalism During a Crisis," *Social Science Quarterly* 104, No. 2 (February 2023), 59–68; on immigration, see Emily M. Farris and Mirya R. Holman, "All Politics Is Local? County Sheriffs and Localized Policies of Immigration," *Political Research Quarterly* 70, No. 1 (March 2017): 142–54; and on domestic violence, see Emily M. Farris and Mirya R. Holman, "Public Officials and a 'Private' Matter: Attitudes and Policies in the County Sheriff Office Regarding Violence Against Women," *Social Science Quarterly* 96, No. 4 (December 2015): 1117–35.

103. Frank Figliuzzi, "This Is How Biden Should Respond to Sheriffs Who Won't Enforce Gun Laws," MSNBC, March 16, 2023.

104. Julia Harte and Alexandra Ulmer, "U.S. Police Trainers with Far-right Ties Are Teaching Hundreds of Cops," Reuters, May 6, 2022.

105. Jessica Pishko, "Here's the Secret 'Sheriff Fellowship' Curriculum from the Country's Most Prominent MAGA Think Tank," *Slate,* September 21, 2022.

106. Robert Snell and Kara Berg, "Two Ringleaders Convicted on Whitmer Kidnapping Conspiracy Charges," *Detroit News,* August 23, 2022; Hannah Knowles, "Wolverine Watchmen, Extremist Group Implicated in Michigan Kidnapping Plot, Trained for 'Civil War,'" *Washington Post,* October 9, 2020; Nicholas Bogel-Burroughs, Shaila Dewan, and Kathleen Gray, "F.B.I. Says Michigan Anti-Government Group Plotted to Kidnap Gov. Gretchen Whitmer," *New York Times,* October 8, 2020.

107. Nils Kessler quoted in "Jury Convicts Two Men of Conspiring to Kidnap Michigan Gov. Gretchen Whitmer," CBS News, August 23, 2022.

108. "Jury Convicts Two Men of Conspiring to Kidnap Michigan Gov. Gretchen Whitmer."

109. Richard Hofstadter, "Reflections on Violence in the United States," preliminary chapter in

Richard Hofstadter and Michael Wallace, eds., *American Violence: A Documentary History* (New York: Alfred A. Knopf, 1970), 10–11.

110. *Meet the Press with Chuck Todd,* October 30, 2021, NBC.

111. Anissa Herrera and Mark Stroeher quoted in Brent Burgess, "Threats, Stalking Lead to Election Office Resignation," *Fredericksburg Standard–Radio Post,* August 10, 2022.

112. Lindsey Brown, interview with the authors, Fredericksburg, Texas, October 27, 2022.

113. Amy Gardner and Patrick Marley, "Trump Backers Flood Election Offices with Requests as 2022 Vote Nears," *Washington Post,* September 11, 2022.

114. Brennan Center for Justice and Bipartisan Policy Center, *Election Officials Under Attack: How to Protect Administrators and Safeguard Democracy,* report, Brennan Center and BPC, June 16, 2021.

115. U.S. Census Bureau "Quick Facts" entry for Boundary County, Idaho.

116. Nick Watt, "Conservatives Join Liberals in 'Quiet and Polite' Idaho Protest to Protect Their Library from Book-Banners," cnn.com, September 5, 2022.

117. James Wesley Rawles quoted in G. Jeffrey McDonald, "Secession Theology Runs Deep in American Religious, Political History," *St. Louis Post-Dispatch/Religion News Service,* November 30, 2012.

118. Anthea Butler, in interview with Jared Holt, host of *Posting Through It* podcast, Episode 180, December 19, 2022.

119. Jillian Cheney, "Trump-Supporting 'Jericho March' Ends in Protest, Burning of BLM Banners," Religion Unplugged, December 14, 2020; Emily Davies et al., "Multiple People Stabbed After Thousands Gather for Pro-Trump Demonstrations in Washington," *Washington Post,* December 12, 2020.

120. Annie Grayer and Kristin Wilson, "21 Republicans Vote No on Bill to Award Congressional Gold Medal for January 6 Police Officers," CNN, June 16, 2021. Categories for the twenty-one members voting "no" were drawn from CityLab's 2010 district classifications, as follows: ten "purely rural"; eight "rural-suburban"; two "densely suburban"; and one "sparsely suburban."

121. "The Harassment Faced by Jan. 6 Witnesses After Trump's False Claims," *Washington Post,* June 21, 2022.

122. IOP National Online Study No. 220265.

123. Robert A. Pape, "21 Million Americans Say Biden Is 'Illegitimate' and Trump Should Be Restored by Violence, Survey Finds," The Conversation, September 23, 2021.

124. "Deep, Divisive, Disturbing and Continuing," Slide 23 in presentation by Dr. Robert Page, Chicago Project on Security and Threats, January 2, 2022.

125. Economic Research Service, "Rural America at a Glance, 2021 edition," U.S. Department of Agriculture, n.d.

126. Zeeshan Aleem, "America's Growing Problem with Political Violence, Explained," interview of Lilliana Mason, MSNBC, November 23, 2021.

127. Rachel Kleinfeld, "The Rise of Political Violence in the United States," *Journal of Democracy* 32, No. 4 (October 2021): 160–76.

CHAPTER 7. RACE AND RURALITY

1. Andrew DePietro, "Richest Cities and Poorest Cities in Every State in 2021," *Forbes,* December 22, 2020.

2. Michael Chameides, "Rural Voters Surge to Polls—Elect Progressive Leader in Enfield, NC," Rural Democracy Initiative blog, May 31, 2022.

3. Mondale Robinson, interview with the authors via email, May 30, 2023.

4. D. W. Rowlands and Hanna Love, "Mapping Rural America's Diversity and Demographic Change," *The Avenue,* a publication of the Brookings Institution, September 28, 2021.

5. C. M. Figueroa et al., "Healthcare Needs of U.S. Rural Latinos: A Growing, Multicultural Population," *Journal of Rural Nursing Health Care* 21, No. 1 (2021): 24–48, see Table 2.

6. Emily Walton, "What's It Like to Be a Person of Color in Rural New England? Basically Invisible," WBUR, November 4, 2019.

7. Don Davis, interview with the authors, Greenville, N.C., February 16, 2023.

8. Brian Murray Walter, "Nostalgia and Precarious Placemaking in Southern Poultry Worlds: Immigration, Race, and Community Building in Rural Northern Alabama," *Journal of Rural Studies* 82 (2021): 542–52; Susan Hartman, "How Utica Became a City Where Refugees Came to Rebuild," *Literary Hub,* June 9, 2022; Maria Sacchetti, "A Rural County in Iowa that Supported Trump Turns to Latinos to Grow," *Washington Post,* May 14, 2022.

9. Kenneth Johnson and Daniel Lichter, "Growing Racial Diversity in Rural America: Results from the 2020 Census," report, Carsey School of Public Policy, University of New Hampshire, May 25, 2022.

10. Mary Logan Wolf, "Yes, Red-State Liberals Exist," *Democracy: A Journal of Ideas* (Winter 2018): 7–23.

11. Johnson and Lichter, "Growing Racial Diversity in Rural America."

12. Economic Research Service, "Rural Hispanics at a Glance," Bulletin No. 8, U.S. Department of Agriculture, December 2005.

13. DelReal and Clement, "Rural Divide."

14. Rowlands and Love, "Mapping Rural America's Diversity and Demographic Change."

15. Mara Casey Tieken, "There's a Big Part of Rural America that Everyone's Ignoring," *Washington Post,* March 24, 2017.

16. "Rural Employment and Unemployment," a report by the Economic Research Service of the U.S. Department of Agriculture, updated May 10, 2022.

17. Economic Research Service, "Rural Unemployment Rates Recovered Faster from 2020 to 2021, Remained Highest for 'Black or African American' Residents," U.S. Department of Agriculture, updated May 2, 2022.

18. Economic Research Service, "Rural Poverty and Well-Being," U.S. Department of Agriculture, updated September 8, 2023, n.d.

19. Teresa Wiltz, "Hispanic Poverty in Rural Areas Challenges States," *Stateline,* August 14, 2015.

20. Economic Research Service, "Rural Poverty and Well-Being."

21. Robin Davey Wolff, "Rural Housing, Race and Persistent Poverty," Enterprise blog, February 5, 2021.

22. Tracey Farrigan, "Rural Poverty Has Distinct Regional and Racial Patterns," Economic Research Service, U.S. Department of Agriculture, August 9, 2021.

23. Alliance for Entrepreneurial Equity, "2023 Vital Signs: The Health of Minority-Owned Small Businesses," January 18, 2023.

24. Alliance for Entrepreneurial Equity, "2023 Vital Signs"; rural Asian American–owned businesses are an exception.

25. "Kaine, Colleagues Introduce Bipartisan Legislation to Support Rural Minority-Owned Businesses," press release, Office of Sen. Tim Kaine (D-Virginia), October 27, 2020.

26. Al Gameros, interview with the authors, November 7, 2022.

27. Mike Feinberg, "Homeownership in Rural America," *Rural Research Brief,* Housing Assistance Council, Washington, D.C., June 2020.

28. Housing Assistance Council, "Race and Ethnicity in Rural America," *Rural Research Brief,* Washington, D.C., April 2012, p. 2.

29. Matt Krupnick, "Economics, Culture and Distance Conspire to Keep Rural Nonwhites from Higher Educations," The Hechinger Report, January 18, 2018.

30. Jon Marcus and Matt Krupnick, "The Rural Higher-Education Crisis," *Atlantic,* September 27, 2017.

31. Maraki Kebede et al., "Segregation Persists in Rural School Districts Despite Rising Ethnoracial Diversity," Center for Education and Civil Rights, Department of Education, Penn State University, August 2021.

32. "Rural Health Disparities," Rural Health Information Hub, November 28, 2022.

33. Carrie E. Henning-Smith et al., "Rural Counties with Majority Black or Indigenous Populations Suffer the Highest Rates of Premature Death in the US," *Health Affairs* 38, No. 12 (December 2019): 2019–26; and Nasim B. Ferdows et al., "Assessment of Racial Disparities in Mortality Rates Among Older Adults Living in US Rural vs. Urban Counties from 1968 to 2016," *JAMA Network Open* 3, No. 8 (August 2020).

34. Probst quoted in Liz Carey, "Study Finds Rural Health Care Access Lacking for Minority Populations," *Daily Yonder*, April 24, 2023.

35. Stacy Grundy and Beth Prusaczyk, "The Complex Intersection of Race and Rurality: The Detrimental Effects of Race-Neutral Rural Health Policies," *Health Equity* 6, No. 1 (2022): 334–37, emphasis added.

36. Sharita R. Thomas, George M. Holmes, and George H. Pink, "To What Extent Do Community Characteristics Explain Differences in Closure Among Financially Distressed Rural Hospitals?" *Journal of Health Care for the Poor and Underserved* 27, No. 4A (2016): 194–203.

37. Whitney E. Zahnd et al., "The Intersection of Rural Residence and Minority Race/Ethnicity in Cancer Disparities in the United States," *International Journal of Environmental Research and Public Health* 3, No. 18 (2021): 1384.

38. Erika C. Ziller, Carly Milkowski, and Amanda Burgess, "Rural Working-Age Adults Report More Cost Barriers to Health," *Policy Brief*, University of Southern Maine, March 27, 2023.

39. DW Rowlands and Hanna Love, "Mapping Rural America's Diversity and Demographic Change," Brookings Institution commentary, September 28, 2021.

40. Rebecca Tippett, "NC in Focus: Black Population," Carolina Demography, February 27, 2015.

41. Jeffrey J. Crow, Paul D. Escott, and Flora J. Hatley Wadelington, *A History of African Americans in North Carolina* (Raleigh: University of North Carolina Press, 1992), 3.

42. Crow, Escott, and Wadelington, *A History of African Americans in North Carolina*, pp. 3–4.

43. David Cecelski, "James R. Walker, Jr., and the Struggle for Voting Rights in North Carolina's Black Belt," blog post, Davidcecelski.com, November 7, 2020.

44. *Lassiter v. Northampton County Bd. of Elections,* 30 U.S. 45 (1959).

45. John Wynne, "Northampton County," Politics in North Carolina, April 2, 2013.

46. Abril Castro and Caius Z. Willingham, "Progressive Governance Can Turn the Tide for Black Farmers," Center for American Progress, April 3, 2019.

47. Andrew Laurence Carter and Adam Alexander, "Soul Food: [Re]framing the African-American Farming Crisis Using the Culture-Centered Approach," *Frontiers in Communication* 5, No. 5 (February 2020).

48. Newsroom, "Senator Reverend Warnock, Colleagues to USDA: We Urge You to Act to Address Historic Discrimination Against Black Farmers," press release, Office of Reverend Raphael Warnock, U.S. Senator for Georgia, June 2, 2022.

49. Ximena Bustillo, "Black Farmers Worry New Approach on 'Race Neutral' Lending Leaves Them in the Shadows," NPR, February 26, 2023.

50. Dan Sullivan, "His Ancestors Were Enslaved People, but Now This Hemp Farmer Owns the Plantation," *Lancaster Farming*, October 16, 2022.

51. Patrick Brown, interview with the authors, July 2, 2023.

52. Mondale Robinson, interview with the authors via email, June 2, 2023.

53. Don Davis, interview with the authors at his district office in Greenville, N.C., February 16, 2023.

54. Geneva Riddick-Faulkner, interview with the authors, Jackson, N.C., February 17, 2023.

55. Rep. Shelly Willingham, interview with the authors, Tarboro, N.C., February 17, 2023.

56. Kandie Smith, interview with the authors, Greenville, N.C., February 17, 2023.

57. Sarah Miller, Norman Johnson, and Laura R. Wherry, "Medicaid and Mortality: New Evidence from Linked Survey and Administrative Data," NBER Working Paper 26081, January 2021.

58. According to the Department of Education, the areas most likely to receive Title I funding were the most densely populated urban areas and the least densely populated rural areas. See National Center for Education Statistics, "Fast Facts," IES/NCES.

59. Emily Walkenhorst, "NC Lawmakers, Controller Want Leandro Back in Front of the State Supreme Court," WRAL, February 10, 2023.

60. Jeffrey S. Passel, Mark Hugo Lopez, and D'Vera Cohn, "U.S. Hispanic Population Continued Its Geographic Spread in the 2010s," Pew Research Center, February 3, 2022; county population sizes drawn from U.S. Census Bureau's "Quick Facts" webpage.

61. Rogelio Saenz and Cruz Torres, "Latinos in Rural America," in David L. Brown and Louis E. Swanson, eds., *Challenges to Rural America in the Twenty-first Century* (University Park: Pennsylvania State University Press, 2003).

62. Jon Shelton, "On, Wisconsin!" *Democracy: A Journal of Ideas* 51 (Winter 2019): 99–105.

63. Salvador Blanco quoted in Fidel Martinez, "Latinx Files: Greetings from Russellville, Alabama!" *Los Angeles Times,* March 24, 2022.

64. Joint Economic Committee—Democrats, "Report Finds Economic Power of Latinos Growing Amid Demographic Shifts," JEC, October 7, 2019; and Joint Economic Committee, "The Economic State of the Latino Community in America," JEC of the U.S. Congress, October 7, 2019, p. 9.

65. Wiltz, "Hispanic Poverty in Rural Areas Challenges States."

66. "Not Enough Food on the Dinner Table: A Look into Food Insecurity Among Hispanics/Latinos Living in Rural Communities in the United States," UnidosUS, January 2023.

67. Pete Rios, interview with the authors, Mesa, Ariz., November 7, 2022.

68. Carmen Huerta-Bapat, "The Racial Profiling of Latinos in North Carolina" (Ph.D. diss., University of North Carolina-Chapel Hill, 2017).

69. Sarah Dewees and Benjamin Marks, "Twice Invisible: Understanding Rural Native America," Research Note #2, First Nations Development Institute Research, April 2017.

70. "Michael Bird," interview by Sampada Nandyala, Public Health Post, August 20, 2018.

71. Reclaiming Native Truth, *Research Findings: Compilation of All Research,* RNT, June 2018, p. 53.

72. Philip Bump, "How Donald Trump's 1993 Comments About 'Indians' Previewed Much of His 2016 Campaign," *Washington Post,* July 1, 2016.

73. The Red Road, "Native American Poverty: An Endless Cycle."

74. The Red Road, "Native American Poverty."

75. Ben Eisen, "Scarce Credit Hinders Homeownership on Tribal Land," *Wall Street Journal,* August 29, 2021.

76. Alana Knudson et al., *Final Report: A Profile of Tribal Health Departments,* NORC at the University of Chicago Public Health Research, June 29, 2012.

77. Indian Health Service, "Disparities" Fact Sheet, IHS, U.S. Department of Health and Human Services.

78. Lisa Wexler et al., "Advancing Suicide Prevention Research with Rural American Indian and Alaska Native Populations," *American Journal of Public Health* 105, No. 5 (May 2015): 891–99.

79. Kristi Eaton, "Report: 113K U.S. Indigenous Individuals Live in Mental Health Care Deserts," *Daily Yonder,* January 24, 2023.

80. Shawna Claw, interview with the authors, Chinle, Arizona, November 8, 2022.

81. Saint Regis Mohawk Tribe, "Belushi's Farm Opens Akwesasne Cannabis Dispensary," SRMT, October 27, 2022.

82. Saint Regis Mohawk Tribe, "Saint Regis Mohawk Tribe Launches Regulated Cannabis Industry," SRMT, December 14, 2021.

83. Douglas Burns, "As Rural Americans We Must See Ourselves as Part of the Nation's Diversity," *Iowa Capital Dispatch,* October 11, 2022.

84. Tieken, "There's a Big Part of Rural America that Everyone's Ignoring."

CHAPTER 8. DESPAIR, DISTRACTION, DISILLUSIONMENT, AND DEMOCRATIC DECLINE

1. Sahil Kapur and Allan Smith, "McConnell Wants to Win the Suburbs by Defusing Cultural Hot Buttons. Trump and His Own Party Have Other Ideas," NBCNews.com, July 4, 2022.
2. We spent a morning with that opponent, Claudia Zapata, while she and some campaign volunteers cleaned a couple of truckloads of junk from the home of an elderly woman who lived alone (with three yapping dogs) in a dusty neighborhood in Kerrville. As they canvassed neighborhoods, rather than just asking people for votes, they would see if there was anything people needed, then do their best to help. It was inspiring to see, but also an extremely inefficient way to assemble the votes necessary to win a congressional race in which a quarter of a million votes were cast. Roy beat Zapata by a twenty-six-point margin.
3. "The reality of the purpose of the Second Amendment," Roy said in a congressional hearing on July 20, 2022, is as a bulwark against the tyranny of the American federal government. That this is a common argument on the right makes it no less vulgar in its insistence that the reason one should have guns is so one can kill officials and overthrow the government should one deem it necessary.
4. Interview with the authors, November 3, 2022.
5. Mettler and Brown, "The Growing Rural-Urban Political Divide and Democratic Vulnerability."
6. Hannah Hartig et al., "Republican Gains in 2022 Midterms Driven Mostly by Turnout Advantage: An Examination of the 2022 Election, Based on Validated Voters," Pew Research Center, July 12, 2023.
7. Chip Roy, interview with the authors, March 24, 2023.
8. Ben Wikler, interview with the authors, January 18, 2023.
9. For instance, after an infrastructure bill was passed in 2022, the Biden administration created a "Rural Playbook" to assist rural communities in accessing funding. The White House, *Bipartisan Infrastructure Law Rural Playbook: A Roadmap for Delivering Opportunity and Investments in Rural America,* last updated April 2022; you can see it at www.whitehouse.gov/build/resources/rural/.
10. Data from the Bureau of Economic Analysis, available at www.bea.gov/sites/default/files/2022-12/lagdp1222.pdf.
11. Pooja Salhotra and Jayme Lozano, "A Boil-Water Notice in Houston Made National News. In Rural Texas, It's a Way of Life," *Texas Tribune,* December 7, 2022.
12. "Georgia Peach Crop Fails Due to Climate Change," *CBS Evening News with Norah O'Donnell,* Thursday, June 29, 2023.
13. Kate Cohen, "My Husband Has Farmed for 4 Decades. Climate Change Might End His Run," *Washington Post,* August 2, 2023.
14. Kathleen McLaughlin, "No OB-GYNs Left in Town: What Came After Idaho's Assault on Abortion," *The Guardian,* August 22, 2023.
15. Tyler Cooper, "Municipal Broadband 2022: Barriers Remain an Issue in 17 States," *Broadband Now,* October 23, 2022.
16. Jon Brodkin, "House Republicans Propose Nationwide Ban on Municipal Broadband Networks," *Ars Technica,* February 18, 2021.
17. Nick Fouriezos, "Rising Cost of Housing and Higher Education Poses Real Problems for Rural Students," *Daily Yonder,* August 31, 2023.
18. Unnamed student quoted in Jon Marcus, "Rural Universities, Already Few and Far Between, Are Cutting Majors," *Washington Post,* December 16, 2022.
19. Liz Hamel, Bryan Wu, and Mollyann Brodie, "The Health Care Views and Experiences of Rural Americans," poll, Kaiser Family Foundation, June 2017.
20. Jacob Bunge and Bob Tita, "Biden Order Takes Aim at Tractor Repair," *Wall Street Journal,* July 10, 2021.

21. Wuthnow quoted in Illing, "A Princeton Sociologist Spent 8 Years Asking Rural Americans Why They're So Pissed Off."

22. Eleanor Krause and Richard V. Reeves, *Rural Dreams: Upward Mobility in America's Countryside,* Brookings Institution, September 5, 2017.

23. As labor historian Gabriel Winant writes, "Within this false class politics, the suffering of working-class people is understood in conspiratorial rather than structural terms. There is no historical logic to class inequality and exploitation, only inexplicable and unique acts of cruelty that bear no useful comparison to anything that has happened to others" (Gabriel Winant, "J. D. Vance Changes the Subject: A Senator from the Unconscious," *n+1* 45 [Spring 2023]).

24. Orbán's undermining of democracy, his attack on the rights of LGBTQ+ Hungarians, his opposition to immigration, and his efforts to make Hungary a more explicitly Christian country have made him a hero to American conservatives. He shares another interest with his U.S. compatriots: gerrymandering. In 2022, Orbán's Fidesz party won 53 percent of the vote in parliamentary elections but controlled 83 percent of the seats. As *The Washington Post* described it, "The districts, drawn with no input from the opposition, spread Fidesz voters across many small districts in rural areas while concentrating opposition voters in much larger districts in the cities, thus giving them fewer chances to win" (Kim Lane Scheppele, "In Hungary, Orban Wins Again—Because He Has Rigged the System," *Washington Post,* April 7, 2022).

25. Andy Westwood and John C. Austin, "To Counter Extreme Politics, Revive Global Democracies' Rust Belts," Brookings Institution, April 8, 2021.

26. The Center for Information and Research on Civic Learning and Engagement found after the 2016 election that 60 percent of rural young people lived in what they call "civic deserts," defined as "places characterized by a dearth of opportunities for civic and political learning and engagement, and without institutions that typically provide opportunities like youth programming, culture and arts organizations and religious congregations," compared with 30 percent of urban and suburban youth. Young people in civic deserts tended to be disengaged from politics, had few if any political opinions, and did not see politics as a means to helping their communities. (Kei Kawashima-Ginsberg and Felicia Sullivan, "Study: 60 Percent of Rural Millennials Lack Access to a Political Life," The Conversation, March 26, 2017.)

27. See, for instance, Patrick Denice and Jake Rosenfeld, "Unions and Nonunion Pay in the United States, 1977–2015," *Sociological Science* 5 (2018): 541–61.

28. James Feigenbaum, Alexander Hertel-Fernandez, and Vanessa Williamson, "From the Bargaining Table to the Ballot Box: Political Effects of Right to Work Laws," Working Paper No. 24259, National Bureau of Economic Research, January 2018.

29. Rowlands and Love, "Mapping Rural America's Diversity and Demographic Change."

30. Johnson and Lichter, "Growing Racial Diversity in Rural America."

31. As one group of political scientists found in its research, "As the share of a county that is non-white increases, urban whites become less racially resentful, while rural whites become more so." And those rural Whites become more likely to vote Republican. Brown, Mettler, and Puzzi, "When Rural and Urban Become 'Us' versus 'Them.'"

32. Richard Hofstadter, *The Age of Reform: From Bryan to F.D.R.* (New York: Vintage Books, 1960), 23.

33. Letter to David Williams, November 14, 1803.

AUTHORS' NOTE

1. National Center for Health Statistics, "NCHS Urban-Rural Classification Scheme for Counties," Centers for Disease Control and Prevention, June 1, 2017; "Federal Office of Rural Health Policy (FORHP) Data Files," Health Resources and Services Administration; Sarah Melotte, "Is Rural America Struggling? It Depends on How You Define 'Rural,'"

Daily Yonder, April 6, 2023; National Center for Health Statistics, "NCHS Urban-Rural Classification Scheme for Counties," Centers for Disease Control and Prevention, June 1, 2017.

2. Melotte, "Is Rural America Struggling?"
3. Kenneth M. Johnson and Dante J. Scala, "The Rural-Urban Continuum and the 2020 Presidential Election," *The Forum* 20 (June 15, 2022).
4. The AHS (American Housing Survey) 2017 Neighborhood Description Survey, Summary Table 1, Office of Policy Development and Research, U.S. Department of Housing and Urban Development; Ruth Igielnik Wieder, "Evaluating What Makes a U.S. Community Urban, Suburban or Rural," *Medium,* November 22, 2019.
5. Parker et al., "What Unites and Divides Urban, Suburban and Rural Communities."
6. Public Religion Research Institute, "Competing Visions of America," Question 34a.

INDEX

media: conservative
  culture war and, 114, 115
  denigration of metro areas on, 119–20, 121
  liberal contempt for rural America on, 108, 115
  portrayal of threats to America on, 6, 7, 16, 116–17
  reinforcement of fear and resentment by, 116
  "replacement theory," 166
  talk radio in rural areas, 115–16
  See also Fox News
Medicaid, 50, 51–52, 55, 213–14, 234–35
Medicare, 50
Meine, Curt, 34
Melotte, Sarah, 55
Mesa County (Colorado), 152
metro areas
  attitudes toward immigrants in, 165
  believers in Big Lie, 174
  childbirth deaths in, 55
  Covid-19 vaccination rates, 57
  culture war and, 105–6
  economic power of, 68–69, 105
  Great Recession and, 31
  gun ownership in, 54
  gun-related deaths in, 53–54
  history of movement to, 247
  median age in, 59
  media portrayal of, 107–8, 119–20, 121, 270n27
  percent of Americans wanting to live in, 104
  percent of residents wanting to move from, 104
  population growth in, 26
  proximity to, and prosperity, 31, 38–39
  Republican Party and, 82–83, 90, 118–19, 231–32
  rural Whites' negativity about, 18, 45–46, 164
  underfunding of, by state legislatures, 85
  white flight and, 27
Mettler, Suzanne, 76, 177–78
Metzl, Jonathan, 49
Mexico, 140–41
Michigan, 81
Miller, Lisa, 266
Miller, Paul D., 183
Mine Wars, 10, 259n3
Mingo County (West Virginia), 10–13, 29–30, 48–49, 53, 136–37, 259n3

Minnesota, 81
"misrecognition," 198–99
Mississippi, 52
Molinaro, John, 69
Moms for Liberty, 111
Monnat, Shannon, 52–53
Morgan, Alan, 40
Morning Consult, 90
Munis, Karl, 162
Muslims, 156–57, 163
"myth of the white minority," 167

Nadler, Anthony, 107–8
Nashville, 105
National Industrial Recovery Act (1933), 259n4
National Labor Relations Act (1935), 259n4
natural resource extraction. *See* coal industry
Nelsen, Matthew, 164
Nevada, 64
New Jersey, 54
New Mexico, 32
New York (state), 24–25, 86
New York City, 54, 106
The New Yorker, 34, 84
The New York Times, 59, 82–83, 175
Niven, David, 84
Norris, Pippa, 179–80
North American Free Trade Agreement (NAFTA), 32
Northampton County (North Carolina), 33, 261n32
North Carolina, 80, 177, 277n66
Nye County (Nevada), 153

Obama, Barack
  attempts to limit agricultural consolidation by, 34–35
  backlash against, as first Black president, 134
  birtherism conspiracy against, 176–77, 277n66
  confirmation of judicial appointees by U.S. Senate, 72–73
  elections and, 83, 112, 121–22, 123
  on malapportionment, 73–74
  rural White belief as illegitimate president, 19
  theme of progress, 139, 270n20
Obamacare, 49–52, 264n91

rural America (*cont'd*):
culture war as used by Republicans in,
102–3
Democratic Party and, 123–24, 230
dependency on federal programs, 45–46
as deserving overrepresentation in Electoral
College, 68
desire to create jobs in new industries in,
36–37
economic conditions in, 7, 26, 36–37
as Edenic, 95
Great Recession and, 31
harmed by delegitimization of government,
232–33
identity of, as rooted in local work, 37
median age in, 59
media portrayal of, 107, 120, 270n25,
270n27, 271n50
moral code of, 151–52, 273n50
percent of Americans wanting to live in,
104
percent of residents wanting to leave,
104
population diversity in, 168, 198, 202
population stagnation, 26
as producer of national wealth, 68
Republican Party's exploitation of, 230, 231,
232–37, 240–41
Republican populism in, 145–48
sheriffs in, 19, 159, 177, 183–86
stereotypes about residents, 105
white flight from, 27–29
as Whitest part of U.S., 162
Rural and Minority Health Research Center
(RMHRC), 206
Rural Health Information Hub (RHIB),
205–6
rural non-Whites
democratic commitment of, 194
economic hardships facing, 16–17, 197, 201,
202–5
as economic lifeline to area, 199–200
education of, 205, 214–15, 282n58
farming by, 33–34
healthcare hardships facing, 16–17, 52,
55–56, 205–7, 213–14
Latinos, 78, 215–19
majority Black areas, 33, 37–38, 196–97, 199,
208–13, 213–14, 261n32
media and, 201
as minority in most counties, 198
Native Americans, 219–24

political power of, 197
population growth, 246
population losses, 30
willingness to work within democratic
system of, 243–44
Rural Objective PAC, 165
rural Whites
belief in conspiracies, 152–54, 158, 174–76,
183, 185, 192–93
beliefs about diversity, 18, 159, 163
birtherism among, 177, 277n66
economic conditions and disconnect with
voting by, 34
election of 2016 as final break with
Democratic Party by, 136
election of Republicans as legitimate, 175
isolation of, 168–69
Jefferson on, 93
as linchpin of Republican and Trump's
power, 12, 230
media stoking of resentments of, 6, 7, 16
minority rule as result of power of, 4
moral latitude given to, 117–18
as most real, best Americans, 4, 15, 94,
95–96, 101, 269n3
need to build coalitions with rural non-
Whites, 224–25
percent evangelical, 183
as percent of U.S. population, 15
prevalence of forces threatening American
political system and, 5
Republican Party exploitation of, 240–41
Trump's appeal to, 127–28, 130–31, 138–39,
142
Trump's support in, 137–38
uninsured rate of, 51
veneration of culture and values of, 15
rural Whites as threats
animus toward immigrants, 18, 20, 159,
165–70
authoritarianism and, 179–80
ballot access and, 178–79
belief in conspiracies, 18–19, 152–54, 158,
159, 171–76, 183, 185, 192–93
Christian nationalism and, 182–83
discomfort with change, 116–17, 162–63
enmity toward metro areas, 18, 45–46
government officials, agencies, or
facilities as targets of violence, 186,
188–90
justification of use of violence by, 20–21,
159, 192–94

ABOUT THE AUTHORS

—

TOM SCHALLER is a professor of political science at the University of Maryland, Baltimore County. A former columnist for *The Baltimore Sun*, he has written for *The New York Times*, *The Washington Post*, and the *Los Angeles Times* and has appeared on ABC, CBS, *The Colbert Report*, and MSNBC, among others. The author of the books *Common Enemies*, *The Stronghold*, and *Whistling Past Dixie*, he is also the co-author of *Devolution and Black State Legislators*.

PAUL WALDMAN is a journalist and opinion writer whose work has appeared in dozens of newspapers, magazines, and digital outlets, including the *Los Angeles Times*, *The Boston Globe*, *Chicago Tribune*, *The Week*, msnbc.com, and cnn.com. He is a former columnist at *The Washington Post* and the author or co-author of four previous books on media and politics, including *Being Right Is Not Enough: What Progressives Must Learn from Conservative Success* and *The Press Effect: Politicians, Journalists, and the Stories that Shape the Political World*.

ABOUT THE TYPE

—

This book was set in Bulmer, a typeface designed in the late eighteenth century by the London type cutter William Martin (1757–1830). The typeface was created especially for the Shakespeare Press, directed by William Bulmer (1757–1830)—hence the font's name. Bulmer is considered to be a transitional typeface, containing characteristics of old-style and modern designs. It is recognized for its elegantly proportioned letters, with their long ascenders and descenders.